The World Is Out of Joint

Fernand Braudel Center Series
Edited by Immanuel Wallerstein

The World Is Out of Joint: World-Historical Interpretations of Continuing Polarizations
Immanuel Wallerstein, coordinator

Alternatives: The United States Confronts the World
by Immanuel Wallerstein

The Modern World-System in the Longue Durée
edited by Immanuel Wallerstein

Overcoming the Two Cultures: Science vs. the Humanities in the Modern World-System
Richard E. Lee and Immanuel Wallerstein, coordinators

The World Is Out of Joint

World-Historical Interpretations of
Continuing Polarizations

Immanuel Wallerstein, coordinator,
and
Ana Esther Ceceña
Roberto Patricio Korzeniewicz and Timothy Patrick
Moran
Peter J. Taylor, Michael Hoyler, and Dennis Smith
Eric Vanhaute, Hanne Cottyn, and Yang Wang
Jorge Fonseca
Ravi Sundaram
Atilio A. Boron and Paloma Nottebohm
Oleksandr Fisun and Volodymyr Golovko
Linda Christiansen-Ruffman
Ari Sitas, Sumangala Damodaran, Weibke Keim, and
Nicos Trimikliniotis

Paradigm Publishers
Boulder • London

Copyright © 2015 Paradigm Publishers

Published in the United States by Paradigm Publishers, 5589 Arapahoe Avenue, Boulder, CO 80303 USA.

Paradigm Publishers is the trade name of Birkenkamp & Company, LLC, Dean Birkenkamp, President and Publisher.

Library of Congress Cataloging-in-Publication Data

Wallerstein, Immanuel Maurice, 1930–
    The world is out of joint: world-historical interpretations of continuing polariza-
tions / Immanuel Wallerstein, coord. and Ana Esther Ceceña and 19 others.
        pages cm. — (Fernand Braudel Center series)
    Includes bibliographical references.
    ISBN 978-1-61205-718-7 (pbk : alk. paper) —
    ISBN 978-1-61205-720-0 (consumer ebook)
    1. Polarization (Social sciences)   2. Social structure.   I. Wallerstein, Immanuel.
II. Ceceña, Ana Esther.   III. Title.
    HN18.3.W35 2014
    301 — dc23
                                                                            2014017352

Printed and bound in the United States of America on acid-free paper that meets the standards of the American National Standard for Permanence of Paper for Printed Library Materials.

19 18 17 16 15   1 2 3 4 5

Contents

Acknowledgments   vii

Chapter 1
Introduction   1
by Immanuel Wallerstein

Chapter 2
Ecology and the Geography of Capitalism   7
by Ana Esther Ceceña

Chapter 3
Economic Inequality, Stratification, and Mobility   23
by Roberto Patricio Korzeniewicz and Timothy Patrick Moran

Chapter 4
Cities   39
by Peter J. Taylor, Michael Hoyler, and Dennis Smith

Chapter 5
Peasantries   55
by Eric Vanhaute, Hanne Cottyn, and Yang Wang

Chapter 6
Large Enterprises and Corporate Power   69
by Jorge Fonseca

Chapter 7
Intellectual Property   83
by Ravi Sundaram

Chapter 8
The States   97
by Atilio A. Boron and Paloma Nottebohm

Chapter 9
Citizenship   111
by Oleksandr Fisun and Volodymyr Golovko

Chapter 10
Women's Spaces and a Patriarchal System   125
by Linda Christiansen-Ruffman

Chapter 11
Deviance   147
by Ari Sitas, Sumangala Damodaran,
Weibke Keim, and Nicos Trimikliniotis

Chapter 12
Conclusion   163
by Immanuel Wallerstein

Bibliography   171

About the Author   191

Acknowledgments

We collectively acknowledge gratefully the assistance of the Fundação Calouste Gulbenkian for its assistance in making possible the annual meetings of the coordinators of the research groups. We also wish to thank João Caraça of the Fundação for attending all of our annual meetings and for his very helpful participation in the discussions.

Chapter 1

Introduction

by Immanuel Wallerstein

Definition of the Intellectual Problem

Over the past two centuries, the dominant view in social science has been that the modern world shows a pattern of linear development in which all positive trends go upward in more or less linear fashion (albeit perhaps at an uncertain speed), and that therefore over time discrepancies between the leaders and the laggards are overcome, eventually resulting in a relatively homogenized world. By leaders and laggards, most analysts have been referring to states.

This view, which we may call the expectation of ultimate positive convergence of all states, reflects the Enlightenment belief in progress as the basic long-term pattern of social life. It was shared by classical and neoclassical economics, by what we now call Whig historiography, and by most of traditional sociology and anthropology. It dominated analysis throughout the world during most of the nineteenth and twentieth centuries.

There were, to be sure, conservative social thinkers who demurred. Some of them insisted that hierarchies were an inevitable (as well as desirable) feature of human social behavior. To the degree that the world seemed to move towards more egalitarianism, these thinkers argued this was a temporary deviation from the norm and that there would be a cyclical return to earlier patterns. However, generally after about 1850, this conservative demurral had little purchase in the emerging world of the social sciences.

Classical (or orthodox) Marxism offered its doctrines as a refutation of liberalism and its *Weltanschauung*. Nonetheless, it shared by and large the same belief in the inevitability of progress and the linear upward pattern of social processes. Marxist differences with liberalism consisted primarily of an argument about the motor forces of this progression as well as many of the details being described.

This widely shared view of ultimate positive convergence of all states grew steadily stronger in the period 1850–1950, and seemed to reach an apotheosis in the twenty-five years following the end of the Second World War. The problem in this last period was the growing empirical evidence that the gap between what was called at the time the "developed" and the "underdeveloped" nations was increasing rather than decreasing as the dominant view had theorized.

As a consequence, in the post-1950 period, a number of analysts began to contest this linear model, but in a new way, not employing the version of the conservative demurral. The linear progress model viewed the modern world as a process of homogenization and therefore one of overcoming the gaps between states or groups of any kind. Against this view, many social scientists began to argue that the modern world was one of heterogenization and polarization. Indeed, they said, the pattern of polarization escalated over time, the result of the way in which the modern world was structured.

The debate of homogenization versus heterogenization extended beyond the confines of social science. The same debate was bubbling in the natural sciences and in the humanities. By the 1970s there had emerged two major knowledge movements seeking to (re)open all the basic epistemological assumptions of the dominant view. The movement within the natural sciences came to be called complexity studies. Its key feature was to deny the ubiquity of linear dynamic models in the physical world. Indeed, these scientists suggested quite the opposite. Complexity scientists argued that natural systems moved inevitably far from equilibrium, and at a certain point entered into a chaotic structural crisis and bifurcated.

The movement within the humanities came to be called cultural studies. The prevailing view within the humanities had been that there were objective criteria of beauty, canons or aesthetic universals, which could be known and taught but not changed. In this sense, the world was homogeneous. The new critics insisted that the canons were simply the self-serving and self-justifying criteria of a particular group. Instead they saw multiple aesthetic criteria grounded in multiple social settings and experiences, all equally legitimate. The cultural world was hetero-geneous, and this was very desirable.

In analyzing the social world, the linear versus polarizing models of historical development became a debate about whether the various zones (or countries) of the world-system would converge to an approximately equal standard of living and similar political and cultural structures, or in fact over time would diverge ever more sharply.

The various researchers who are writing this book all began with a sympathetic inclination for the polarization hypothesis. But we wished to see if a close look at the empirical evidence would sustain the argument seriously. Obviously, we knew we would find some social trends that have been linear upward and some that have been polarizing. We sought to examine and evaluate which trends were linear and which polarizing, and to what degree. We thought that we could then assess the overall mix that the modern world-system has created—whether, as the "linearists" have contended, there has been an overall reduction in differences or, as the "polarizers" have contended, there have been emergent processes that are bringing into question the very continued existence of the present system.

To do this, we felt it necessary to make our empirical analysis large in scale and long in duration. The object of our analysis was the existing world-system as a whole, over the entirety of its effective existence of the past five hundred years. We decided therefore to try to (1) give an adequate portrayal of the historical realities of the world-system, (2) draw a nuanced assessment about this fundamental theoretical debate, and (3) provide the basis on which we can not only envisage probable future trends but also draw conclusions about the policy and/or political implications of our work.

The Research Clusters

After considering various ways we could conduct this research, we decided that the optimal strategy was to divide our work into a series of clusters, each of which defined a locus of research, and the sum of which, we believed, would enable us to respond to the three objectives we set ourselves. We rejected using the standard widely employed categories of variables—political, economic, social, cultural, military, and so on. Instead we drew up a list of what we considered crucial nodes of social activity or organization that often cut across these standard categories. Of course, these clusters are not gated entities. The activities in each cluster overlap in many ways with those of other clusters. But each provides a node of activity and therefore a vantage point from which to assess the basic issues: linearist versus polarizing trends. The clusters we selected are the following:

   a) *Ecology and the geography of capitalism*: colonization of nature and civilizing subversion—natural resources, energy, and infrastructure

b) *Economic inequality, stratification, and mobility*: access to wealth and lifetime income, mobility, and intrastate and interstate inequalities
c) *Cities*: the growth of multiple types of cities and their geographical inequalities, including ports and flows of commodities, transport, in-migration, and the role of both the formal and the informal economy
d) *Peasantries*: trajectories of peasant transformation; the decline of the centrality of rural zones (de-ruralization) and its consequent impact on the rural workforce (de-peasantization and de-agrarianization), the strategies of rural households, out-migration, and the place of the informal economy
e) *Large enterprises and corporate power*: operation of firms—legal, paralegal (informal production), and illegal (mafiosi), including concentration and monopolization
f) *Intellectual property*: patents, copyright, piracy, and the concept of the author
g) *The states*: expansion of state power—military, police, bureaucracy, and taxation
h) *Citizenship*: mechanisms of inclusion and exclusion; claim-making in its multiple forms
i) *Women's spaces and a patriarchal system*: status of women and norms governing sexualities, including shifting concepts of "normality" and institutional constraints
j) *Deviance*: clustering of people (both identities and institutions): households, classes, status groups, and imprisoned/constrained groups

These were, of course, not the only clusters we could have chosen. But we believe this group touches on so many different realities of social life that we feel confident about drawing a general picture from its analysis.

Research Procedures

We constituted a group of individual researchers to be the cluster leaders. This group was deliberately made up of persons located in different parts of the world. Each agreed to pursue and coordinate the research required by a particular cluster. In most cases, each cluster leader created a team of researchers to participate in the work. The ten cluster leaders plus the overall coordinator of the project constituted the scientific network of the project, which met together to oversee the entire project.

The cluster leaders gave each other a difficult charge. Each cluster was asked to provide a worldwide analysis over a long historical time. In terms of space, we left to each cluster the decision of whether to analyze the whole globe or only the part that constituted the capitalist world-economy at different points in time. In terms of time, we left to each cluster the decision as to the most useful and appropriate time scope. We asked the clusters to obtain data at multiple points in time going back several centuries, to the extent possible.

The network of cluster leaders met together at least once a year over a period of five years. The primary purpose of these meetings was for the group to receive a report from each cluster leader about its ongoing research activities and findings. The collective group then discussed these reports and debated what had been omitted or unnecessarily emphasized in the work of each cluster. The objective of these discussions was to ensure that the work on each cluster remained within the spirit of the overall project and would therefore be contributing its share to the overall assessment.

The methods used to collect data were adapted to the realities of what kinds of data were found to be available. This, of course, varied according to the subject matter of the cluster. In most cases the data that could be located or created were both quantitative and qualitative. The data inevitably varied considerably in reliability. The outcome we offer is, we hope, probing and indicative. We do not suggest that it is definitive.

We consider the project to be a single unified one. This book is not a collection of separate (and disparate) papers about the various clusters, but each cluster produced its own conclusions. The final chapter attempts an overall assessment of the modern world on the basis of the evidence provided in the reports of the multiple clusters.

We shall not anticipate that final chapter here except to summarize the heart of the conclusion: the polarizing thesis has enough supporting evidence that it needs to be taken very seriously by historical social scientists. Consequently, in the final chapter we shall assess whether there are secular trends visible in the overall data, and whether there is reason to believe that such trends as are visible could continue to operate in the near (and/or indefinite) future. Finally, we shall formulate, in light of the patterns discerned, possible policies to move the systemic patterns in desired directions.

Chapter 2

Ecology and the Geography of Capitalism

by Ana Esther Ceceña

The Divorce with Nature

Over the long history of humanity, the world has known many distinct ways of conceiving the cosmos. Most, possibly all, civilizations that existed before the fifteenth century appeared relatively humble when facing the greatness of the creation of life and the cosmos. The dominant mode of thinking implied a complex universe in which human beings were perceived in their relation to life, land, and the existing material world.

Some civilizations considered an isolated being as an impossible emptiness. In their perception, a tree is at the same time "the rain that falls on its leaves, the wind that moves it, the land that feeds and sustains it, the seasons, the climate, the moonlight, and the light of the stars and the sun" (Sogyal 1996: 19). In such a conception, no hierarchical separation between the diverse forms of life exists. Society and nature form a unity that, when violated, ends the harmony of the whole, affecting all its parts.

For the nonanthropocentric civilizations the organization of life implied a respect for nature that the modern world has considered to be pre-scientific and superstitious. Such respect generated, however, not only the conservation of nature but also its development and, in certain cases, its production[1] (Mann 2006). Trees, plants, animals, and human beings were considered as forming a creative and interactive totality, which made possible the diversification and growth of life on Earth.

For millions of years, life evolved, reaching very high levels of complexity and refinement. Species multiplied and enlarged their combinations and imbrications. For human beings, there is much evidence that this process meant improved conditions and the increased variability of human beings. Barbarism, which obviously existed, never reached levels of destruction that could not be absorbed by nature. The intrinsic richness of each ecosystem expanded and diversified in accordance with the cultural expressions of their inhabitants, leading to a growing biodiversity, a great accumulation of knowledge, and wide horizons of reflection about the world and the cosmos.

However, even if that seems to have been the dominant feature before the onset of capitalism and the modern world, it is possible to identify within that diversity and richness two great civilizational perspectives, coexisting but contradictory in their conceptions of life and social development. Those two perspectives had conflicting visions of reality that have deepened their divergence ever since. The two were the self-centered utilitarian and the solidary decentered civilizations, generating otherness versus complementarity.

The self-centered perspective was based on the conception of humans as superior beings in relation to all the others. It transformed nature into an object, separating nature and society. The role of subject was attributed exclusively to the human species. All the rest were relegated to the role of objects capable of being manipulated, appropriated, and converted into instruments for the benefit of humanity. This view became widespread probably since the fifteenth century. Norbert Elias, however, argues that it became definitive only in the sixteenth century. For him, its foundational moment was when Galileo started his reflections about "real facts, tangible and objective" (Elias 1996).

Galileo's innovation, although he was a deviant in his own context,[2] constituted an essential contribution to the conception of objectivity immanent in the capitalist ethos. It became shaped, slowly, in the "long sixteenth century" (c.1450–c.1640), "during which our modern world-system came into existence as a capitalist world-economy" (Wallerstein 2004: 10).

The conceptualization of the human species as superior to all the other species and destined to submit them broke with the logic of social

---

1. Research about Amazonia has shown that human beings have produced, to a certain extent, their environment by developing the jungles. One of the most eloquent examples is the way that Amazonian people invented the "black earth" (the *terra preta*) in order to extend the possibilities of nature to develop in those lands. The same can be said about other peoples of the world. A good synthesis about all this for the Americas can be found in Mann (2006).

2. See Chapter 11, "Deviance," in this volume.

organization based on the previous macrovisions still dominant at that time in most Asian, African, and Amerindian cultures. It opened up the way to the great transformation represented by the creation of a truly planetary world-system, capable of promoting progress, the world market, development, and monopolization. It arrived in the form of anthropocentrism and Eurocentrism. The new dualism between subject and object became a dangerous epistemological starting point.

This conceptualization made possible an expansive world-system that swallowed and subjugated everything in its course. The relation, subject-object, entered into the framework of life. It was expressed by a new territoriality that became competitive rather than being solidary and favoring coexistence.

There are historical records of destructive peoples before the emergence of capitalism, but none of them was able to destabilize the planet and threaten life itself. This was because their technological, appropriative-transformative, and consequently depredating capacities were much below the level at which they become irreversible. Capitalism is the first system of social organization able to turn the forces of nature against themselves through a technology that explicitly aims to dominate and correct nature. Capitalism has been shaping the planet to meet the immediate, but historically unsustainable, appetites of capital.

The Original Asymmetry

Fernand Braudel (1979: 352–353) insists on the importance of asymmetry as a starting point in the establishment of the capitalist world-economy. Asymmetry offers privilege, and Europeans achieved this by combining advanced navigation technology with the use of gunpowder for their warlike objectives. It is in this achievement that we find the key to European supremacy in overseas expansion (Braudel 1979) and the formation of the world market. Chinese ships were superior in nautical technology, but the Chinese intent was trade. The Arabs moved in a huge regional space, but not one spanning the whole planet. Europeans had inferior ships but the Castilians had cannons, muskets, and the whole power of the Catholic Church behind them, pushing for their worldwide expansion.

The rationale of capitalist accumulation became a growing and unstoppable force that was able to unleash knowledge and human ability to guarantee the greatest possible accumulation, with the least time and effort. It quickly developed communication and war technologies in an interrelated way. Greed and power, communications and guns fed one another in each voyage of the ships that arrived in the Indies, intent on looting wealth. In a distinct way but with a similar objective, European traders, sailors, warriors, and evangelists, with the support and authorization of the monarchies, burst into Asia, Africa, and America in what became the great and definitive foundational act of the modern world.

Asymmetry and Disproportion

The history of the last five hundred years, announced as the epoch of the progress of humanity, was initially marked by plunder, violence, and pillage. The human capacity to know and transform matter, places, and human beings themselves developed ample and complex technological instruments and made possible improvement of the quality and duration of life. But this was achieved in a deeply contradictory register that generated well-being for some but denied it to others.

The conquest of the Americas combined with importing slaves from Africa was the first act in the construction of an ever-deepening polarization. The technology of communications that never ceased to improve and to surprise us went hand in hand with increasing sophistication and advances in war industries.

The strategy was to use force in order to achieve superiority by creating disproportions in the conqueror's favor. The Europeans were intruding in culturally unknown lands where great civilizations were flourishing. They did not arrive to discover the world. Their adventure was, rather, inspired by the imaginary promise of wealth and power. It was confirmed as soon as they encountered humans with tan skin and adorned with gold as described in the chronicles. It was not enough for them that they were received as envoys or as great lords, which they were far from being. The important thing for them was to eradicate, from the outset, any other space or entity of power.

The military strategy used for the first expansion was the same used in our day—a strategy of overdimensionality, of domineering disproportion based on shock and awe as an initial measure of discipline and hierarchic structuration. In a parallel way, the technological strategy was to create the required tools to make possible that disproportion and subjugation. Europe and, later on, the United States became the generating and profiting center of a process in which the whole planet, with all its components (nature and society), was being placed—voluntarily or not—at the disposition of capital, the only recognized subject in this history.

This was established principally by the combination of three things: (1) the conversion of small-scale exchange into large-scale trade, (2) the massive extermination of previous societal structures, and (3) the relocation of whole peoples, with a consequent loss of their cultural and geographical referents, knowledge, and technologies.

Capitalism commodified an ever-increasing number of products— many more than those initially offered in the markets. The idea of progress destroyed the compensating circularity of the relations between society and nature, and established in its place a dynamic of endlessly appropriative growth that had to appeal to war as an instrument of control and that kept on undermining the societal and ecological constructions in which it penetrated.

The immense territories in which gold and silver mines were found, whose extraction were based on slave or tributary labor, were constantly called upon to increase their production. The wealth sources expanded beyond precious metals to other minerals, fibers, and various natural elements that, with the advance of capitalist technology, became raw materials for the processes of production of goods. Nature became resources (Scott 1998) and people became workers or, even worse, just a labor force.

This was how the linear, abusive, and unbalanced use of nature under all its forms pushed the planet towards a tragedy of great proportions. For the moment would arrive at which the levels of human looting and exploitation went beyond their capacity to recuperate, beyond the elasticity of the environment. Capital's destructive forces have been much bigger than its constructive or generative forces, as Marx showed.[3]

The construction of a new territoriality, a new way of life, started then. It changed radically the social relations as well as the conception of intersubjectivity with which the environment is forged. Interactions changed from subject-subject to subject-object.

The Foundational Genocide

Before 1492 [America] was, in the current view, a thriving, stunningly diverse place, a tumult of languages, trade and culture. . . . Much of this world vanished after Columbus, swept away by disease and subjugation. So thorough was the erasure that within a few generations neither conqueror nor conquered knew that this world had existed (Mann 2006: 31).

The wealth from those regions and the establishment of hierarchical and discriminatory cultural relations served to legitimate the original violence and the implementation of tutelary relationships, a pattern that afterwards was incessantly repeated in all processes of subjugation of populations. According to this view, domination fulfilled a civilizational mission based on the symbolic creation of the margins, a kind of social emptiness to be redeemed or filled. Peoples, cultures, and geographies

---

3. In addition to Marx, many critical voices within modernity worried about the ecological predatory nature of capitalism. There were many contributions in the social sciences and in literature and art, but also among those with some practical experiences. See, among others, Charles Fourier (1772–1837), William Morris (1834–1896), Robert Owen (1771–1858), and, more recently, André Gorz (1923–2007).

were placed in a position of inferiority or exteriorization to be subjugated. Physical extermination was combined with moral and cultural extermination.

As opposed to the view defended by many historians that Europe was the locus of the birth of capitalism, it seems to us essential to test the hypothesis that it was rather in the geosocial nodule formed by the violent and conflictual articulation between Europe, America, and Africa that the complex scenario of capitalism as a planetary organizing system was created. There a perverse relationship between the center and its margins or peripheries appeared. Also there, a polarity was forged allowing the creation of the double circuits of exploitation that took away wealth to impose the consumption of goods whose manufacture it made possible.

The first major environmental tremor in the capitalist world-system occurred when the Europeans arrived in the Americas. The most important component in that environmental tremor was the destruction of local populations by the abusive use of their labor energy, and through an underground biological war. The latter was not planned but arrived with the bacteria and viruses brought by the conquerors and the rats that accompanied them. Two-thirds of the almost sixty million inhabitants estimated to have been living in the Americas in 1492 were eliminated in the following fifty years (Mann 2006).

The environmental dynamics that followed the first genocide will never be repaired because in those killings and in the burning of books and other cultural instruments containing the inventory of the accumulated knowledge about nature and the cosmos, a great part of the history and of the experience related to the knowledge and care of the environment was forever lost. Tenochtitlán was the center of a flourishing civilization that kept under its control a vast territory with twenty-five million people. The number was reduced in a very few years to about six to eight million. The new scarcity of the indigenous population was remedied by the settlement of populations brought from Africa, with other life experiences, originally from other environmental conditions, and with different knowledge, which was not easily adaptable to the new milieu. This provoked new discrepancies at all levels.

A second component of this environmental tremor was the vertiginous greed with which the conquerors plundered the riches of the American continent. The new settlers eagerly extracted mainly gold and silver but also plants, animals, natural dyes, and so many other wonders that America gave to the world. They did not hesitate because of collateral losses that were the costs of the objectivation of nature, a process that continued to redesign the environment.

The enormous mining of gold and silver—about 100,000 tons of silver and 50,000 tons of gold (Garner 1988; Macleod 1990)—created space to perceive the existence of other types of riches that, bit by bit, were incorporated into the world market. The effect on the invaders of the splendor they found in the places where they arrived leaves no doubt of the cultural greatness of the American peoples and of the exuberance of the environment, something that would be repeated with their specificities in other continents.

The more remarkable the invaders found the cities, the more aggressive and depredating was their arrival. Whole peoples and nature were destroyed and with them their own environmental technology. The creative relationship with nature; manipulation of microclimates and ecological diversities; the small units of floating agriculture (*chinampas*) to supply Tenochtitlán and other similar cities; the networks of aqueducts that are still visible in Mesoamerica and the Andean regions; medical, nutritive, and decorative use of plants and animals; terraces to guarantee a nondepredating agriculture capable of saving water; the work of metals, ceramics, and dyes not known in Europe; channels for internal navigation; the knowledge of the stars; mathematics; and many other discoveries that had generated a very different technological complex than that of the Europeans and that, usually, was based on care for Mother Earth or *Pachamama*, on which are contained not only the human beings, but all the other beings. Almost nothing of all this received the attention of the conquerors. Their objective was the improvement of their status in their remote lands, far away from America, in an arrogant and ignorant Europe.

The sensation of abundance and the results of the illegitimate appropriation implanted the logic of looting at all levels. To snatch the riches of the earth, to change nature—including human nature—into objects of enrichment, impeded the valuation of the benefits of a complementary technology, which would not yield as much revenue in either the short or the long term. The reorganization of the population promoted by the conquerors, which consisted in the concentration of the different peoples the better to control them and made them abandon the seminomadic practices that allowed adaptation to the various ecological conditions of their surroundings, was a third component of harm to the environment. The relationship with nature changed, the yearly cycles broke down, and the extraction started to be devastating due to the disproportion with which it was made. The intersubjective complementary relation that made possible the mutual creation of nature and society in the process began to be lost.

Unidimensionality and the unique subject was combined with the specialization of the territories. Without any versatility, territories became designated by each one's exclusive use: mining, farming, livestock. This resulted in even greater and quicker environmental erosion.

The mental image is that of a carved-up and disintegrated territory that was to be rearticulated through the market, communication networks, and geopolitics to achieve a controlled, disciplined, and directed integration.

Geography of World Domination

The conquest of the Americas was coincident with a process in Africa that evolved in a different manner. The difficulties of entering the African territories were mainly a consequence of the high density of the forests and the implacability of the deserts, as well as the difficult navigability of the biggest rivers. It took a long time for the explorers to determine the water courses of those rivers. Moreover, they were mysteriously attacked without even knowing in the beginning where the arrows were coming from or how to protect themselves against their poisons (De Gramont 1975; Forbath 1977). To this it is necessary to add the strong competition to seize the African coasts and territories between the Portuguese, British, French, and Spaniards, and later the Belgians, to mention only the Europeans.

For quite a long time, Europeans had to limit themselves to kidnapping or buying Africans near the coasts. The sale of slaves became a huge business associated with the looting of the Americas, making easier the subjugation of the peoples of the so-called New World. African slaving was one of the major instruments in the destruction-destructuration of the previous civilizations in Africa and the Americas. According to explorer Stanley's estimates, for each 50,000 enslaved Africans, another 33,000 died (Forbath 1977).

The dimensions of the slave trade increased steadily, reaching its maximum of about ten million in the eighteenth century (Forbath 1977). As a business, slavery complemented that of the precious metals. It was the carnal gold of the time, materialized by millions of Africans sacrificed to its process. It is estimated that the population of Africa oscillated around sixty million, approximately the same quantity as in the Americas. The estimate of losses varies between one- to two-thirds, including those who died during the capture and the voyage. An average of between 27,000 and 40,000 African slaves arrived in America each year (James 1963).

The Full Spectrum Dominance

The discovery that the world is round made it clear that there was not a *beyond* that was indefinite or impossible. Everything could be known and controlled. It was necessary only to create the required technological tools to make possible the great capitalist utopia—the "full spectrum dominance" (Joint Chiefs of Staff 2000)—that is, the submission of all the materiality of the world to the law of value.

Means of penetration over land, through the air, under the sea, and across space followed the interoceanic means of communication. Once ships reached all coasts, the capitalist scheme was implemented with railways opening up the veins of all continents to spread the sap to all centers of processing and power. The territories were delineated with a new logic. They were drawn with functional hierarchical criteria, social relations assuming a new order based on new specialties. The continents were broken up to allow the construction of diverse kinds of pathways for trade, investment, and plunder. The reproduction of capital became more important than life and subjugated it. Everything in the world became abstract and acquired the form of value flowing to the center.

War became an industry. It ceased to be an extreme situation of relations among peoples or social groups, and instead became a vertebral characteristic of the expansion of capitalist relations and one of the pillars of its transformative strength. The world incorporated the progress brought about by repetitive and self-reproducing violence at all levels, as in the relation between the so-called center and its margins.

The spectacular development of the productive forces and of the capabilities of production accomplished by capitalism made it the articulator of all the production processes of material life, which were thus incorporated into the dynamics of extensive reproduction. The capitalist blossoming that made possible the development of the sciences as well as the growth and diversification of production and communications had, however, feet of clay. It swallowed the chicken of the golden eggs and destroyed its sources of life. It was a King Midas.

The huge scales of production-appropriation-objectivation attained were oriented to dominating everything. They were also disproportionate in relation to the capacity of nature to regenerate itself or to that of human beings to contribute to their creation. In a paradoxical way, they were and are coexistent components of the historical rise and decline of the first world-system at the level of the whole planet.

During the sixteenth century the geography of capitalism was formed. But it was only in the nineteenth century that the world productive base deepened and made irreversible the trajectories of evolution of the system within the system itself. The industrial revolutions opened up the way for growth and abundance, improved life expectancy, and made it possible to reach the cosmos and the microcosms. But this resulted as well in a trajectory of suicide, into what the World Wildlife Fund (WWF) called an "ecological overshoot" (WWF 2010: 10) that "occurs when humanity's demand on nature exceeds the biosphere's supply, or regenerative capacity" (Global Footprint Network 2009).

As capitalism reached its technological maturity, the proposal became the grand-scale appropriation of nature. The territory had been converted into an object, the simple base for that appropriation, and as such it was fragmented, reticulated, and shredded. The objective was to individualize each one of its components, potential goods or raw materials, to appraise and order them as a first step to their massive exploitation. The same happened at the end of the twentieth century with the internal structures of human life that were transformed into sequences of genes that could be individually manipulated, reaching the extreme of trying to convert them into private property.

The building of railways, the transformation of iron into machinery of communication and production, was built over the metal skeleton on which capital advanced with its civilizing proposal. Grand-scale mining extraction and the metal-mechanic industry became the foundation and simultaneously the beneficiaries and the lever of one of the strongest moments in the development of capitalism. They were also at the same time the sequential circle that marked the guidelines for the future—to extract more metals to be used in the production of more machinery needed to extract more natural materials in order to transform them into tools for new appropriations or cheap food to make the workers' army able to manufacture more machinery. All this was mediated by the suction of the energy, nerves, and brains of Black, Amerindian, Yellow—and White—human beings.

The problem is not in the iron, but rather in capitalism itself. When iron started to be replaced by plastic, ceramics, or polymeric materials, when the communication networks began to be made with optical fiber, when the great machines changed into integrated circuits, and when the nanotechnologies lightened the industrial weight, capitalism did not become less harmful. It multiplied its depredation and damages.

The capitalist mode of doing and going beyond its specific materiality, supported by science and by the new instruments of war, became ever more dangerous due to the damage it did to life and the environment. Despite the creation of the so-called clean technologies, the period from 1950 to today has been catastrophic. Since 41 percent of CO_2 emissions come from energy generation (Earth Policy Institute n.d.), electricity consumption has increased 342 percent between 1965 and 2008, while oil production has increased 822 percent between 1950 and 2008 (Intergovernmental Panel on Climate Change 2009a: 39).

According to the Global Footprint Network (2009), "Since the 1970s, humanity has been in ecological overshoot with annual demand on resources exceeding what Earth can regenerate each year."

Ecological damage grew exponentially in this same period. In its 2011 climate behavior study, the Berkeley Earth Organization confirms a dangerous and maybe irreversible planetary trend of global warming, with all the ecological changes that follow. Their data permit us to present the graphic on the following page (Figure 2.1), quite eloquent about the acceleration of that process and its link to industrialization, energy overuse, and the modern way of life. It is interesting to see in this graphic the noticeable decrease of the temperature of the earth in the postwar periods (those wars being the US Civil War, WWI and WWII, the Korean War, and the Vietnam War), after the destruction of a big portion of the productive structure of the planet. After its reconstruction, an accelerated and dangerous recovery is observed.

Figure 2.1 Decadal land-surface average temperature.

Historical Climate Change

The world reached a critical ecological stage as it progressed. James Scott (1998) showed how capitalism disarranged nature to reorder it again according to its interests. It destroyed whole forests to remake them but in a rational, administrated, and alienated way. The species that were unnecessary from a productive perspective were eliminated while the profitable species, defined as necessary, were strengthened. It ignored the fact that the species that at first sight seemed to be harmful were in many cases those that defined the limits of growth and helped to maintain the proportionality of the whole.

Nature was re-created, conserved, and protected with a predatory-utilitarian objective that paradoxically ended up destroying it, because unilateralizing the natural behavior cancels its complex dynamics, despite science's efforts to recuperate complexity.

Ecological overshoot began in the 1970s, when "the Earth's human population began consuming renewable resources faster than ecosystems can regenerate them and releasing more CO_2 than ecosystems can absorb" (WWF 2010: 36). In fact, the productive overdimensioning was born in the period between wars, with the introduction of "Fordism," and was expanded worldwide after the Second World War, where Americanism and mass production become generalized in the capitalist world-system.

In the last decades of the twentieth century damage grew exponentially, as did production. If in the past the increase in damage could be counted in centuries or decades, it is now counted by years or even by months. This is the case of the situation of risk to the Amazon forest, Earth's greatest ecological reservoir, which every year loses, only on the Brazilian side, around 20,000 hectares.

According to the World Wildlife Fund (2010), in 2007 the ecological footprint exceeded by 50 percent Earth's capacity of recuperation. The giant Gangotri Glacier—whose ice melt supplies 70 percent of the Ganges flow—is decreasing thirty-five meters per year, twice as quickly as it was twenty years ago. Mount Kilimanjaro, Africa's tallest mountain, lost 33 percent of its ice cap between 1989 and 2000. The glaciers in Peru and Bolivia lost one-third of their surface between 1970 and 2006 (Earth Policy Institute n.d.). Between 1990 and 1997, between 4.1 and 6.9 million hectares of humid tropical forest were lost each year, with a further 1.6 to 3.0 million hectares of forest visibly degraded (Achard et al. 2002: 999). Madagascar, biologically one of the richest areas of Earth, lost half of its rain forest (3.8 million hectares) between 1950 and 1985 (of 7.6 million that existed in 1850 and of an original surface of 11.2 million before the arrival of Europeans). In conclusion, the average ratio of overall deforestation was 111,000 hectares annually (Green and Sussman, 1990), and each year an average of 700,000 hectares of jungles and forests is lost.

The populations of wild vertebrate species decreased on average about one-third (31 percent) in the world between 1970 and 2006. The decline was particularly acute in the tropics (59 percent) and in freshwater ecosystems (41 percent) (Convenio sobre la Diversidad Biológica 2010: 26):

> Species in all groups with known trends are, on average, being driven closer to extinction, with amphibians facing the greatest risk and warm water reef-building corals showing the most rapid deterioration in status [for their proximities to oil deposits, among other reasons].
>
> Among selected vertebrate, invertebrate and plant groups, between 12% and 55% of species are currently threatened with extinction. Species of birds and mammals used for food and medicine are on average facing a greater extinction risk than those not used for such purposes. Preliminary assessments suggest that 23% of plant species are threatened.

In less than one century capitalism has been able to reverse what the planet was able to create only in millions of years. There is no doubt that this points to the immense power achieved by science and technology but, more than that, to the perversion with which this system understands and confronts nature.

Because the tropics are the sites of more genetic concentration, diversity, and variability, the ecological overshoot made them contract 60 percent in less than forty years (WWF 2010). Recent studies concerning the Amazon show the accelerated deterioration within the region. Highways, train tracks, and hydroelectric power plants are built, while pastures for cattle are being enlarged and monoculture and similar endeavors are encouraged in the name of progress. Between 2000 and 2010, this development destroyed 240,000 square kilometers of forest. If the economic plans continue as expected, it is estimated that in twenty years only 45 percent of the forest that exists today will remain (Red Amazónica 2012). The higher footprint, however, is in North America and Europe. These regions are relying on the biocapacity of the other areas of the world (Global Footprint Network 2009: 37).

> If everyone in the world lived like an average resident of the United States or the United Arab Emirates, then a biocapacity equivalent to more than 4.5 Earths would be required to keep up with humanity's consumption and CO_2 emissions. Conversely, if everyone lived like the average resident of India, humanity would be using less than half the planet's biocapacity (WWF 2010: 38).

Capitalist development leads the planet into a fatal disaster, apoptosis. Never before in history has capitalism developed the technological capabilities it has today. Never before has science registered so many and such important advances. And, in a paradoxical way, never before has capitalism found itself incapable of ensuring the perdurability of life and of the planet it has brought to the edge of a terminal catastrophe.

Catastrophe is here to stay as the capitalist system continues to foster it. All the so-called solutions proposed up to now reinforce the commodification of nature. This is the case with environmental services, which stimulate a relationship of profitability or unilineal benefit between humans and nature and justify the extended global predatory behavior with some few elements of nonpredatory care. The sense of competence, the objectivation, and the negation of alterity have pushed the world to unsustainability. It is the capitalist way of life. It contains the seeds of its own destruction. Capitalism is producing the unlivability of the planet. The snake has bitten its tail.

The Systemic Challenge

System unsustainability has created a permanent and insoluble crisis that shows different faces, offering a confused picture of isolated or independent phenomena, hiding its internal connection and integrality. Systemic instability, manifested in the multiple and overwhelming crisis, is the signal both of capitalism's incapacity to restore its conditions of possibility and systemic alternatives' capacity to weaken and overcome capitalism.

The capitalist system is irretrievably declining, but it is still strong enough to destroy any other attempt of social organization on its way down. Evidence about the contradictory systemic apoptosis is clear and overwhelming, but evidence of the possible emergence of another systemic social organization of life is proportionally rather slender and not sufficiently visible.

Nevertheless, it is possible to recognize some diverse, dispersed, and shy attempts to dislocate the logical basis of dominant prevailing global society, and to create or re-create some other noncapitalist organizational forms.

Capitalist relations are the cohesive force of this world-system, but there are no homogeneous societies. They are always a convergence or a warp of different visions in a circumstantial mode of collective self-organization, even if most of the time one implemented by those in power. All societies contain contradictory impulses that have their origin in different, confrontational conceptions and historical practices.

With a vast diversity, with nonstatist imaginaries that are decentered, unlike the current dominant ones, it is possible to glimpse, in the proposals for plurinational states—which means pluricultural and multisocietal and recognized as part of an overwhelmed totality that transcends and includes them—those other perspectives of the world that were subdued but alive and have not been updated for more than five hundred years. Today they are assuming political force and visibility in the face of the suicidal absurdity, the apoptosis, in which capitalism has placed the planet.

Polarized and mostly thrown to the margins both by the growing general precariousness to which capitalism has condemned the dominated of the world and by the obstinacy of their *pachamámica* consciousness, they are today the spearhead in what is a possible socio-civilizing bifurcation, with many different faces. These incipient potential systemic alternatives carry the contradictions of modernity in which they have been forged. But they have the strength of their ecological appropriateness and a new meaning of life. Modernity, and not only capitalism, is being criticized.

One of the most relevant spearheads of these potential ways of bifurcation may be found in the experiences of transformation processes in Latin America, with a wide spectrum of proposals. The Zapatista movement postulates the "world that contains all the worlds," and the Suma Qamaña and the Sumak Kawsay developed in Bolivia and Ecuador reconceptualize social and biological relations, understanding totality as an integrated complex in which humans are not superior but rather one piece in the whole assembly. For them, complementarity is the main concept, accumulation is inappropriate because time is circular, and material production is submitted to reproduction of integral life.

The planet has come to a moment of enormous crisis but also historical opportunity. Capitalism is declining, but nothing permits us to presume what will be the outcome. What is sure is that ecological disaster has no solution without a reformulation of the relation of humans and nature.

The modern material civilization, despite the great discoveries in science and the spectacular nature of its accomplishments, is not sustainable. There are multiple hints of the upcoming of a new material civilization in which society and nature interact and complement each other. In this new scheme, society and nature would not interact by a relationship of power and domination in any sense. This very complex issue will have to be forged as it is put into practice.

So far there are no reasons to assume that this new material civilization will actually become real or that capitalism will be replaced by another scheme of general organization of life. The few certainties that we have, however, indicate that this material civilization has reached its limits and is leading to the destruction of life. Moreover, life struggles to survive through subverting the fundamentals of modernity and reinventing itself in as many diversified ways as possible. The complexity of life keeps adjusting and creating passageways suitable for the development of new civilizing horizons.

Chapter 3

Economic Inequality, Stratification, and Mobility

*by Roberto Patricio Korzeniewicz
and Timothy Patrick Moran*

Most studies of inequality, stratification, and mobility assume that national boundaries delineate the relevant units of analysis. They then proceed to draw universal conclusions from the patterns found in very specific areas of the world—most often (probably 90 percent) in high-income nations. Moreover, the methodological assumptions guiding this literature generally preclude it from seriously addressing theoretically, or even empirically, a key question: What, how, and why has the relationship been between globalization and inequality, as experienced over time by different populations across the world?

Of course, if we seek to address this question from a world-historical perspective, we face the constraint that often adequate empirical information is lacking. Relevant data on *world* income distributions are not easily forthcoming. Even contemporary income data are collected primarily by national statistical offices that presume that national boundaries delineate the only possible unit of analysis. Furthermore, such national income data have seldom been collected over sufficiently long periods of time. The systematic collection of such data is largely a post-1945 phenomenon, and even then mostly limited to high-income countries.

Keeping in mind these constraints, we shall try to advance from a world-historical perspective nine propositions, which we believe can help theorize social stratification, mobility, and inequality. We have developed some of these arguments in *Unveiling Inequality: A World-Historical Perspective* (Korzeniewicz and Moran 2009), and more extensive empirical analyses of worldwide income and inequality data that propel these propositions can be found there. We argue that inequality should be understood as a world-historical phenomenon. Accounts of inequality that focus on discrete populations of the world are bound to miss the key global interactions that shape this phenomenon, even within those discrete populations.

Proposition 1

Levels of inequality within countries over the last one hundred years show two clusters. Some nations have been characterized by relatively high inequality and others by relatively low inequality.

Contemporary data indicate that most countries are located in one of the clusters. One is characterized by relatively low levels of inequality, with Gini coefficients below 0.340. The second cluster has Gini coefficients above 0.500—that is, significantly higher levels of inequality. The high-income low-inequality nations cluster has in recent history included all of western Europe, as well as countries such as Japan and, frequently, the United States. Much of eastern Europe falls within this cluster as well, and so do several of the East Asian nations that have experienced high rates of growth in recent decades. The countries that are low income and high inequality tend to be located in Latin America, Africa, and Asia. There has been considerable stability in the composition of both these clusters, even during the recent decades of "globalization."

Of course, not all nations fit neatly into one of the two clusters. There are several "hybrid" cases (such as Argentina), and there are instances of countries that have shifted in and out of one particular cluster (such as the United States). However, there are virtually no examples of countries shifting over time from one cluster into the other.

Proposition 2

The origin of patterns of high and low inequality within the current geographical state boundaries can be traced back in time to at least before the eighteenth century.

In areas characterized by high inequality, institutional arrangements selectively excluding large sectors of the population from access to wealth and power historically were imposed by the primarily European elites that benefited from such arrangements, and generally entailed between-group hierarchies—what Tilly (1998) terms "bounded categories"—organized around the ascribed characteristic of race. Fredrickson (1982) has summarized such arrangements as regimes of "white supremacy." Through the past two centuries, White supremacy provided one of the most powerful frameworks for justifying, maintaining, and defending the institutional-arrangements characteristic of high inequality within countries.

A very different early pattern is found in areas with lower inequality that (later on) became characterized by high levels of income, such as New England and other areas of European settlement. According to one line of interpretation, the main difference between these areas and those where high inequality prevailed had to do with endowments. De Ferranti et al. (2004: 110) argue about New England, for example, "Land was cheap and labor was costly. Such circumstances were radically different from those found elsewhere in the hemisphere, and fostered a remarkable degree of equality."

In the case of high-inequality countries, institutional arrangements can most often be traced back to slavery. It is less clear how far back we can trace the institutional origins of low inequality in Continental Europe or the relative significance of changes in inequality in these latter areas prior to the nineteenth century. The available historical literature, just like contemporary studies of inequality and stratification, largely does not discuss trends and patterns of income distribution in a world-historical perspective, but limits its focus to specific (and again most often high-income) sets of nations.

Proposition 3

The persistence of such distinct patterns of within-country inequality for such a long period of time suggests situations of equilibria, in which opposing forces are balanced. We designate these as high-inequality equilibria (HIE) and low-inequality equilibria (LIE).

We do not mean to imply that HIE and LIE arrangements are entrenched in unchanging institutional arrangements. There are multilayered and shifting constructions of solidarities, cleavages, and social identities that regularly challenge these arrangements. However, such challenges, while sometimes successful in inducing change, generally are followed by counterresponses and institutional transformations that over longer periods of time generate continuities in income distributions.

Proposition 4

While much of the literature conceptualizes situations of high and low inequality as representing independent institutional paths, a world-systems perspective calls attention to the ways in which HIE and LIE are relational and interact over time.

From a world-systems perspective, the eventual competitive advantages of the institutions involved in LIE since the nineteenth century emerged precisely in response to certain rigidities that came to characterize the coercive institutions characteristic of HIE.

We must reject the preconception that the institutional arrangements of HIE have been intractably tied to inefficient forms of organization of production and markets. In fact, after European colonization and until the nineteenth century, the areas characterized by HIE (e.g., Latin America and the Caribbean) where coercive labor arrangements (e.g., slavery or the forced recruitment of indigenous populations) were used in high-yielding activities (e.g., commercial agriculture and mining) constituted in their time a world epicenter for the creation and accumulation of wealth.

Coercive strategies of labor control, including but not limited to plantations, represented in their own time what Joseph Schumpeter (1942) would characterize as innovative activities, yielding extraordinary levels of wealth. The "extractive institutions" associated with HIE provided crucial competitive advantages to the elites benefiting from such arrangements. In addition, they did so by simultaneously providing a very effective basis for wealth maximization and economic growth for several hundred years.

By contrast, many of the areas that contained within themselves the type of arrangements we would today characterize as constituting LIE (particularly those in the Americas) were relatively marginal and perceived at the time as fairly impoverished. Perhaps due to these difficulties, the entrepreneurial activities developed in these areas sought to exploit the interstices left open by mercantilist arrangements, such as smuggling and filling commercial niches not easily met by colonial empires.

From a comparative perspective, then, it is important not to extrapolate from the logic of economic arrangements that subsequently became successful criteria of rationality for evaluating HIE and LIE (criteria that were simply not in operation at the time). Rather than retrospectively evaluating "design" according to some standard that emerged hundreds of years later, we are on better ground if we consider different institutional paths to be the outcome of processes of conflict and negotiation between social forces that enjoyed different degrees of relative bargaining power, and note that the consequences of specific institutional paths have changed over time precisely due to their interaction.

Proposition 5

Between-country inequality can be understood best as involving a HIE over at least the last two centuries.

The overall level of inequality between nations—as expressed by a Gini coefficient that measures dispersion of gross national income (GNI) between countries—has been both extremely high and persistent for the past two centuries. The available empirical data on national incomes unequivocally show that inequality between countries in the twentieth century is higher than the inequality exhibited within any single nation-state. In fact, if we were to construct a global map of inequality, showing where each household or individual stood vis-à-vis everyone else in the world (that is, combining information on within- and between-country inequality), the relative standing of each household or individual would be shaped most heavily by location in a poor or wealthy nation; that is, by between-nations inequality.

Figure 3.1 shows two different estimates of population-weighted between-country inequality over the last two centuries. We use GNI adjusted alternatively by purchasing-power parities (PPP) and exchange rates (FX)—see the statistical appendix at the end of this chapter for further explanation. According to both estimates, between-country inequality remains today above the boundary demarcating within-country HIE. Moreover, the data based on exchange rates place countries with high between-country inequality above those with the highest observed within-country inequality.

Over the 1820–2007 period, there have been major shifts in the organization of production and consumption, the rise and fall of very different patterns of state/market interaction, two world wars, and revolutionary change among large swaths of the world's population. Despite the turbulence implied in these transformations, which observers might expect to have a significant impact, overall inequality between countries as an

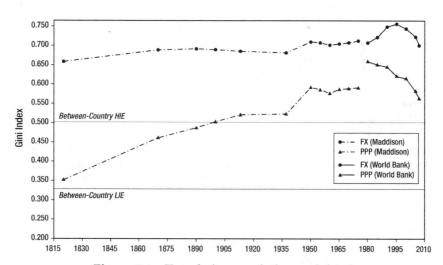

Figure 3.1   Trends in population-weighted between-country inequality, 1820–2007.

Sources: Authors' calculations based on two samples: 1820–1975 Maddison (1995), 1980–2007 World Bank (2008).

output of global interaction showed remarkable stability. This stability is indicative of a high-inequality equilibrium similar to the kind we established regarding patterns of within-country inequalities.

Of course, to say that interactions between countries have constituted a system that reached equilibrium through most of the nineteenth and twentieth centuries is not to say that the trajectories of all individual countries showed rigidity and stability. We know that during the same period there was a considerable amount of mobility for individual states (e.g., from Canada and the United States in the nineteenth century to China and India today). But over time, such cases of "successful" upward mobility were accompanied by the stable persistence of high inequality between nations, resembling the HIE that characterizes divergent patterns of within-country inequality.

Proposition 6

The HIE characterizing the current distribution of wealth between countries emerged only gradually before the nineteenth century.

The existing empirical data are sparse and much more work is required to reach robust conclusions, but the evidence suggests that until the eighteenth century the overall gap between wealthy and poor populations was not as pronounced as it would become in the nineteenth and the twentieth centuries. To an important extent, this was because the vast majority of people faced similar conditions. At one end of the social spectrum, "the world between the fifteenth and eighteenth centuries consisted of one vast peasantry, where between 80% and 90% of people lived from the land and from nothing else" (Braudel 1981: 49). The extent of disparities within this vast majority of people (for example, between African slaves in the Americas or peasants in continental Europe) was probably not very pronounced. Moreover, even between skilled and unskilled workers within Europe, wage differentials were not very great.

At the other end of the distribution in the eighteenth century we find what Braudel (1982: ch. 5) describes as a small oligarchy (often less than 1 percent of a population) in which wealth and power were concentrated. But the relative command over wealth of this small elite probably did not differ significantly among various areas of the world-economy. As we noted earlier, much of the raw-material production carried out under coercive forms of labor organization yielded very high levels of wealth for elites.

Between a small aristocracy and the peasantry, during the fifteenth to eighteenth centuries, there were developing middle strata, often called bourgeoisie. Braudel (1982: 476) estimates that even in France, this bourgeoisie (*honorables hommes*, such as merchants, legal advocates and notaries, doctors, apothecaries, and other professionals) constituted roughly 8 percent of the population. Colonial areas, again, had their own equivalent of this stratum in the form of government officials and bureaucrats, professionals, and merchants. Skilled workers in many areas were an additional component of this stratum.

To assess the relative level of inequality prior to the nineteenth century, we have assembled Gini coefficients for the 1500–1820 period in Table 3.1. To be sure, data on per capita national incomes and within-country income distributions are virtually nonexistent. We are therefore forced to carry out such an exercise using very speculative figures. Despite such caveats, the stylized data presented in Table 3.1 allow us to make some important points about the relationship of the between- and within-country distributions for the period under consideration.

The first scenario of Table 3.1 shows the Gini coefficients calculated on the basis of the average per capita incomes estimated by Maddison (2006) for thirty-one regions of the world. As registered, these Gini coefficients are quite low, ranging from .095 in 1500 to .155 in 1820. This pattern is compatible with the notion that overall inequality between countries was not yet very pronounced for the period under consideration. The average per capita incomes of various areas of the world-economy were not yet

Table 3.1 Historical Gini Coefficients Measuring World Inequality

Scenario 1
> between-country inequality

1500	0.095
1600	0.103
1700	0.119
1820	0.155

Scenario 2
>(a) assuming a high polarization distribution in noncore areas

1600	0.342
1700	0.351
1820	0.372

>(b) assuming a high polarization distribution in noncore areas
    but not in India or China

1600	0.264
1700	0.269
1820	0.303

Scenario 3
> assuming a high polarization distribution everywhere

1600	0.364
1700	0.373
1820	0.393

Source: Authors' calculation based on Maddison (2001) and Braudel (1981, 1982).

very far apart from one another, and became much more polarized only by the nineteenth century.

In the other three sections of Table 3.1, we have calculated Gini coefficients for various hypothetical scenarios that combine data on within- and between-country distributions. To carry out this combination, we have used Maddison's data on between-country distributions and Braudel's estimates on within-country patterns of stratification.[1] The overall level of inequality is low in any of the relevant scenarios, ranging from a low of between .264 and .364 in 1600 to a high of between .303 and .393 in 1820, depending on the assumptions of each of three scenarios. This indicates that most of the existing inequality during the period under consideration reflected the patterns found in within- rather than between-country distributions.

To some extent, this is a consequence of the relatively small volume of surplus being generated above subsistence. Milanovic, Lindert, and Williamson (2007) argue that as long as this surplus and the size of the elite population are relatively small, summary measures of inequality will move within a narrower range than when either or both undergo significant growth.

In short, for much of the period between the fifteenth and late eighteenth centuries, the national boundaries of states had not yet become the crucial criteria organizing categorical inequality. We illustrate these patterns, in Figure 3.2,[2] with a stylized representation of the three populations that eventually became contemporary Brazil, Portugal, and the United States.

The basic notion represented in Figure 3.2 is that, early on, nation-states were only an incipient marker of inequality, as illustrated in the figure by the dotted line demarcating state boundaries. State boundaries became crucial only over time, illustrated in Figure 3.2 by the accentuation of the line demarcating national state boundaries over the three represented "moments." On the other hand, other boundaries (cities and towns at one "moment," or the expansion of empires at another) were probably more significant markers of inequality in the earlier "moments," illustrated by the accentuated lines representing such boundaries in the figure. These nonstate boundaries became relatively less significant over time, represented by the fading away or even the disappearance of the lines stylistically representing such boundaries in Figure 3.2.

---

1. Braudel's estimates for seventeenth-century France are that elites comprised 1 percent of the population, the middle strata 9 percent, and the poorest strata 90 percent of the total. Of course, these data might underestimate the extent of the polarization characterizing some areas at the time. According to Braudel (1982: 490), in 1600 Naples elites "might have 100,000 crowns a year, while their subjects were lucky to have three crowns to rub together." However, for the purposes of this exercise, the next three scenarios extend such a distribution of income to various populations of the world-economy.

2. The authors thank Jessica Giovachino for the design and construction of Figures 3.2 and 3.3.

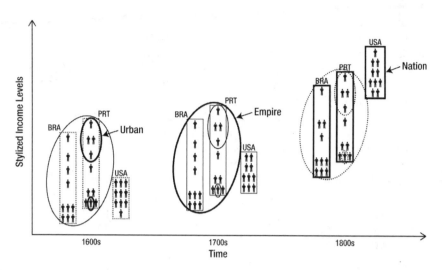

Figure 3.2 Stylized historical trends of inequality, 1600s–1800s.

♀ = Stylized country income deciles.
The three income distributions within each "moment" are stylized representations of what will eventually become Brazil, Portugal, and the United States.

Proposition 7

Over the last two centuries, the establishment of within-country LIE and the emergence of between-country HIE are not two separate processes. Rather, they are the outcome of the institutional arrangements undergirding world inequality.

The institutional arrangements of selective exclusion and categorical inequality that are the most salient distinguishing characteristic of HIE are just as central to the development and persistence of LIE.

In HIE, institutional arrangements enhance economic opportunities for elites while restricting the access of large sectors of the population to various forms of educational, political, or economic opportunity. Enhanced opportunities for elites and the restricted access of the majority are related. Selective exclusion serves to reduce competition among elites through institutional arrangements that simultaneously enhance competitive pressures among excluded populations in the arenas or markets to which these populations are restricted. In HIE, this selective exclusion operates fundamentally *within* national borders.

The role of selective exclusion is less evident in situations of LIE. In fact, the institutional-arrangements characteristic of LIE appear to differ from HIE precisely by the extent to which they enhance a broader access to educational, political, and/or economic opportunity for their overall population. Whereas HIE countries are most manifestly characterized by exclusion, ascription, and categorical inequality, LIE countries claim to be the very embodiment of universal opportunity, facilitating the possibility of success through individual achievement.

However, the institutional arrangements actually characteristic of LIE do restrict access to opportunity for large sectors of the population, but these excluded populations now are located primarily outside national borders. Selective exclusion, in the case of LIE, operates fundamentally through the very existence of national borders, reducing competitive pressures within these borders while enhancing competitive pressures among the excluded population outside those very same borders in the arenas or markets to which *these* populations are restricted.

When focusing only on wealthy nations, institutional arrangements indeed appear to be characterized primarily by inclusion, and economic growth and markets seem to constitute virtuous spheres where gain is fundamentally an outcome of effort. From such a perspective, success appears to be the outcome of individual achievement, as measured by universal criteria, via relatively unrestricted access to education and labor markets.

The relation of such virtuous inclusion with processes of selective exclusion can be observed only when we shift our unit of analysis to encompass the world as a whole. Such a shift reveals that the prevalence of "achieved" characteristics in today's wealthy nations has been attained through between-nations processes that hide how the institutional arrangements characteristic of LIE simultaneously reestablish privileges based on exclusion and "ascribed" characteristics.

Thus, while portrayed as inclusive in comparison to HIE, the property and political rights characteristic of LIE were generated through often-violent imposition over other arrangements that might have been characterized by even lower inequality. The very creation of national states in "nations of recent European settlement" required the subordination and/or elimination of indigenous populations. LIE in areas such as the United States or Canada eventually developed via two kinds of changes. Some institutional arrangements incompatible with LIE, such as slavery in the South of the United States, were abolished. Other arrangements entailing even higher inequality were forcibly ended. This is the case of indigenous populations in the "open frontiers" of areas of recent settlement, or of analogous groups in the cases of China and India during the nineteenth century.

Protectionism and restrictions on immigration in wealthy countries in the late nineteenth and early twentieth centuries had a similar effect, and were key to reversing the rise in within-country inequality across many of the wealthier countries. The "backlash" against global markets in the early twentieth century and the responses to within-country inequality among wealthier countries in following decades revolved around strengthening the nation-state as a basis upon which to organize categorical differences. Constraints on migration and the rise of the welfare state involved the consolidation of identities constructed around the nation-state and citizenship (Wright 2006).

The institutional arrangements of LIE and the national regulation of international migration in the twentieth century reduced competitive pressures among workers within wealthy nations and thereby contributed to the declining income inequality in wealthier nations at the time. But the institutional arrangements and market mechanisms that served to reduce inequality within high-income countries simultaneously generated or strengthened constraints that accentuated inequalities between countries. Constraints on international migration, for example, accentuated competitive pressures in labor markets elsewhere in the world, and in the process eliminated for much of the twentieth century the possibility of reducing the income gap between countries by the transfer of populations from poor to wealthy nations.

To resume: in LIE, institutions function in ways that restrict within-nations competitive pressures by selectively excluding important sectors of the population of other countries from some markets while including them in others. Over the twentieth century, restrictions on international migration or trade have been crucial forms of exclusion. Simultaneously, the same institutional arrangements moved towards pushing for inclusion in other markets, such as intellectual property. The institutional arrangements underpinning LIE detach the improvements and dislocation in a different way than in HIE. In LIE countries, the arrangements enhance the access of the overall population within a nation to improvement by using exclusion of populations residing outside the country, thus deflecting to other parts of the world any dislocation inherent in the process. As race became a crucial ascriptive criterion sustaining within-country HIE, national identity and citizenship constituted the central ascriptive criterion shaping between-country HIE.

Proposition 8

The single most immediate and effective means of global social mobility for populations in most countries of the world has been to migrate.

In particular, over the last two centuries, given the crucial role of nationality in shaping global stratification, "jumping" categories by moving from a poorer country to a wealthier one became a highly effective strategy of mobility (illustrated by Figure 3.3).

Figure 3.3 takes the relative global standing of country deciles of six nations that have considerable migration flows among them: the United States, Mexico, and Guatemala on the left side of the figure, and Australia, Malaysia, and Indonesia on the right side. Mexico is a receiving country for migrants from Guatemala, and a sending country to the

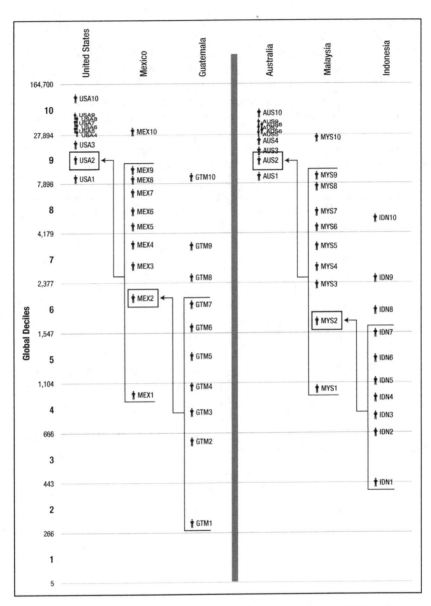

Figure 3.3 International migration as social mobility.

United States, just as Malaysia is a receiving country for migrants from Indonesia, and a sending country of migrants to Australia. The main point of the figure is to illustrate how global stratification produces strong incentives for migration for individuals and/or groups of people in relatively poorer countries.

In the case of Guatemala, for example, anyone belonging to the poorest seven deciles would be engaging in upward mobility by gaining access to the average income of the second poorest decile in Mexico. In the case of Mexico, the incentives are even more striking, as all but the wealthiest decile would find upward mobility in gaining access to the average income of the second poorest USA decile.

In Indonesia, anyone belonging to the poorest seven deciles would be engaging in upward mobility by gaining access to the average income of the second poorest decile in Malaysia. In the case of Malaysia relative to Australia, the incentives are even more striking, as all but the wealthiest decile of Malaysia would find upward mobility in gaining access to the average income of the second poorest decile in Australia.

Of course, migration is not merely the product of differentials in income incentives. Engaging in migration requires access to manifold resources—from those needed to meet the costs of transportation and entry into a foreign country, to those involving social networks that can facilitate access to housing and jobs—and these resources are not equally available to all populations within a given country. Furthermore, decisions to migrate are also based upon broader considerations regarding security, safety, well-being, and personal attachments. But migration, while often requiring a high level of courageous determination, tends to offer immediate and certain returns in economic upgrading. Migrants, in their crossing of such borders, reveal the boundaries of stratification to be global.

Proposition 9

Recent trends in globalization, characterized by a reduction in between-country inequalities, might represent a challenge to prevailing forms of categorical exclusion.

The very success of within-country LIE among wealthy nations through the twentieth century eventually led to the emergence of significant challenges to established patterns of selective exclusion in the between-country HIE. These challenges have revolved around the key institutional feature linking within-nation LIE and between-nation HIE—the exclusion of labor from poorer countries by the rich—and have taken two forms: increased migration (both documented and undocumented) and the rise of India and China.

The very growth of between-nation inequality through most of the last two centuries has become a driving force for the migration of labor and capital. Growing income disparities between countries over time have generated strong incentives (e.g., drastically lower wages in poor countries) for both the migration of workers to higher-wage markets and the outsourcing of skilled and unskilled jobs to peripheral countries. Both trends exercise a market bypass that in effect overcomes the twentieth-century institutional constraints on labor flows that characterized the development of LIE. Such are the processes at hand in the recent decline of between-country inequalities suggested earlier, in Figure 3.1.

As we have noted, between-nation inequality always has been characterized by the mobility of individual countries, such as Sweden in the late nineteenth century, Japan in the immediate post-1945 era, and South Korea in the 1970s and 1980s. But in the past, as we show, the upward mobility of individual countries took place within a setting whereby systemic inequality continued or became even more pronounced. The large populations of China and India make today's story different than before, as their effective mobility, even if limited to any one of those two countries, implies a potentially dramatic shift in patterns of between-nation inequality.

Current patterns of social stratification, mobility, and inequality might be transformed in the future as a consequence of the very opportunities generated by the growth of between-nation inequalities through much of the twentieth century. On the other hand, the interests challenged by such a transformation might engage in the type of protective reaction experienced in the early part of the twentieth century (although the size of India and China, together with their linkages to other countries in Asia and elsewhere, might contribute to producing very different outcomes than those of the twentieth century). Which forces become more significant, and at which rates, is less predictable.

Statistical Appendix

Figure 3.1

We measure inequality using the most popular measure, the Gini index. This summary measure provides a single statistic intended to capture the fluidity of income along the entire distribution. The Gini index ranges from zero (when a distribution has complete equality, every unit shares the same amount of income) and one (when a distribution has total inequality, one unit has all the income). The coefficients shown here are population-weighted.

The historical trends in between-nation inequality are based on our calculations employing two datasets. For the 1820–1975 series, we estimate inequality between twenty-four countries using the population and per capita gross domestic product data in Maddison (1995). Maddison's data are presented in a form of PPP dollars. So to obtain comparable FX figures we index Maddison's trend line to a base year

(1992) and apply per capita GNI, Atlas method data (World Bank 2008). Maddison indexes his own trend line to a base year's PPP-adjusted data, so our procedure is essentially the same as his. For the contemporary 1980–2007 series, we estimate inequality between 107 countries using the population and per capita GNI; again, Atlas method data published by the World Bank (2008).

Long-standing debates exist as to the relative merits of converting national income currencies to a comparable metric, and more specifically around the use of exchange rate (FX) vis-à-vis purchasing-power parity (PPP) data. While intuitively appealing because of their promise of better capturing differences among countries in access to welfare, PPP data have serious problems that are not usually acknowledged by their users, and we have provided considerable discussion elsewhere of many technical aspects that render such measures much less precise than usually assumed (Korzeniewicz and Moran 2009).

Despite our reservations about the PPP data (and especially in using them to capture longitudinal trends), and the theoretical considerations we use to justify our methodological decision to privilege FX conversions throughout the chapter, we do report both historical trend lines in the figure.

Figure 3.2

This figure uses highly stylized estimates of approximate income distributions within and between the relevant locations, as drawn from the arguments developed in greater detail in Korzeniewicz and Moran (2009).

Figure 3.3

The procedures to conceptualize global stratification and mobility employ the country income shares by population decile data from a large cross-national dataset (n=85 countries) we assembled (Korzeniewicz and Moran 2009). For each country, we calculated "country deciles"—the average GNI per capita income accruing to each 10 percent group. For example, the income share accruing to the richest 10 percent of the United States (USA10) is 27.6 percent, translating into an average income for the decile of $127,517 based on the GNI per capita for the United States in 2007. We then ranked these country deciles from poor to rich to establish global deciles (that is, each with 10 percent of the sampled population), their income boundaries, and their composition. For example, in the figure the average incomes of USA10, MEX10, and AUS10 are all in the wealthiest global decile (G10), while the average incomes in GTM10 and MYS10 are in the second wealthiest global decile (G9).

This exercise on global stratification and mobility is difficult to execute due to the lack of appropriate comparable income data for people and households around the world. While we fully recognize the shortcomings of these procedures, including the use of per capita GNI as a proxy for the "average" income for people in a given country, our goal is to start an empirically driven discussion around the reconceptualization of stratification and mobility as global phenomena. As we note, a more world-historical approach to these issues will require the collection of truly global income and distribution data.

Chapter 4

Cities

by Peter J. Taylor, Michael Hoyler, and Dennis Smith

Bringing in Cities

The transition towards a modern world-system in the "long sixteenth century" (c.1450–c.1640) can be interpreted as a social transformation in the relations between political ruling groups and commercial economic groups. In previous world-systems, the two groups were definitively separated and hierarchically ordered, with commerce cast into a secondary mode. These previous systems are defined by Wallerstein (1979) as *world-empires*. The modern world-system is an interloper amongst these political worlds. It is based upon a *modus operandi* between ruling and commercial groups that Wallerstein calls a *world-economy*. In this system the relative powers of the political and the economic groups are more balanced. There is a recognized mutuality not found in world-empires. This change is generally referred to as the rise of mercantilism in the seventeenth and eighteenth centuries—states embarking on commercial-economic policies to augment their military-territorial policies.

Mercantilism came in many forms and can be measured in terms of different balances between the economic and the political. The United Provinces were located at one end of this scale. This "merchant's state" was based on "a high-voltage urban economy" (Braudel 1984: 180) that created the "Dutch golden age" during what was for the rest of Europe "the crisis of the seventeenth century." With an exceptionally high level of urbanization, this first modern "economic miracle" developed a republican political philosophy that lauded commercial activity and therefore specifically valued the economic benefits of city networks. This is clearly expressed in Pieter de la Court's (1972) *The True Interests and Political Maxims of the Republic of Holland,* first published in 1662 as a guide for Holland's rulers. He interpreted Dutch cities as "intertwined one with another" (p. 30) so that according to Braudel (1984: 180) "together they formed a power bloc." One of de la Court's key maxims was that "the overthrow of great and prosperous cities may be attributed to monarchs and princes of all times but never to republics" (p. 4) so that "it follows then to be the duty of the governors of republics to seek for great cities, and to make them as populous and strong as possible" (p. 5). Without acceding to the historical veracity of the maxim, we can see that de la Court recognized the production and productivity of cities as central to Holland's success and future while casting rival monarchical states—initially the modern ideological successors of world-empires—as wasting the wealth created by cities for the selfish "glory" of the king (Taylor 1999: 72). De la Court has been called "Adam Smith a century before *The Wealth of Nations*" (Caton 1988: 233), but his precocious focus on how growing cities generate new work (de la Court 1972: 57–59) makes him sound more like Jane Jacobs three centuries before *The Economy of Cities* (1969). We follow de la Court's cities-centered political economy in this analysis.

We use the "urban cluster" concept of modern scholarship to investigate the spatial polarization represented by the core-periphery structure of the modern world-system. The focus is on cities within the system and how these are implicated in the development and reproduction of this uneven economic development. Our approach has one very important advantage. Estimates of the population size of cities are available for all the times and spaces of the modern world-system. This provides the opportunity to generate comprehensive quantitative measurement of social change and produce a customized comparative analysis of cities. The beginning assumption is that a fast-growing city is an economically successful city and therefore demographics can chart this success across the time and space horizons of the modern world-system.

We begin by describing our methodology for achieving this aim. The demographics are extremely useful but require careful interpretation to relate them to polarization. We therefore follow this with a conceptual discussion of city processes in core-making and consequent periphery-making. Jumping forward from de la Court to recent developments in urban theory, seven basic processes are introduced to make sense of the geohistory of demographic descriptions of city growths. Next we discuss the results of this exercise in terms of polarization versus convergence over the long term (i.e., the years 1500 to 2000). Superficially the demographics appear to suggest an urban convergence as the cities in non-core zones are growing into "megacities" and rates of urbanization are catching up to those of the core. But our city processes indicate a much more complex outcome unfolding. In a short conclusion our findings are related to overall world-systems thinking.

Methodology: City Demographic Changes, 1500–2000

We offer here a basic summary of our methodology, which is described and justified in detail in Taylor et al. (2010). The purpose is to create an inventory of rapid city population growths for the whole time and space of the modern world-system. Certain arbitrary decisions were made in order to achieve this in a manageable way. The results do not necessarily include all such growth but do provide a reasonably comprehensive and representative set of successful cities in the system. For our purposes it is especially important that a large number of cities are so identified. We successfully produced an inventory of 342 cases of rapidly growing cities.

The steps taken towards this end were as follows:

1. We used de Vries (1984) for populations of European cities up to 1800 and Chandler (1987) both for non-European cities before 1800 and for all cities after 1800 up to the most recent period, for which we used Brinkhoff (2007).
2. City populations were inspected for five century dates: 1600, 1700, 1800, 1900, and 2000.
3. In line with Wallerstein's model of the expansion of the modern world-system, cities were included just for Europe and the Americas in 1600 and 1700. Indian, Ottoman, and Russian cities were added from 1800 onwards. Chinese and Japanese and some other cities were added from 1900 onwards.
4. Rosters of cities for these dates were produced by averaging the population of the largest three cities and then including all cities with 10% or more of this average. This was to make the numbers of cities comparable over time while also being manageable in quantity. These five rosters are shown in the first line of Table 4.1. The universe of cities in the study is 373.
5. Additional populations of roster cities were then collected for 1500 and half-century points: 1550, 1650, 1750, 1850, and 1950. Note that, following Wallerstein, Indian, Ottoman, and Russian cities were included only from 1750, and Chinese and Japanese cities from 1850.
6. Annualized rates of change over fifty-year intervals were computed for each of the five rosters of cities. For instance, using the 1600 roster, demographic changes were found for 1500–1550 and

Table 4.1   Cities Included in the Study Over Time

Classifications of Cities	1500–1600	1600–1700	1700–1800	1800–1900	1900–2000	Total Total
City rosters for each century	72	39	60	49	153	373
City change measures for each half century	144	78	120	98	306	746
Of which: Sum of rapid-growth cities for each half century	29	16	30	70	197	342
Of which: Cities with growth rates above 5% per annum	0	2	6	30	161	199

1550–1600. This provided 746 city growth measures in ten lists, one for each fifty-year period.

7. All demographic changes of 1 percent per annum and above were designated rapid-growth cities. These were aggregated into century sums and shown in the second row of Table 4.1. Note that a roster city may occur twice as a rapid-growth city if it has growth above 1 percent per annum for both half centuries covered by the roster (e.g., Birmingham in 1700–1750 and 1750–1800). The result is an inventory of 342 rapid-growth cities out of the total of 746 city growth measures. This inventory is the empirical base of the remainder of this analysis.

We can note the following in Table 4.1. The crisis of the seventeenth century is clearly shown as the only downward blip in the data. Otherwise there is a trend of increasing numbers of cities over time, indicating both intensive change (new and more cities in the existing land area) and extensive change (incorporation of new land areas). The trend accelerates immensely in the twentieth century. This feature is especially reflected in the fourth row of Table 4.1, where cities experiencing growth rates of over 5 percent per annum are numbered. Such *very*-rapid-growth cities become numerous only in the nineteenth century and become commonplace in the twentieth century. This latter feature will be discussed in some detail after we have the conceptual tools to interpret variations of what is happening amongst our inventory of 342 rapid-growth cities.

Cities in Core-Making and Periphery-Making

The specificity of Wallerstein's (1979) core-periphery thinking comes in two key ways. First, he treats core and periphery as processes—core-making, periphery-making—that are system-wide but that differ greatly in their geographical concentrations. Hence there is the spatial polarization into core zones and periphery zones. Second, Wallerstein adds a new category, semi-periphery, which in itself is not a process but rather a consequence of places where the two opposing processes are relatively balanced. In such circumstances particular states can harness core processes in a drive to become part of the core zone. This is the political mechanism for semi-peripheral states to rise (or fall if the drive fails) in the spatial hierarchy of the capitalist world-economy. This way of thinking can privilege a territorial spatiality of the modern world-system, what Castells (1996) calls spaces of places. By focusing on cities we privilege a network spatiality of the modern world-system, Castells's spaces of flows. Through using cities as a vehicle for understanding core-periphery, we hope to provide new insights into the changes in spatial polarization of the modern world-system across its half-millennium existence. We base our ideas on the seminal works of Jacobs (1969) and Castells (1996), who both interpret cities as process.

How does this distinctive urban process relate to Wallerstein's "systemic process"? Introducing cities to center stage in world-systems analysis is problematic because Wallerstein (1984b) has created a tight, rigorous argument building on classes, states, ethnicities (nations, races), and households, with their associated political movements.

There is no place for cities in this world-systems analysis except as sites where events take place. Although Wallerstein is sensitive to the importance of space in his social processes (hence core-periphery), especially in relation to time (what he calls TimeSpace), he gives no recognition to the special places that are cities. Urbanization is treated as an outcome of economic, political, and cultural processes undermining the rural world (Wallerstein 1984a). Although for most of the history of the modern world-system such processes have generated large numbers of important cities in core zones, with few or no such cities in periphery zones, in Wallerstein's argument cities remain essentially inert. Core-making does not depend on cities. His position contrasts with a growing urban literature that interprets cities as the key generators of economic change. As Jacobs (1969) tells it, cities are themselves the fundamental process through which economies expand. Let us briefly rehearse this argument. As a form of human settlement, cities exhibit several unique features. Recently Ivan Turok (2009: 14) presented these very clearly and succinctly:

> Cities are complex adaptive systems comprising multitudes of actors, firms, and other organisations forming diverse relationships and evolving together. Frequent face-to-face contact and other cooperative and competitive interactions enabled by proximity help to increase people's knowledge and skills, to improve their capacity to respond creatively to economic challenges, and to develop new and improved products, processes and services. Other places cannot easily replicate these conditions.

Accepting this position, we can add a further dimension: cities are constituted as networks interlocked by commerce and trade (Taylor 2004). Such linking creates an incessant turnover of nonlocal actors who join in the processes that Turok describes. The effectiveness of the density of interactions he identifies is hugely enhanced by the cosmopolitan nature of a city's residents and visitors. Thus the complexity of cities includes both internal links (clusters/agglomeration) and external links (networks/connectivity). It is this combination that makes cities so special.

This special character—Jacobs's city as process—is the prime mechanism of core-making. Jacobs (1969) describes city process as a generic form, but we will argue that it is given a specific momentum within the modern world-system (Taylor 2013). The operation of this process in world-empires was evident but restricted by the precedence given to political ruling groups. Making money could not become a prime end in itself, only a means to other (political) ends. But with the more balanced relation between political and economic groups in the modern world-system, restrictions on the commercial growth potentials of cities were lessened in the development of a capitalist world-economy, whose primary objective was the endless accumulation of capital. Money had now become a prime end in itself. This is what Pieter de la Court was grappling with in his new understanding of Holland and what in the next two centuries was to be expressed as the intimate relation between urbanization and industrialization, the twin processes of modernization.

The first major statistical comparison of modernity's unusually large cities was made by Adna Weber in his 1899 study of the growth of great nineteenth-century cities. The study of the modern world-systems' association with ever larger cities continues today under conditions of economic globalization in the analyses of global cities (Sassen 2001) and world city networks (Taylor 2004). Cities are at the economic cutting edge, continually reproducing the core zone of the world-economy. We call this the *dominant economic process*.

However, Jacobs's economic process is not the only city-formation mechanism in the modern world-system. In world-empires the largest cities were where political power lay—capital cities. Thus the three nonmodern cities that unequivocally reached a population of at least a million were centers of great world-empires with immense redistributive powers: Imperial Rome, Caliphate Baghdad, and Qing Beijing.

In the modern world-system this sovereign political power is divided among polities in an interstate system initially defined legally in the Treaty of Westphalia of 1648. This was the culmination of political centralizations of the fragmented governance of medieval Europe in the transition to the modern world-system. Capital cities of these new territorial states attracted wealth and consequent population to become large cities in their own right. We shall call this continuing political importance in city-making in the modern world-system the *political privileging process*.

As centers of consumption, many large political cities often developed important commercial functions, including sizable production to meet political and military needs. This is an important category of the modern city related to the mercantilism in the core that we shall label *mixed economic/political competitive process* because it encompasses roughly balanced political and economic city functions in the interstate system.

There is another political economy process that modern cities possess—the power to mold distant economic landscapes to their particular market demands. This is described by Jacobs (1984) in her "five great forces" that create simple dependent economies. She calls them "economic grotesques." These can come in different formats—from plantation agriculture to provide sugar for European cities to peasant agriculture to provide cocoa or coffee to accompany the sugar in consumption. Other primary economic sectors (resource regions—oil, ores), secondary economic sectors (transplanted industry—the "new international division of labor"), and tertiary sectors (back-office services) can all form economic grotesques.

It is not what is produced that matters, but the relation of these economic activities to the core cities. The fluctuation of the demands of the core zone's cities controls the "success" of these fragile economies. There are urban places that function to facilitate the transmission of wealth production to the core, ports, and local political centers, but these cities ultimately serve to replenish cities in core zones, not the local economy. In world-systems terms this is dependency theory. Andre Gunder Frank's (1969) "development of underdevelopment" process links what he calls the "metropole" (core zone of cities) to "satellites" (dependent facilitating places) through which wealth is drained from the periphery. We call this the *dominant peripheral economic process*. But there is an additional process featuring capital cities of noncore states that combines economic and political processes. Where states are instrumental in devising semi-peripheral strategies (such as protectionism) this may lead to the growth of a primate city structure with immense economic centralization in the capital city. This mercantilism in the periphery we call *mixed economic/ political development process*.

Finally, there are two city processes directly related to the geographical expansion of the world-economy, one that expands the periphery and one that expands the core. First, some of the world-empires that have been incorporated into the modern world-system themselves had thriving cities, both political and economic. Therefore there has been an *inheritance by incorporation process* whereby large cities that grew outside the modern world-system become part of the system. Many declined in the new circumstances (for instance, resulting from Britain's policy of de-industrializing India in the nineteenth century) but others prospered relatively (for instance, serving as the economic impetus for some Chinese treaty ports).

Second, there has been European settlement that has been able to reproduce itself in sparsely populated regions on other continents. Belich (2009: 70) describes the most successful example of this as the "settler revolution" of Anglophones after about 1800 that manifested itself in two movements—the expansion of the United States westward and "Greater British" expansion in its Dominions, "the white un-coerced part of the British Empire." Further, he shows (p. 85) that these Anglo expansions "grew at a staggering demographic growth rate with economic growth to match." By 1920 the American West had sixty-two million people and the British Dominions had twenty-four million. Between them their "white majorities were, on average, the richest peoples in the world." And these multiple expansions were based upon numerous "boom cities"—the "precocious sprouting . . . of nineteenth century settler cities" (p. 2). This settler revolution was city-based, involving the "mass transfer" of transportation technologies, financial instruments, information, technical skills and knowledge, and people so that Anglos were able "to reproduce . . . their own society" in these new lands (p. 127). The result is a "new form of settlement" that Belich calls "explosive colonization" and describes as "human history's most rapid form of societal reproduction" (p. 183). We will call this multiple creation of boom cities *core frontier expansion process*. These seven city processes are summarized in Table 4.2 in their world-systems context.

The seven city-making processes within the modern world-system account for the great rise in the sizes and numbers of cities that typifies this system. In Table 4.3 we have listed the three cities with the highest growth rates for each of the ten fifty-year periods to illustrate the processes through extreme cases of each. Thus there are classic examples of each process. For instance, the list for the early modern period (1500–1700) shows Antwerp, Augsburg, and Amsterdam as dominant core economic; Potosí as dominant peripheral economic; Lisbon and London as mixed core competitive; and Berlin and Dublin as political privileging. The inheritance by incorporation process is represented by Lucknow, and the first example of mixed peripheral development is early Philadelphia. At the end of the nineteenth century the two fastest-growing cities are Chicago and Melbourne, coincidently the two cities Belich (2009: 1–2) features at the beginning of his book to illustrate his explosive colonization. This core frontier expansion continues into the early twentieth century, when it is replaced by the dominant peripheral economic process in the final fifty-year period. But to understand such trends comprehensively, we need to move on to considering the whole inventory of 342 rapid-growth cities.

The Increasing Complexity of the Core-Periphery Relation

In Table 4.4 the 342 examples of rapid-growth cities are ordered by century and process. This summarizes the basic quantitative findings

**Table 4.2   City Processes in Producing and
Reproducing the Capitalist World-Economy**

City Processes	World-System Process
A. Dominant core economic B. Dominant peripheral economic	These are the two basic processes that have produced and reproduced the capitalist world-economy as a core-periphery structure, with commercial metropoles in the core (A) and dependent urban facilitators in the periphery (B).
C. Political privileging D. Mixed core competitive E. Mixed peripheral development	Early state centralization created important capital cities as centers of political power in the core (C). This was sometimes mixed with basic commercial functions, producing a balance of political and economic power that has become increasingly common (D). More recently this mix has developed outside the core, where state centralization is integral to a semi-peripheral development strategy (E).
F. Inheritance by incorporation G. Core frontier expansion	These are two historically specific processes. Where the capitalist world-economy expanded into city-rich empires, successful cities were initially incorporated (F). In contrast, where the capitalist world-economy expanded into territories devoid of cities, large-scale urban settlement created frontier cities (G).

of this research. To aid interpretation, sums for core-making (dominant core economic, mixed competitive, political privileging, and core frontier expansion processes) and periphery-making (inheritance by incorporation, dominant peripheral economic, and mixed peripheral development processes) are presented. Interpretation proceeds in two stages: first, overall patterns are described, and second, these are used to address the question of polarization or convergence in the core-periphery structure of the modern world-system. As will be seen, this cities-based analysis does not provide a simple answer to this question. Increasing complexity makes this question intriguingly open.

The first point to make is that overall the half-millennium trend in Table 4.4, as shown in rows 5 and 9, is towards convergence between core-making and periphery-making processes. In the early modern world-system (first two centuries in Table 4.4), city growth is almost absent outside the core zone. The two exceptions are Potosí with its silver mountain and Mexico City with its colonial administrative functions.

Table 4.3   **Fastest-Growing Cities and Their City Processes**

City	Period	Percent Change per Annum	City Process
Lisbon	1500–	4.53	Mixed core competitive
Seville	1550	3.20	Dominant core economic
Antwerp		2.50	Dominant core economic
Augsburg		2.50	Dominant core economic
Potosí	1550–	3.24	Dominant peripheral economic
London	1600	3.00	Mixed core competitive
Rome		2.67	Political privileging
Dublin	1600–	4.80	Political privileging
Amsterdam	1650	3.38	Dominant core economic
Leiden		3.36	Dominant core economic
Berlin	1650–	7.17	Political privileging
Dublin	1700	5.06	Political privileging
Copenhagen		4.09	Mixed core competitive
Liverpool	1700–	5.33	Dominant core economic
Birmingham	1750	4.86	Dominant core economic
Cadiz		3.22	Mixed core competitive
Lucknow	1750–	7.60	Inheritance by incorporation
Manchester	1800	5.78	Dominant core economic
Philadelphia		5.19	Mixed peripheral development
New York	1800–	18.48	Dominant core economic
Baltimore	1850	11.00	Dominant core economic
Philadelphia		10.53	Dominant core economic
Chicago	1850–	120.64	Core frontier expansion
Melbourne	1900	25.71	Core frontier expansion
Buenos Aires		19.78	Mixed peripheral development
Los Angeles	1900–	72.50	Core frontier expansion
Houston	1950	29.82	Core frontier expansion
Jakarta		23.25	Mixed peripheral development
Lagos	1950–	69.98	Dominant peripheral economic
Dacca	2000	52.83	Dominant peripheral economic
Khartoum		43.78	Dominant peripheral economic

The growth of noncore cities in the middle century (1700–1800) is mainly due to inheriting cities from the incorporation of India and the Ottoman and Russian world-empires. This is a "geographically mixed" category of growth across pairs of world-systems, but it does inaugurate the rise of cities in periphery-making in the modern world-system. Both core-making and periphery-making increase immensely in the nineteenth century. This feature is further greatly accentuated in the twentieth century when periphery-making city growth processes exceed core-making for the first time, and by a large margin. Thus by the twentieth century rapid-growth cities are to be found across all zones of the modern world-system. Given

Table 4.4 City Growth Processes, 1500–2000

City Growth Process	1500– 1600	1600– 1700	1700– 1800	1800– 1900	1900– 2000
Dominant core economic process	16	7	12	30	54
Political privileging process	4	6	9	4	0
Mixed economic/political competitive process	7	3	1	15	17
Core frontier expansion process	0	0	0	4	4
Total Core-Making	27	16	22	53	75
Dominant peripheral economic process	1	0	2	5	75
Mixed economic/political development process	1	0	1	8	47
Inheritance by incorporation	0	0	5	4	0
Total Periphery-Making	2	0	8	17	122
Total Demographic Expansion	29	16	30	70	197

that the periphery zone always constitutes a majority of the world-economy's population, we can say that the distribution of rapid-growth cities has come to reflect approximately the overall demographic pattern of the world-system. Therefore at this level of analysis, there can be no clearer example of core-periphery convergence.

But the role of cities in the modern world-system is not so simple. We can add to the analysis in both detail and complexity. Taking the detail first, we can note the interesting variations between the trends of the seven processes individually. We have already mentioned the *inheritance by incorporation process*. This occurs only in the eighteenth and nineteenth centuries when the modern world-system experiences two major expansions.

In addition we can see that political processes in core-making are concentrated in the seventeenth and eighteenth centuries. The seventeenth century is the only time when dominant core economic processes do not constitute a majority of core-making processes. The rise of Madrid as the new capital of Castile/Spain and Berlin as the capital of the rising power of Prussia are two classic examples of political rapid-growth cities at this time.

However, in the last two centuries political processes are over-whelmed by economic processes, with the seventy-five cases of dominant economic peripheral processes in the twentieth century being the outstanding feature. But there are also forty-seven examples of mixed development process, with cities like Buenos Aires and Mexico City as primate centers of powerful semi-peripheral states. In other words, it is periphery-making city growth processes that dominated the twentieth century, and with extremely large rates of growth per annum.

In Table 4.5 we have extended the top three cities for 1950–2000 from Table 4.3 to show the top fifty rapid-growth cities in this period. This confirms both the concentration of these cities outside the core zone of the world-economy and the very high growth rates. The only four cities in the list that are from the core zone are all in the United States (Phoenix, Miami, Dallas, and Atlanta) and reflect bringing the southern United States into core status through their cities in a variety of ways. But the really interesting rapid-growth cities are the other forty-six in poorer countries of the world. This represents a crescendo of urbanization in the late modern world-system and requires specific consideration.

The great advantage of thinking in terms of processes is that we can handle the fact that there are always multiple processes operating in the same place. Hence process research can encompass complexities. We saw earlier that Wallerstein used this facility to define semi-periphery as coinciding core and periphery processes within states. This situation is replicated in urban processes and cities. Dominant core-making and periphery-making processes can and do occur simultaneously as important components of contemporary cities outside the core zone. For instance, Mumbai, Mexico City, Caracas, Johannesburg, and Bogotá feature in the top fifty cities in terms of business connectivity in the world city network in 2008, which is a measure of dominant core economic process (Taylor et al. 2011). These cities are also listed by Davis (2006: 28) as housing the "largest megaslums" in a list for 2005, the epitome of a peripheral city process.

These are two very different processes operating simultaneously in these cities. In fact, this is typical of cities beyond the core zone. Such cities are important enough economically to be linked into the world city network but are also burdened by great swaths of poverty. The latter is the result of unprecedented levels of rural-urban migration in the twentieth century as city-based core processes have reorganized the global economic landscape for their food and resource needs.

The resulting massive population growth rates represented by Table 4.5 have produced this new category of city commonly referred to as megacities. In poorer countries these have two demographic components. Up to about a quarter of the population is economically integrated into the world city network and life is consumption-led just as it is for all who make a living through dominant core economic process. At the same time at least three-quarters of the population lives in abject poverty, residents of Davis's megaslums. Therefore in a city like Mexico City its population is unequally divided—about five million within core processes and twenty million in periphery processes. Because of the former group, Mexico City is approximately as important as Amsterdam and Zurich in the world-city-network process (Taylor et al. 2011). Because of

Table 4.5   The Top 50 Rapid-Growth Cities, 1950–2000

Rapid-Growth Cities	Population Change per Annum
Lagos	69.98%
Dacca	52.83%
Khartoum	43.78%
Kinshasa	41.32%
Phoenix	33.54%
Surat	29.43%
Fortaleza	28.84%
Chittagong	28.53%
Belo Horizonte	28.09%
Delhi	27.13%
Karachi	26.13%
Shantou	24.94%
Seoul	24.73%
Taipei	24.37%
Bogotá	23.25%
Ankara	22.02%
Medellín	22.00%
Lahore	21.49%
Rawalpindi	20.84%
Kabul	20.79%
Izmir	20.08%
Tehran	19.71%
Miami	19.51%
Monterrey	19.32%
Dallas	19.24%
Guadalajara	18.95%
Istanbul	18.25%
Porto Alegre	17.89%
Manila	17.79%
Atlanta	17.28%
Baghdad	17.18%
Jaipur	16.95%
Cali	16.92%
Kaoh-siung	16.90%
Jakarta	16.49%
Taiyuan	16.37%
Bangalore	16.03%
Poona	15.88%
Algiers	15.69%
Guangzhou	15.47%
Medan	15.46%
Tel Aviv-Jaffa	15.32%
Addis Ababa	14.98%
São Paulo	14.47%
Pyongyang	14.36%
Lima	13.93%
Bangkok	13.81%
Damascus	13.43%
Chengdu	13.02%
Ibadan	12.64%

the latter group Mexico City is very, very different from its core zone network peers. This city as process is visibly semi-peripheral in outcome. The idea of a growing multinodal semi-periphery does not support our initial interpretation of core-periphery convergence. Rather it seems that spatial polarization is alive and well in the late modern world-system, albeit packaged into a more complex geography.

Coming Full Circle

It is perhaps ironic that Wallerstein (1974b) initially derived part of his analysis of the modern world-system from a series of Marxist debates, in one of which (that on the transition from feudalism to capitalism) cities were the main issue of contention. In the Dobb-Sweezy debate (Hilton et al. 1978) the two positions were (1) that feudalism was undermined by its own class contradictions and (2) that it was undermined by the growth of bourgeois cities within. Wallerstein comes down on the latter side because it provides a broader systemic approach to the transition than the more restricted national class interpretation. But he does not fully embrace the importance of the role of cities that we have traced from Pieter de la Court onwards.

However, with the recent urbanization crescendo finally making city dwellers the majority of humanity and with this ongoing urbanization likely to lead to perhaps three-quarters of the world living in cities later in the twenty-first century, this emerging multinodal semi-periphery in the modern world-system requires special attention.

There are two basic interpretations of the contemporary megacity mix of core-making and periphery-making city processes as they relate to material polarization or convergence. For Mike Davis (2006), cities are sites of increasing divergence. In his *Planet of Slums* he emphasizes the despair of these grossly unequal cities and the future potential instability of a new, disconnected, "informal urban proletariat." In contrast, for Robert Neuwirth (2006) cities are sites of potential convergence. In his *Shadow Cities* he emphasizes the social creativity of the megacity residents in their struggles for survival. Dominant core economic in practice but not in outcome due to the severe constraints, cities remain places of opportunity in this more optimistic account. This disagreement tells us that the modern world-system is entering its demise through a newly emerging urban politics of polarization and convergence in cities in the semi-periphery. We are only beginning sketchily to discern and understand this "urban revolution" where, according to Brugmann (2009), both past core proletariat and peripheral peasantry are being superseded as the potential progressive agents of change by the global urban dispossessed. One thing that is certain is that this great wave of urbanization, concentrating billions of people in close proximities, is creating ever more complex world-making processes of powers, flows, legitimacies, entwinings, and creativities. Amongst the turmoil of polarizations and convergences there exists a possibility for a new progressive politics through cities, as promoted by Pilon (2010: 5): "It is not only the right to urban resources, it is the right to change ourselves by changing the city: the kind of city we have is linked to the kind of human beings we are willing to be." This means moving the focus of progressive urban politics from promoting inclusion (extending current ways of living) towards transition to new ways of living together.

Chapter 5

Peasantries

by Eric Vanhaute, Hanne Cottyn, and Yang Wang

Research Questions and Strategy

A comparative and global analysis of the position of peasant societies
within the expanding capitalist world-system from 1500 to 2000 must address three different but interrelated global questions: de-agrarianization,
de-ruralization, and de-peasantization.[1] We try to understand the different
roads of transition via a comparative research design, looking for similar
and divergent trajectories of peasant transformation, both in space (zoning within the world-economy) and over time (phases of incorporation).
We do this by focusing on three cases: northwestern Europe (North Sea
Basin), the east coast of China (Yangzi River Delta), and Latin America
(Central Andean Highlands). They are analyzed via four successive
snapshots: circa 1600, 1800, 1900, and 2000.

The choice of the three regions reflects the zoned division within
the modern world-system:

---

1. Our analysis is based on a larger project, *The End of Peasant Societies? A Comparative and Global Research into the Decline and Disappearance of Peasantries and Its Impact on
Social Relations and Inequality, 1500–2000*, a research project coordinated by Eric Vanhaute
and funded by the Flemish National Science Foundation. The project is summarized
in Vanhaute (2008, 2011). Our analysis here sketches the general outline of the project.

- *North Sea Basin (England and the Low Countries)*: a predominantly core region from the late Middle Ages onwards within the (western European) interstate system and the capitalist world-economy (incorporation through core-making processes)
- *Central Andean Highlands (southern contemporary Peru and the western areas of Bolivia)*: from the core of an Andean world-system (Inca empire) to an incorporated and increasingly peripheralized region within the modern world-system since the sixteenth century (incorporation through periphery-making processes)
- *East coast of China (Yangzi River Delta)*: from being a core region in the East Asian world-system to becoming primarily a peripheral (late nineteenth century) and then a semi-peripheral (late twentieth century) zone within the modern world-system (incorporation by inheritance)

Three interlocked dimensions constitute the trajectories of transformation of these rural zones: (a) the (re)constitution of the peasant societies—household organization, village systems, regional networks; (b) the relations of these rural zones to broader societal structures—trade and commerce networks, fiscal systems, power and property relations; and (c) the transformation of these societies and the effects on their social relations, survival, and income levels. To understand the interaction between these three dimensions, we analyzed three interlocked research themes: political and economic organization and social power relations; regulation of and access to labor, land, and natural resources; and household and village strategies.

An integrated analysis of these themes allows us to address the following questions: What were the trajectories of incorporation of rural zones into the capitalist world-system? How did this incorporation affect the spaces and edges of peasant subsistence systems? Did and do these processes of peasant transformation create a more homogeneous world, or do they feed new trends of heterogenization?

Hypotheses and Definitions

Historical capitalism has been at the heart of the permanent (re)creation and marginalization of peasant societies. We define peasants as members of rural, agrarian households who have direct access to land and natural resources. They are organized in family groups and village communities that meet a large part of their subsistence needs (production, exchange, credit, protection), and they pool different forms of income from land, labor, and exchange. They are ruled by other social groups that extract a surplus via rents, via (unbalanced) market transfers, or through control of state power (taxation). The key analytic issues are the degree of household and local autonomy, the flexible strategies of income-pooling, the household-based village structures, and the surplus extraction that is outside local control.

The long-term decline of the centrality of rural zones has been framed within three interrelated concepts: de-ruralization, de-agrarianization, and de-peasantization. De-ruralization refers to the decline of rural spaces and the growth of "urbanized" zones. De-agrarianization refers to the decline of reliance on agriculture as the principal source of livelihood. De-peasantization refers to the erosion of the family basis of their livelihoods and the commodification of subsistence (see *inter alia* Bryceson 1999; Johnson 2004; Bernstein 2010; Vanhaute 2011).

The common use of de-peasantization as a unilinear vector of modernization is misleading, ignoring the diversified effects of capitalist expansion on rural societies. Peasantries as a social group are a dynamic social process in themselves. They are "the historical outcome of an agrarian labor process which is constantly adjusting to surrounding conditions, be it fluctuations of climate, markets, state exactions, political regimes, as well as technical innovations, demographic trends, and environmental changes" (Bryceson et al. 2000: 2–3). This implies that processes of de-peasantization and re-peasantization are the outcome of changing strategies of peasant livelihood diversification. As Van der Ploeg has argued, the re-emergence of twenty-first-century peasantries follows the same historical patterns of survival ("self-provisioning") and autonomy ("distantiation"), albeit in different societal settings: "Today's peasantries are actively responding to the processes that otherwise would destroy, by-pass and/or entrap them" (Van der Ploeg 2010: 2, 21).

The long-term process of capitalist development has both widened (expansion) and deepened (intensification) relations of commodification. Commodification refers to the commercialization of goods sold to or bought from external markets. However, the central tendency of capitalism towards generalized commodity production does not mean that all elements of social existence are necessarily and comprehensively commodified (Bernstein 2010). Over time, uneven incorporation has been creating new frontier zones, in which the commodification of subsistence goods is followed by an increasing social and spatial differentiation.

The gradual incorporation of vast rural zones has subjugated, transformed, and sometimes (re)created peasantries. It has put increasing pressure on their bases of existence through the alteration of peasant access to the essential means of production—land, labor, and capital. In general, the survival margins of the former majority of small-scale, diversified, community-based agricultural systems have significantly decreased.

However, we cannot understand the position of the rural zones in the modern world-system in a singular manner. Peasantries over the world have followed different trajectories of change and have developed divergent repertoires of adaptation and resistance. Throughout its history the expansion of the capitalist world-system has been fueled by the creation of new social and ecological frontier zones, spaces that generated new sources of cheap land, labor, and natural resources (Hall 2000; Moore 2010).

Peasantries have always been a vital frontier zone. The process of incorporation created flows of surplus extraction, without necessarily dispossessing rural producers of their land and other means of production. These dynamic zones of uneven commodification led to new forms of struggle and resistance. That is why trends of homogenization on a macro level can generate new forms of heterogenization on the micro level. The expansion of the global division of labor triggered different paths of de-peasantization and re-peasantization. These differences are a consequence of different balances between internal dynamics (processes of internal change) and external pressure (changes caused by actors outside local society), and/or between peasant modes of extraction (exploiting family labor) versus capitalist production modes (creating capitalist labor relations) (McMichael 2009).

The three cases illustrate the three basic models of the transformation of peasantries in the last five centuries: as internal frontier zones in the core of the modern world-system (incorporation through core-making processes), as newly incorporated frontier zones in the periphery of the modern world-system (incorporation through periphery-making processes), and as external zones to the modern world-system (incorporation by inheritance). In the North Sea region the expansion of zones of capitalist agriculture initiated strong processes of regional and social differentiation. The violent incorporation of the Andean peoples created new intra-regional and inter-regional relationships as part of a process of peripheralization. In the highly commercialized Yangzi River Delta, the trend of growing differentiation was slowed down by the persistence of both a redistributive state system and kinship and clan networks.

Sixteenth Century: Regional Incorporations

The sixteenth century marked the beginning of fundamental divergences in the development paths. On the eve of the sixteenth century we find a polycentric world with thriving agrarian civilizations all around the globe—from East Asia, India, the Middle East, and Europe to West Africa and Central and South America (Marks 2007). Most of these regional world-systems were interconnected in supra-regional networks. For thousands of years all these regions were characterized by cyclical changes in climate and population, linked to long-term transformations in political and social organization, economic production, and living standards.

This biological ancien régime was organic. It depended on solar energy to grow crops and on wood for fuel. Overall progress was limited due to the physical constraints on such solar energy–based agrarian societies. That is why agrarian systems all over the world lived at more or less the same level. This world of about 450 million people was an overwhelmingly rural one, in which 80–90 percent of the population lived as peasants. Nearly all of them were located in a handful of civilizations occupying only a small proportion of the earth's surface. These civilizations or empires, and above all the ruling elites, survived on the extraction of surpluses from those who worked the land, mostly via rents to landowners and taxes to the states.

Three of the most important regional systems were the (western) European interstate-system, the Inca empire, and the Chinese empire. On the eve of the sixteenth century, the core areas in these regional systems (North Sea Basin, Central Andean Highlands, and Yangzi River Delta) were all expanding economically and demographically, and increasing their supra-regional interconnectedness. In all three regions, regional autonomy was combined with a continuing integration in broader commercial networks. They were developing complex societies, with elaborate city networks, advanced levels of intensive agriculture, and expanding exchange networks.

In the *North Sea Basin* this expansion was related to accelerated processes of market integration and state formation (Dyer 2005; Hoppenbrouwers and Van Zanden 2001; Thoen 2001; Van Bavel 2010; Van Bavel and Hoyle 2010; Vanhaute et al. 2011). Historically, England and the Low Countries constituted the core area of the North Sea Basin. From the twelfth to thirteenth centuries onwards they formed the central area of structural transformations in the economy (commercialization), demography (urbanization), and politics (state-building). These regions were comparatively densely populated and highly urbanized. They had a strongly commercialized agriculture, a growing interregional and intercontinental trade system, and intensive industrial production. The transformation in the rural societies generated strong regional differentiation. Zones with capitalist agriculture, dominated by commercial farms and wage labor, developed in the regions bordering the North Sea. These zones were bounded by two types of peasant societies. The first combined small-scale family farming with an expanding protoindustry, thus creating a commercial subsistence economy. More distant, but still integrated in a regional division of labor, we find more autarchic peasant zones with a significant labor surplus.

At the time the Spanish *conquistadores* arrived, the (relatively) densely populated highlands and intermountain valleys of the *Central Andes* constituted the core region of an expanding Inca world-empire. In response to altitudinal zoning, a system of direct (diffusion of colonists) and indirect (long-distance trade) "vertical ecological control" and community-based reciprocal traits, rather than markets, structured the access of communities to complementary resources (Larson and Harris 1995; Lehmann 1982; Masuda et al. 1985; Mayer 2002; Murra 1975; Hirth and Pillsbury 2013). Highly reliant on previous developments, the Incas managed to unify this patchy landscape around a central bureaucracy and a redistributive division of goods and labor (Andrien 2001; Collier, Rosaldo, and Wirth 1982). In the sixteenth century the region was incorporated as a peripheral zone in the new European-Atlantic system. This incorporation into the capitalist world-economy and the accompanying Columbian exchange led to a new regional and sectorial differentiation. Serving as the economic backbone of the Spanish metropolis, the mines of Potosí gave rise to a network of regional markets and trade circuits that linked local communities to a silver-export economy (Assadourian 1982; Garavaglia 1983; Glave Testino 1986; Larson and Harris 1995). In response to the drastic decline of the native population and in order to facilitate efficient evangelization and labor and tribute extraction, the scattered kin-based ethnic groups were concentrated into Spanish-style villages under local control and cut off from their outlying lands. Local peasant production modes shifted substantially as labor was absorbed by agro-exporting estates (hacienda system) and obligatory service in the mines (mita system) (Aylwin 2002; Carmagnani et al. 1999; Hoberman and Socolow 1996). Although the shift from an autosufficient society marked by reciprocity and redistribution into a tributary and mercantile society deeply affected rural Andean life, the integration of the countryside was a process of dynamic encounters rather than of unidirectional imposition.

Since the beginning of the second millennium the *Yangzi River Delta* has been one of the most developed and densely populated regions in East Asia, becoming the agricultural and industrial center in China (Shiba 2000; Fan 2008). For this region, the final phase of the Ming Dynasty in the sixteenth century was a period of economic and commercial growth based on a well-integrated commodity economy with high land productivity, cash crops, and livestock farming (Fan 2005; Li 1998; Liang 1980; Pomeranz 2000). Cities grew and rural industries flourished. Regional differences were caused by ecological factors (plains, mountains) and reflected a differentiated agricultural output (grains, rice, cotton, mulberry) (Feng 2002). The international trade network, lubricated by silver imported from Japan and the Americas, increased inland commerce and led to a diversified industrial production around Taihu Lake, the Grand Canal, and the Yangzi River (Atwell 1982; Qian and Zheng 1998).

As in most rural societies, families in these regions were organized in small households, knit together in kinship/clan/village systems. These rural and peasant families pooled the fruits of their land with income from a wide range of labor activities. Village communities acted predominantly as informal exchange and credit networks. In the North Sea Basin a growing part of this income came from commodified labor, either in the form of protoindustrial activities or as wage labor outside the farm and village (including migrant labor). The integration in broader economic systems put local exchange networks under growing constraints, resulting in more unequal economic and power relations. Along with a gradual decrease of the commons, land rights became more individualistic (family-based). Proletarianization promoted polarization, with the concentration of village power and the control over village institutions such as poor relief in the hands of land-based oligarchies.

The growth of a flexible and extravillage labor market was much more limited in the Inca and Chinese world-empires. In the Andes, the import of the Spanish village system after the *Conquista* cut through interecological and intracommunity solidarity systems. Although increasingly under pressure, communitarian support systems still relied primarily on precolonial mechanisms in the hands of rotating village leadership. Clan loyalties remained strong in the Yangzi River Delta. In periods of social unrest they replaced failing state engagements (Fuma 2005; Huang 1990; Li and Jiang 2000).

In the sixteenth century rural zones in all three areas were subject to new processes of political and economic incorporation, albeit of fundamentally different types. In the North Sea Region the direct impact of (internal) integration in an expanding interstate and capitalist system resulted in the growing commodification of land, labor, and capital. This accelerated a process of regional and social differentiation. These regional zones and social groups with different production and labor regimes were interconnected through unequal power relations. The North Sea Basin is a typical example of transformation via the establishment of new internal frontiers, frontiers that fed the expanding capitalist world-system. In the Andes, the (external) process of incorporation was much more sudden and violent. Processes of commodification were inserted into a village and kin-based rural society. This was accompanied by a regional reorganization of the rural economies, which created a new, external frontier zone. In both western Europe and the Andes, new flows of commodities, capital, and labor reorganized the rural zones with new spatial and social boundaries. The Yangzi River Delta encountered successive processes of increasing and decreasing political incorporation within the context of the Chinese world-empire. The sixteenth century was marked by processes of agricultural and commercial expansion in combination with the dissolution of Ming state structures and a strengthening of local clan systems (Hillman 2004). Structural transformations remained limited.

1800: Global Incorporation

In the three centuries after 1500, world population doubled and tensions between peasant producers and ruling elites increased. Shifting power relations sharpened regional differentiation. In general, peasants became more subordinate to landlords and/or the growing power of governments (Tauger 2011). This coincided with an unprecedented expansion of long-distance markets, creating a remarkable differentiation in labor relations—from tributary labor (slavery and indentured labor) to different forms of commodified labor, from sharecropping to self-employed market production (Van der Linden 2008). In Europe, increasing pressures of commodification spurred social differentiation in peasant societies. In the Americas, Western explorers, rulers, and investors created a strongly polarized "plantation complex." Chinese Manchurian rulers tried to soften tensions by protecting peasant rights (Goldstone 2009).

In the *North Sea Basin* agrarian capitalism was firmly established by the early nineteenth century (Allen 2009; Hoppenbrouwers and Van Zanden 2001; Overton 1996; Van Bavel and Hoyle 2010; Vanhaute et al. 2011). The combination of labor-employing capitalist farmers and wage laborers was widespread in much of England and in some parts of the European continent. In other regions, peasant market-economies based on household farmwork and protoindustrial activities remained predominant. They were based on local credit networks that linked the logic of subsistence farming with the logic of external market production. The economic transformations accompanying industrialization resulted in a massive contraction in the proportion of the workforce employed in agriculture, and in a sharp rise in agricultural labor productivity. Around 1800, one agricultural laborer in England and the Low Countries produced enough to support two workers in manufacturing and services. In the nineteenth century the share of nonagricultural population rose to 60–65 percent, followed by rapid urbanization.

This process of de-agrarianization started in the areas around the maritime ports of the North Sea area and, from 1800 onwards, followed the spread of industrialization. By the early nineteenth century, population pressure and economic transformations increasingly affected the fundamentals of the rural economy in western Europe (subsistence farming, commons, village autonomy). This coincided with a deepening social polarization. After 1800, ever larger portions of the rural population could secure their survival only via a deeper exploitation of family labor on small pieces of land, in old and new putting-out industries (such as the clothing and lace industries), and by seasonal agricultural and industrial activities.

In the eighteenth and nineteenth centuries, the *Central Andean region* experienced sharp processes of peripheralization. Since the sixteenth century the silver economy organized around Potosí was the centerpiece of the peripheral connection of the Central Andes to core zones and the main shaping force of the Andean peasant (socio-ecological) space (Bonilla 2007: 108; Moore 2010; Tandeter 1995). Colonial reforms initiated a major reconfiguration of the Central Andean rural space towards an incomplete and uneven model of capitalist organization. Peasants were subjected to tribute payments in money, species, and labor, and to evangelization. Indigenous tribute and labor extraction eroded the village community, instigating market participation and shaping the space for new community survival systems (Larson and Harris 1995). In late colonial times, peasant economies faced increasing levels of surplus extraction by an interventionist Bourbon state, a system of coerced commodity commerce (*reparto de mercancias*) and ethnic authorities (*kurakas*), erupting in the great Andean rebellions of 1780–1781 (Andrien 2001; Garrido 2001; Golte 1980; Stavig and Schmidt 2008; Stern 1987). Indigenous groups were gradually pushed to the margins of the markets to which they had adapted as traders and transporters, initiating a long transition phase until the second half of the nineteenth century (Langer 2004; Larson 1995; Larson and Harris 1995). From the 1780s on, the declining silver economy and the chaotic transition to independence shifted further the position of the Central Andes, which became a periphery of the periphery. State revenues would continue to depend almost exclusively on indigenous contributions until the export boom of the second half of the nineteenth century, indirectly contributing to a ruralization of Andean national economies (Langer 2004; Larson 2004; Platt 1982).

During the Ming Dynasty the peasants in the *Yangzi River Delta* strongly increased agricultural outputs by reclaiming new land, planting new crops, and adapting labor-intensive techniques (Huang 1990; Pomeranz 2000). After 1644, Manchu rulers promoted a massive change in class structure and power relations, followed by rapid economic and demographic growth (Gao 2005; Goldstone 2009; Ho 2000). Many peasants acquired property rights, strengthening Qing autocratic rule. This agricultural and demographic expansion increased pressure on the use of public goods, such as water and commons management, market infrastructure, public relief, social safety, and education. The local clan elites played an important role in safeguarding village credit networks, in preserving the environment, and in land redistribution. This did not prevent the decay of rural institutions in the nineteenth century, leading to peasant bankruptcies and to the dismantlement of village communities. The local gentry left for the cities and rural common interests were neglected (Qian and Zheng 1998). This implosion of Chinese peasant societies preceded the process of the incomplete incorporation and peripheralization of China.

1900: Imperialist Intensification

As of 1900 only about 15 percent of the world's population were living in urban areas. Twelve cities had more than one million inhabitants. By 1950 the ratio of urban population had doubled to 30 percent and the number of cities with over one million people had grown to eighty-three. This overall trend is the outcome of divergent paths of transformation. From the 1870s, a "first global food regime" based on a settler-colonial model created a new global division of agricultural labor (McMichael 2009). The colonial/imperialist project implied control over labor in the rural zones in the global South. This required a direct intervention in the rural institutions and practices of land allocation and use, sometimes destroying them, sometimes modifying them. Rural regions specialized either in grain and meat production (extra-European settler economies) or in tropical export crops (colonial Asia and Africa, and former colonies in Latin America), both via plantations and via forced peasant production.

This imposed the commodification of peasant and settler farming and facilitated the creation of industrial plantations. In Latin America's process of brutal peripheralization, peasantries adapted to encroaching processes of commodification, while in China the implosion of rural societies foreshadowed the painful process of an indirect incorporation. In the western European core, peasant societies crumbled and were absorbed by "modernized" economic and political structures.

By the 1870s markets in the *North Sea Region* were liberalized. Large-scale grain and food imports provoked a fall in market prices, and the number of farmers started to decline (Overton 1996; Van Bavel and Hoyle 2010; Vanhaute et al. 2011). Surviving family farms were reoriented towards commercial crops and raising livestock. In these farming households, family labor was more and more restricted to the nuclear household, gradually excluding all forms of labor exchange with other family and nonfamily relations. Ever more inputs came from outside the farm and the village, making farmers more dependent on external factors. New types of farmers' organizations succeeded in filling the gap, via cooperatives for the purchase of fertilizers and livestock feed, savings and loan cooperatives, cooperative dairy farms, and mutual insurances.

The farmers' unions presented themselves as the political representatives of the farmers and efficiently supported their members through the process of modernization. Nonagricultural alternatives, such as subcontracting production, commuting, and new industrial activities, relieved the growing tension between labor and income. Expelled surplus labor could largely be absorbed by urban and rural industrialization and by the new service sectors. Rural society separated into a smaller fraction of market-oriented specialized family farmers and a growing number of households pooling their own farm income with outside agriculture and other employment outside the village economy. Villages in these regions suburbanized, becoming part of bigger systems of employment, transport, and provisioning. Regional differences were gradually blotted out in favor of a much more uniform sub-rural/sub-urban society. In the longer run, the fact that the majority of rural households broke their ties with agriculture paved the way to a continuous rise in economic welfare in twentieth-century western Europe.

In the post-independence *Andean Highlands*, colonial power relations were reproduced at the local level by new rural provincial elites, at the national level by oligarchic and new capitalist elites basing their power on land and mining, and at the international level by foreign capitalist entrepreneurs. The attempts to create a land market and convert indigenous commoners into a smallholder class in the late nineteenth century, however largely frustrated, substantially altered Amerindian-State (tributary) relations and heightened rural unrest (Jackson 1997; Larson 2004; Mallon 1995; Platt 1982; Stern 1987; Thurner 1997; Yepes del Castillo 1972). Liberal reforms and the shift to free-trade policies went accompanied by pressures towards the enclosure, displacement, and absorption of rural communities by the world market and its local agents (Larson 2004). However, the indigenous community was able to negotiate, escape, and resist these commodification projects rather than yielding to one-sided incorporation or isolation (Grieshaber 1980; Jacobsen 1993; Klein 1993; Langer 1989; Mallon 1983; Moreno and Salomon 1991; Platt 1982; Rivera Cusicanqui 1987).

After the 1840s, the process of indirect incorporation confined China to a peripheral position in the capitalist world-economy. Agricultural and industrial performance deteriorated in the *Yangzi River Delta*. In the early twentieth century, a new wave of innovation launched the modernization of China's agriculture. A cooperative rural reconstruction movement filled the gap left by failing state power. This could not stop rising social vulnerability and polarization (Wang 2003). The rural areas were not able to absorb the growing supply of labor. Social differences in the villages increased, and a rural exodus loosened community ties.

2000: Neoliberal Intensification

In 2000 almost half of the earth's population resided in urbanized settings. Only 42 percent still lived predominantly from agricultural labor. One is tempted to see this as a central vector of convergence in the contemporary world, incorporated in a single capitalist world-system. However, beneath the overall trend of contraction of rural/peasant zones, one discerns striking regional differences. Between 1950 and 2000 the disparity in agricultural population ratios between highest-income and lowest-income countries increased from approximately 1:4 in 1960 (19 percent and 78 percent) to about 1:20 in 2000 (3 percent and 59 percent). This went along with opposite trends in land/labor intensity. While in the global North the long-term trend was one of labor saving, in the global South more agricultural workers were employed per unit of farmland in 2000 than in 1950. These divergences are part of a shared experience of a more global and more entangled corporate food regime, shrinking the margins for peasant and family farming. While peasant farming in the global North virtually disappeared, in the global South large parts of rural and urban populations clung to small-scale agricultural production. Neoliberal globalization included a shift towards a corporate regulation of the global food economy, with an increasing concentration of global firms in both agri-input and agri-food industries, and an ongoing and deepening commodification of peasant subsistence in the global South.

In the *North Sea Region*, the development of a European agricultural policy in the 1950s sealed the breakthrough of a highly commercialized, industrialized, and interconnected agricultural sector (Van Bavel and Hoyle 2010; Vanhaute et al. 2011). The remaining small farmers were pushed out, except for those who switched to producing high-value, capital-intensive crops and livestock. Labor was replaced by machinery. Increasing farm sizes required farmers to have more capital resources at their disposal.

While in Europe farmers as a social group disappeared from the social radar at both the village and national levels, in the *Andes* the socio-economic and political emancipation of indigenous peasants gained major impetus (Gotkowitz 2007; Larson 2004; Stern 1987). Peasant mobilization was triggered by servile labor relations, extreme land concentration, and syndical organization around the middle of the twentieth century. Land and constitutional reforms enhanced formal and individualizing land and civil rights, but failed to halt land fragmentation, extreme poverty, and marginalization, and generally favored capitalist production (Kay 1998; Mayer 2009 for Peru; Urioste et al. 2007 for Bolivia). Although the majority of the Andean population still lived in indigenous peasant communities in the Altiplano and valleys, demographic pressures in combination with large-scale mining and small-scale agriculture prohibited further expansion of the agricultural frontier. This led to de-ruralization, intra-/inter-community conflicts, and massive migration towards the lowlands, coastal and urban areas, and abroad. Environmental degradation, climate change, and migration were changing the face of the Andean countryside. There was a widening socio-economic gap, particularly between the rural and the urban zones. Social conflicts marked the enduring processes of peripheralization.

After 1950 the communist state apparatus in China tried to speed up the processes of de-ruralization and de-peasantization in the *Yangzi River Delta* (MacFarquhar 1997). The household-based peasant system was replaced by a collective production system. Landlords were eliminated after a process of mass collectivization. Through highly centralized social institutions, the rural cadres of the Chinese Communist Party controlled social and economic resources, which greatly strengthened the state's social mobilization capacity. After the 1980s, peasants gradually privatized land-use rights in practice, and an agricultural marketing system was gradually rebuilt. The people's communes were replaced by a "town-level government plus village-autonomy" (Carter et al. 1996). However, social and economic stress on the rural society increased heavily during the last decades of the twentieth century. Local governments were trying to raise land-based revenues by enlarging farms and increasing mechanization. Massive migration flowing from villages to cities fuelled the most radical process of de-ruralization up to then. The imbalanced rural/urban growth fundamentally undermined the basis of social order in rural areas, increasing social inequality and social protest.

Trajectories of Peasant Transformation: Distinct Stories in a Single Narrative

The incorporation of rural zones in the capitalist world-economy has thoroughly redefined and re-created the spaces and boundaries of peasant survival systems. The decline of both its agrarian organization as its family and village basis has fundamentally altered the strategies of livelihood diversification. The uneven nature of the processes of incorporation and commodification has fuelled divergent trajectories of peasant transformation and created new social and ecological frontier zones. All world regions encountered between the sixteenth and twentieth centuries new and more intensive forms of social and geographical polarization, albeit in strongly different manners. The breakthrough of commercial and agricultural capitalism in the North Sea area and of a trans-Atlantic trade system in the "long sixteenth century" thoroughly reconfigured peasant zones in both the core and peripheries. Inequality increased, within and between regions. Core processes of incorporation in western Europe could eventually absorb the impact of uneven economic and social growth. Peasant zones differentiated into a small fraction of commercial farmers and a large nonagricultural labor force. Peripheral processes of incorporation, such as in the Andean Highlands, had a disastrous impact on the regional rural systems, brutally redirecting them towards the needs of the metropolis. This process was not at all unilinear or equal. Although it gradually weakened the capacity of peasant livelihood diversification, it also created new spaces of interaction, survival, and resistance.

The long-term transformation of peasant communities in the Yangzi River Delta was rooted in the gradual decline of the inclusive and protective policies of the Chinese empires. This process was amplified by the indirect, unequal incorporation of China. This triggered new forms of social tension, to which the new republican and communist states responded inadequately. The rural-urban gap has become a crucial determinant in the fast-growing inequality in China.

The "long twentieth century" corporate food regime globalized through waves of imperialist and neoliberal intensification the North Sea geo-model of a core of capital-intensive market production with peasant-based export-cum-survival zones at the edges. This restructuring and intensification of core-periphery relations created new divergences both in the rural economy as in peasant societies.

The disappearance of peasantries in Europe, the reconfiguration of rural societies in China, and the struggle to formulate new peasant responses to peripheral positions in Latin America are all part of the changing global geo-system of the early twenty-first century. This has greatly strengthened global inequality.

Contrary to the (semi-)urbanized labor force in the global North, the rural workers of the global South have to pursue their reproduction through increasingly insecure, oppressive, and scarce wage employment and/or a range of precarious small-scale and "informal economy" survival activities, including marginal farming. Peasant livelihood strategies remain a central part of twenty-first-century global capitalism, both as a means of survival and as ammunition for new forms of resistance.

Chapter 6

Large Enterprises and Corporate Power

by Jorge Fonseca

> In democratic countries, the violent nature of the economy is not perceived; in authoritarian countries, it is the economic nature of violence which is not perceived.
>
> —*Bertolt Brecht*

The Role of the State

The main role of the capitalist state is that of guaranteeing the cohesion and stability of its capitalist strata via protection rent, laws, rules, incentives, pressures on other governments, and wars. It seeks to repress the conflict derived from the class struggle and to favor the distribution of the social surplus in such a way that the class struggle does not provoke a fall in the profit rate that might interrupt the process of capital accumulation (Lane 1979; Wallerstein 1974b).

In periods of crisis, the states have on the whole defended the interests of the big corporations and of the richest sectors of the capitalist class, thereby favoring the concentration and centralization of capital (Mandel 1972). Therefore, in order to study how corporate power emerged and evolved, we need to analyze it within the capitalist process as a whole.

Corporate power comprises a set of economic-financial, labor, social, political, institutional, environmental, and cultural aspects, which together may secure quasi-monopoly power for the companies. This benefits those countries that have many large companies, resulting in growing world polarization.

Financial and economic power—the ability of corporations to affect trade, finance, taxation, and other economic conditions, and to profit from concentration, technology, property rights, and the ability to pressure governments—is the most important, visible, and measurable aspect of corporate power. Regrettably, there are no homogeneous and complete international data on market concentration or centralization of capital. Indeed, for periods before 1900 they are almost nonexistent. One substitute indicator of the corporate power of all enterprise from a country as a whole, and therefore of the hegemonic economic role of that country, is the share of transnational capital it owns, measured by the ratio of foreign direct investment (FDI) outward stock to world gross domestic product (GDP). Consequently, the variation of the grade of dispersion or concentration of world FDI (outward stock) reflects convergence or polarization in the world economic development.

Therefore, its full significance of corporate power is understandable only in the context of the historical capitalist economic process as a whole.

The Capitalist Enterprise at the Initial Stage of Capitalism

The European world-economy came into existence in the "long sixteenth century." It included large parts of western Europe, parts of eastern and southern Europe, and European colonies in the Americas. It included what had been two smaller world-economies and launched a new historical system based on the capitalist mode of production (Wallerstein 1974a, 2004).

Family Firms and Large Public Companies in Venice, the Pioneer of Capitalism

From the eleventh through the fifteenth centuries there were two small world-economies, one centered in Flanders and the Hanseatic states and one centered in the north of Italy (Venice, Milan, Florence, Genoa, and Pisa). In the early fifteenth century, the Venetian Republic constructed an empire in the Aegean Sea, becoming a pioneer state of commercial capitalism. Although the typical Venetian enterprise was the small or medium-size family firm, the Arsenal was a large public shipyard, which in the fifteenth and sixteenth centuries was the largest European enterprise and forerunner of the modern large company. It employed several thousand workers—in banking, carpentry, metallurgy, and armaments.

It played a very important role in the overseas expansion of Venice and it transferred important income to private enterprises.

Its practices resulted in an unequal distribution of the surplus between Venice and other states. In this foundational period, other large European enterprises were private companies administered by their owners, but with strong links with the state, as was the case of the Florentine company of the Medici, which had subsidiaries in the main European cities and great influence in business between the fourteenth and sixteenth centuries (Lane 1992).

The State-Entrepreneur in the "Business of Conquest"

The discovery and conquest of the Americas was decisive in the primitive accumulation of capital and very important for the evolution of Europe towards capitalism, but not yet for the large capitalist enterprise. Conquest, based on violence and the extermination of native populations, allowed agricultural production to be diversified on both sides of the Atlantic Ocean, and the trade of food was very important to increase the level of profit. The main sources of wealth that stimulated the development of European enterprises were the extraction of the silver of Mexico and Peru and plantation agriculture, much of it using African slave labor (Wallerstein 1974a).

In 1494 Spain and Portugal agreed to a division of the newly colonized lands. In the sixteenth century, Portugal replaced Venice as the leader in worldwide trade, due to geographical advantage, military power, monetization of the economy, investment of capital from Genoa, and mainly the strong entrepreneurial role of the state, dominated by the large landowners. Portuguese expansion, based on guns and butter, gave to Portugal and its companies the monopoly of trade in slaves and goods. The Portuguese were the main proprietors of sugar plantations, and plundered gold and diamonds. This allowed a great accumulation of private wealth and converted Portugal into a great maritime monopoly, with an empire stretching from Brazil to much of Asia, including a large area on the coast of Africa (Wallerstein 1974a).

The advantage of Portugal in the "business of colonization" favored the revenue of the state, the aristocracy, the commercial bourgeoisie, and the urban semi-proletariat, expelled from agrarian activities and expecting that the overseas expansion would be a source of jobs. This "capitalist social solidarity" produced unequal development in both the core and the periphery of the European world-economy.

The Portuguese landowning class and firms also developed unequally. The profit rate obtained in the colonial monopoly controlled by the state was double or triple that in the domestic markets. The merchants in foreign trade bought from the producers before the goods were produced, at fixed prices, selling them at a previously fixed price (Lane 1979).

Therefore, the private companies were dependent on the state, which played a central role in the distribution of surplus. As collector and administrator of income, it was the main entrepreneur, which allowed it to be very strong until the eighteenth century and to be essential to the development of capitalism (Wallerstein 1974a).

The Large Capitalist Company as a Delegate of the State in the Mercantile Era (1600–1770)

In northern Europe in the sixteenth century, Holland grew stronger than Flanders and Brabant, and in the next century built the largest fleet in Europe, opening up space to the sea and enlarging its territory. It developed industrial activities (production of raw materials for the textile industry and dairy products), banking, shipping, weaponry, and infrastructure. After its independence in 1581, the Dutch Republic (United Provinces) blocked Antwerp for two centuries in the Spanish Netherlands, enriching the Dutch. Between 1600 and 1800 the Dutch had the highest per capita income of Europe, combined with high taxes (Maddison 2001). Dutch colonial expansion overseas in a few decades snatched from Portugal the trade in gold and slaves, its military bases in Africa, the monopoly of trade with Asia (silver, coffee, sugar, textiles, and spices), and its colony of Brazil, with sugar plantations based on slave labor (de Vries and van der Woude 1987; Wallerstein 1980).

The Dutch East India Company (VOC) was born in this context and was the first public limited company, created by the Dutch state in 1602 with a legal commercial monopoly. It was authorized to mint money and exercised diplomatic and military authority in its zones of activity. The VOC was a large company that built its own large merchant-warship fleet, reinforced with mercenaries and pirate fleets, which was used against local populations, as in the Spice Islands in 1621, where large groups were exterminated (de Vries and van der Woude 1987; Maddison 2001).

The VOC had a central role in Dutch colonial expansion, built a great empire, and centralized Dutch foreign trade. It also helped to develop an internal market through the construction of a network of river channels, producing a major transformation of transport and a new expansion of shipping. Beginning in 1651, however, English and French protectionist laws led to wars over more than a century. The wars resulted in the loss of the VOC monopoly in India and, finally, to its bankruptcy. This reduced Dutch production and exports, increased unemployment, and accelerated the decline of Holland, which demonstrates the important role of VOC in the Dutch economy. The fall in profit levels provoked an outflow of foreign investment, doubling the Dutch national income and generating a high return for a few investors. This process, combined with unemployment and the bankruptcy of small firms, led to strong internal polarization (de Vries and van der Woude 1987; Maddison 2001).

In the Core of the World-Economy, the States Give International Monopoly Power to the Companies (1770–1880)

In this period, England/Great Britain was the most advanced country in the world-economy. Its expansion overseas in Asia and Africa was accomplished by a combination of the British East India Company, pirates, and the Royal Navy. Even in the River Plata, where the British were defeated militarily, their banks and corporations soon ended up dominating the region. The United States in the first half of the nineteenth century underwent a profound economic restructuring with a combination of agricultural and industrial transformations, technological innovation, profits amassed through its role as neutral transporter in the war between Great Britain and France, exports of cotton produced with slave labor for England, and territorial expansion obtained by occupation, purchase, and annexation. This includes its annexation of Mexican territories, which multiplied the US territory three and one-half times and allowed it access to a large amount of natural resources (Fonseca 1993; Niveau 1966).

In the period 1850–1873, there was an expansion of the world-economy. Great Britain had a strong international hegemonic role, which gave corporate power to its companies as a whole. During this period, there were scarcely any monopolies. Market concentration was low, and the majority of enterprises were small or medium-sized and oriented to the domestic market. However, this was also the period of the construction of the first transnational enterprises, as a few banks and industries set up subsidiaries abroad (Pollard 1989; Wallerstein 1989).

Large Companies Became Transnational Corporations and Capitalism Turned into Monopoly Capitalism (1880–1929)

The recession in Europe (1870–1876) led to a political crisis and war between Germany and France, from which Germany emerged as a new military and industrial power while France sank into a deep crisis that intensified the class struggle (the Paris Commune government in 1871). The crisis stimulated the merging of thousands of companies and the purchase of manufacturing firms by banks, thus strengthening financial capital by the merger of banking and industrial capital. In the United States, the previous accelerated growth of production and demand created an important surplus of domestic savings, consolidating the banking system and reducing to a minimum the need for foreign capital. Between 1870 and 1900 the United States doubled its national income and became the world leader in per capita income, productivity, and industrial production, accounting for 30 percent of the worldwide total (Fonseca 1993; Niveau 1966), but with a strong concentration of capital. Three hundred industrial corporations accounted for 40 percent of total industrial investment in 1904 (du Boff 1989).

The result was European and US financial and colonial expansion abroad. In two decades the European powers divided Africa to plunder its natural resources. Great Britain also extended its colonies in Asia, the British Empire at that point governing a quarter of humanity. The United States invaded several countries in Central America where it pursued a policy of creating semi-colonial enclaves. Other countries were "colonized" by private enterprises. The search for new markets led the corporations to set up subsidiaries and became large monopolies. The majority of them are still today among the top one hundred transnational corporations (TNCs). US firms included Singer, Morgan Guaranty, Chase Bank, Citibank, Exxon, GM, Ford, Chrysler, IBM, Goodyear, Otis, Merck, Kodak, Standard Electric, General Electric, Portland Cement, Johnson & Johnson, Pfizer, Dow Chemical, Procter & Gamble, Coca-Cola, and United Fruit. Other multinationals included German firms (Deutsche Bank, Dresdner Bank, Wella, Telefunken, Bayer, and BASF), other European firms (Anglo-Persian Oil or later British Petroleum, Royal Dutch Shell, Total, Nestlé, and Roche), and Japanese firms (Mitsui and Mitsubishi) (Andreff and Pastré 1981; Fonseca 1992; UNCTAD 2010).

In 1914, the totality of FDI outward stock in the world reached an unprecedented 9 percent of the world's gross domestic product, of which 45 percent was by transnational corporations based in the United Kingdom, 15 percent in the United States, and 35 percent in Germany, France, and the Netherlands. Twenty-four percent of the total was invested in the European/North American industrialized countries, 33 percent in Latin America, 21 percent in Asia, 7 percent in Russia, 6 percent in Africa, 4 percent each in Australia and in South Africa, and 3 percent in the Middle East. Two-thirds of the total investment was in new productive installations, mostly related to oil, mining, and agriculture (55 percent), railways (20 percent), and manufacturing (15 percent) (Dunning and Lundan 2008).

After the First World War, the United States became the financier and supplier of weaponry and equipment of both Great Britain and France, and replaced them in areas they had previously dominated. Thereupon, the "military-industrial complex" occupied the center of the US economy and by 1919 the United States had also become the net creditor of the rest of the world (Fonseca 1993; Niveau 1966). In 1929 the one hundred biggest US enterprises concentrated 38 percent of industrial sales while a smaller number of holdings controlled internal markets (du Boff 1989).

The international expansion of enterprises provoked a differentiation within the capitalist class, increasing the role of the state in economic regulation because it had to articulate internal and external interests of local and foreign corporations. In the core of the world-economy, the state is financially sustained from within through taxation. The state combines the direct action in defense of its capitalist enterprises with a delegation of powers to corporations.

In the periphery, the states were economically and financially sustained more from the outside through debt and foreign investment than from the inside. And a part of the ruling capitalist elite is located outside the country. Therefore, the role of the states was more complex because of the need to reconcile local and foreign interests, often under the direction of the latter. Consequently, in both core and periphery, states strengthened the corporate power of the companies, which were increasingly represented in state and supranational institutions, increasing their financial, political, and social power.

Boom of Foreign Investment by Industrial Transnational Corporations (1929–1972)

In 1929 Great Britain and the United States were the major investors in the world—40 percent for Great Britain and 28 percent for the United States (Dunning and Lundan 2008). In Latin America the United States had 50 percent of the total, and their industrial corporations were the world's biggest. After the crisis of 1929 and during the Second World War, FDI declined (Berberoglu 1987; Fonseca 1992). Meanwhile, many US corporations continued their expansion abroad, often leaping protectionist barriers, sometimes also breaking other rules. Such is the case of General Motors, which in 1929 bought Opel in Germany. This firm later produced for Hitler's regime during the Second World War, while in the United States it was producing for the allies. Many other firms, such as Ford, Chase Bank, IBM, and ITT, were also accused of collaboration with the Nazis. This was true as well of German companies, such as Daimler Benz, Bayern, BMW, Krupp, Volkswagen, and Siemens, all of which used the slave labor of prisoners. Many firms from other countries have also been the object of denunciations for collaboration with the Nazis (Black 2001; Higham 1993; ISSOCO 1976; Sampson 1973).

After 1945 there was a long period of growth led by metal-mechanical industries and with strong public spending and incentives, both in the Western capitalist countries and in the large zone of centrally planned economies. It included a new boom in FDI, mainly in manufacturing, which reached 35 percent of the total in the 1960s. Also there were further cross-border mergers and acquisitions (M and A), and the large enterprises became diversified transnational corporations. Two-thirds of FDI were invested in the wealthier countries. In 1914 and 1938, it had been only 24 percent. And half of the investments in the global South were in Latin America. The United States was the hegemonic power and the greatest world investor, with a share of almost 60 percent of the world's FDI in 1950 and still almost 50 percent in 1960 (Berberoglu 1987). Between 1950 and 1970, FDI from the United States multiplied by seven while the number of affiliates of its TNCs increased four times.

This investment was made by reinvesting profits from foreign affiliates. Although most TNCs were small and medium-sized enterprises, a few dozen large companies had monopoly power in almost all markets of the world (Fonseca 1992; Vaupel and Curhan 1974).

Financialization, Centralization, and Leadership of TNCs in Neoliberal Globalization (1973–2011)

In the mid-1960s the postwar economic expansion ended, causing a sharp drop in the average rate of profit. There was a currency crisis with the abandonment of the gold-dollar standard and a global recession in the 1970s, aggravated by rising oil prices. The increase in public spending to curtail the decline in demand resulted in fiscal crises, debt expansion, and rising interest rates, which encouraged the recycling of petrodollars into the indebted countries. In turn there was an outflow of productive capital in search of higher returns in the financial system. From the 1970s, currency and debt securities speculation in Eurocurrency and in the offshore banking centers created worldwide financial speculation that was much more profitable than any productive investment. It also accelerated the expansion of transnational banking and the speculative activities of nonfinancial corporations (Fonseca and Martínez Gz.-Tablas 2008).

The 1970s marked the beginning of what has come to be called the era of neoliberalism. One principal feature was the so-called structural adjustment programs. These programs made receipt of financial assistance, primarily from the International Monetary Fund (IMF), conditional on reductions of wages, public spending, and taxes; financial liberalization; privatizations of state-owned enterprises; and other measures consistent with the primacy of the market.

The pioneer state to implement such requirements was that of the Chilean dictator Augusto Pinochet, with the direct advice of Milton Friedman and his associates. Margaret Thatcher in Great Britain and Ronald Reagan in the United States implemented programs in the same spirit in the 1980s. And gradually many European governments applied similar policies. These programs resulted in high levels of debt, and for many countries de-industrialization and drastic reduction of the welfare state. This led to a transfer of income from workers to the capitalist class, particularly to bankers and others financial speculators. It also led to the worldwide transfer of public assets to private monopolies through privatizations, deepening productive transnationalization and the centralization of capital (Fonseca and Martínez Gz.-Tablas 2008).

The volume of banking transactions in 2007 reached thirty-two trillion dollars, three hundred times greater than in 1970. Banking assets also increased to more than 50 percent of the total value of the global GDP. In addition, the concentration of global banking capital in the fifty largest banks increased from 42 percent to 60 percent between 1996 and 2007, while the top one hundred of banks increased their share from 55 to 75 percent. In the first decade of the twenty-first century, speculation in financial derivatives reached extraordinary levels. The market in credit derivatives was multiplied by forty between 2001 and 2007, reaching US$45 trillion. Moreover, daily foreign-exchange transactions reached $3.4 trillion in 2007 and daily operations with over-the-counter derivatives reached $4.2 trillion. This means that the sum of both exceeded the total currency reserves of the world-economy and explains the permanent financial turmoil (Fonseca 2008; Fonseca and Martinez Gz.-Tablas 2008).

The financial bubble of 2007, caused by speculation in mortgage-backed securities, gave rise to a worldwide capitalist crisis, causing a further wave of M and A, which reached a new record of more than 10,000 operations worth $1.6 trillion. Seventy-one percent of this value was concentrated in three hundred megamergers of more than $1 billion each, which increased the flow of FDI to $1.8 trillion and the FDI outward stock to twenty-seven times that of 1982, reaching the equivalent of 28 percent of global GDP in 2007 and 35 percent in 2009, the highest in history (Fonseca 2008; UNCTAD 2010).

However, given that almost 90 percent of the FDI was made through M and A of existing companies, it contributed neither to the formation of gross fixed capital nor to the creation of jobs. This, in combination with the concentration of origin of investment, contributed to the further centralization and polarization of capital.

Moreover, this expansion of FDI was supported by the high profits generated by the FDI itself in the host countries—70 percent of the total FDI and up to 90 percent of M and A in 2005–2007, with local savings.

In turn, the source of FDI continued to be very polarized. The United States remained the largest investor, with 18 percent of FDI outward stock in 2007, but also the major beneficiary of FDI inward stock, with 13 percent, although in decline.

Together, the United States, Great Britain (13.3 percent), France (11.2 percent), and Germany (8.4 percent) accounted for half the total outward stock of FDI. Italy, Spain, and Japan accounted for 14.2 percent and seven other developed countries 22 percent. Developing countries together accounted for 15.2 percent of total FDI outward stock (China 7 percent, Russia 2.3 percent). Moreover, TNCs were also the main agent of trade globalization because two-thirds of world trade was conducted by transnational corporations and about 40 percent of this was between affiliates of the same firm (Fonseca 2008; UNCTAD 2010).

In the long term, the currency outflows from peripheral zones by TNCs via interest and royalties have been much higher than inflows by investment. Consequently, TNCs contributed further to polarization in the world-economy, extracting capital in net terms from peripheral zones to accumulate it in core zones. Corporations seeking to control markets with high purchasing power have concentrated their investments geographically both in developed countries with high income and in the large "emerging" markets. In 2007, the United States (13 percent), Great Britain (10 percent), France (9 percent), Germany (3 percent), and the BRICS with 16.3 percent (Brazil 2 percent, Russia 3 percent, India 1.3 percent, and China 10 percent) totaled 51.3 percent of inward stock of FDI. The industrialized countries concentrated 68 percent and underdeveloped countries 32 percent (Asia 17 percent, the Middle East 4 percent, Latin America 7 percent, Africa 3 percent, and the Commonwealth of Independent States, including Russia, 5 percent). In 1914, the global South had received 72 percent of total FDI (Table 6.1).

Between 1914 and 2009, the transnationalization of capital, measured by a ratio of FDI outward stock to world GDP, was multiplied fourfold, going from 9 to 35 percent. In 1914, FDI was mainly into new productive installations. In 2007, 90 percent was in buying existing shares of companies. Sectorially, in 2007 FDI was primarily in financial activities (20 percent of total), services to enterprise (14 percent), and others with large infrastructures. The services sector totaled 56 percent. The exception is East Asia, where there was investment in manufacturing. In 1914 90 percent of FDI was in the primary sector and manufacturing, which by 2007 declined to 36 percent (Table 6.2).

The relative importance of the world's largest corporations is very impressive. The one hundred largest global companies (financial, nonfinancial, and diversified conglomerates) listed in the Fortune Global 500 accumulated in 2006 total assets of US$45 trillion, which amounted to 92

Table 6.1   Evolution of Transnationalization of Capital, 1914–2007

Location of FDI Outward Stock	Percentages			
	FDI Outward 1914	FDI Outward 2007	FDI Inward 1914	FDI Inward 2007
Global North	100	85	28	68
Great Britain	45	13	—	—
United States	15	18	—	—
France, Netherlands, Germany	35	21	—	—
Seven others	5	22	—	—
Global South	0	15	72	32
Russia	0	2	7	5
Asia	0	9	21	17
China	0	7	—	10
Middle East	—	2	3	4
Latin America	—	2	33	7
Africa	—	0	8	3

Sources: For 1914 Dunning and Lundan 2008; for 2007 Fonseca 2008; for data UNCTAD 2010.

Table 6.2   Evolution of Transnationalization of Capital, 1914–2007/2009

	World FDI Stock as percent GDP and Sectorial Distribution		
	1914	2007	2009
FDI percent GDP*	9	28	35
percent FDI:			
NPI[1]	66	10	
M and A[2]	34	90	
O, M, and A[3]	55	8	
Manuf./rail	35	28	
SERVICES	—	62	
Financial	—	20	
Not rated	10	1,5	

*FDI outward stock
[1]New productive installations ("green fields")
[2]Mergers and acquisitions
[3]Oil, mining, and agriculture
Sources: For 1914 Dunning and Lundan 2008; for 2007 Fonseca 2008; for 2009 UNCTAD 2010.

percent of the global gross domestic product (GDP) in the same year. The value of assets of the largest five hundred exceeded 75 percent of world GDP. The assets of the one hundred largest nonfinancial companies exceeded the world's gross fixed capital, and the income of the two hundred largest firms was nearly equivalent to the whole value of world exports.

Geographically, in 2007 340 of the 500 largest companies in the world (almost 70 percent) were located in countries of the G5 (the United States, Great Britain, France, Germany, and Japan) plus the Netherlands, all countries that had been hegemonic or sought that position since the sixteenth century. China, with twenty-five of those five hundred companies (Fortune 2007), ranks sixth and is the emerging power in the global quest for resources and control of markets through an accelerated development of large corporations. It is trying to regain the place it occupied until the fifteenth century.

By 2011, four years after the beginning of the worldwide financial crisis, the TNCs, especially the financial enterprises, had more than recovered their initial value. The TNCs based in the United States maintained their hegemony, although China already was the second power in the ranking of largest world TNCs. Five of the top ten and seven of the top twenty-three largest financial corporations are from the United States. Four of the top ten and five of the top twenty-three are from China. An important difference is that the US corporations are highly internationalized while the Chinese corporations have a low grade of internationalization, which gave them less world corporate power.

The United States has six of the top ten and twenty-four of the top fifty largest nonfinancial TNCs, with a predominance of information and communication companies. China is second, with four of the top ten and five of the top twenty-three, but with a predominance of oil companies, which indicates the continuing technological hegemony of the United States (Forbes 2011).[1]

The Consequences of Corporate Power

Historical evidence shows that the power of corporations has been a determining element in achieving geopolitical and economic hegemony, and this resulted in global polarization. In the mercantile era large colonizing companies gave economic hegemony to their home countries. In the monopoly era most large enterprises with thousands of affiliates around the world were based in a handful of developed countries that have increased their share of foreign outward stock in relationship to global production (from 8.5 percent in 1914 to 30 percent in 2009).

They were able to extract savings and wealth from countries in which they invested, accumulating this wealth in their home countries. This polarization is based on an international division of labor stemming from uneven development and a social system that penalizes severely those who seek to modify it, but tolerates or protects serious violations of fundamental rights by the same powerful corporations.

Great enterprises have strong corporate power because they are integrated in holdings and monopolistic associations that allow them to control distribution networks as well as give them access to strategic raw materials. In these conditions the decisions of the corporations have come to be made at a worldwide scale capable of creating integrated global systems of raw materials, production, financing, commercial distribution, and after-sales service. This allows them to make the most of advantages at each and every link in the chain of worldwide value to obtain control of the world market as a whole. Therefore, the corporations take advantage of the skilled manpower in high-tech industries and the low cost of wages in mature industries, of the scale in industries of intensive fixed capital, and of the control of strategic raw materials (or of a combination of these).

The negative effects of current account-of-balance of payments in a large number of countries creates the need to seek external capital to finance their deficits, and the large corporations have developed a great capacity for imposing extraordinary conditions of monopolistic profits and protection as conditions for their investment. This leads to a vicious circle, in which inflows always end up increasing external imbalances. The need for more capital by the host country is exchanged for better conditions for the investing corporations. They receive subsidies, tax exemptions, and special rules governing labor, as well as changes that

---

1. For the debate concerning the outcome of a US-China rivalry, see the contrasting views of Jacques 2008, Shirk 2008, and Bustelo 2010.

affect the whole economy, such as the exchange rate, general taxation, and general labor regulations. This gives even more corporate power to the enterprises.

The states of the core countries where most enterprises have their headquarters and where the major international institutions of global capitalism are located, in combination with the great corporations, impose the global economic and financial rules to be followed by the peripheral countries as well as the conditions for them to be able to finance their external debt, or to receive "development assistance." They must, consequently, accept the imposition of asymmetric rules of "free trade" and regressive labor regulations. The final conclusion is that the large corporations are an important factor in favoring unequal development and the social polarization within and between different regions and countries of the capitalist world-economy.

It follows that, since the formation of the modern world-system, the handful of countries that were hegemonic combined the power of the state with corporate power. Initially the state was the entrepreneur; then it became the official protector of the companies, to which some powers were delegated. In the nineteenth century companies assumed their autonomy, and in the twentieth the great enterprises began to exercise forms of global hegemony previously the purview of the state. In the neoliberal era, the power of large corporations established an authoritarian world regime, officially democratic but in which the rules are enforced by them, not by the citizens.

Chapter 7

Intellectual Property

by Ravi Sundaram

The discussion/debates about media piracy, copyright, and the so-called knowledge economy have taken a central place in the rhetoric of the contemporary global crisis. This discussion exposes the dramatic and widespread acceleration of the transformation of the domain of culture into property after the arrival of mechanical and digital forms of media in the twentieth century. It also sets up the contours of current skirmishes between the United States and China, and between US media industries and European regulators.

The twentieth-century debates reflect the high point of a long-term historical process by which cultural forms like print were transformed into property. We seek to present some of the issues at stake in this process and raise questions about long-term polarization. We use copyright as a vantage point of tracking the movement of culture into property, in turn linked to four hundred years of secular movement in media history.

Copyright offers a clear site to understand and measure key systemic shifts. We shall track the media-property regime from print in seventeenth-century England to the current digital era. These systemic shifts in media property parallel but do not necessarily equal the larger polarization patterns in the capitalist world-economy.

We can identify four phases in this long-term movement. Phase one was the patent system in early modern Europe. Patents shaped the copyright regime by creating models of proprietorship and authority, and their relationship to state power. Phase two was the emergence of the copyright system in the early 1700s in England and its coexistence with competing models in mainland Europe and the early United States. Phase three was the establishment of a dominant copyright regime with the rise of US hegemony and Hollywood, and the elimination of most competing systems. Phase four has been the challenge of video and digital piracy, paralleling the decline of US power in the post-1968 era. This phase has also seen the aggressive turn to copyright enforcement by the United States and its agencies, a model that is increasingly ineffective as a mode of managing media property.

Copy/Original/Pirate: An Introduction

Since Plato's time, the relationship between the real and the copy has been framed so as to consider the simulacrum almost entirely as a negative comparison, a false claimant to the real. Plato's distinction became significant by the seventeenth century when Western modernity refashioned itself through the lenses of creativity and authorship, both tied to an emerging theory of cultural property. The establishment of a widespread discourse on authorship was by no means easy. From the seventeenth century on, mass reproduction techniques inaugurated by print rendered Plato's philosophical distinction increasingly suspect because of the proliferation of multiple versions of the presumed same text.

In his remarkable book on early modern print culture, Adrian Johns suggests that widespread piracy in early Western print culture had both "epistemic" as well as economic implications. Most significantly, piracy localized print reception and undermined the imagined "fixity" and unity of print communities. As readers' access to texts vastly increased, so did the experience of uncertainty about the authority of the printed word.[1]

> Piracy and plagiarism occupied readers' minds. . . . Unauthorized translations, epitomes, imitations and other varieties of "impropriety" were, they believed, routine hazards. . . . From Galileo and Tycho to Newton and John Flamstead, no significant learned author seemed to escape the kinds of practices soon colloquially subsumed under the label of piracy (Johns 1998: 30).

Printed titles with the same "authors" differed from region to region, throwing readers into both confusion and ecstasy.

> Martin Luther's German translation of Scripture was actually beaten into print by its first piracy, and in succeeding years the proportion of unauthorized to authorized versions was roughly ninety to one. . . .

---

1. For the various other debates in early modern print culture in the West, see Chartier (1994), Darnton (2006), and Eisenstein (1979).

A century later, the first folio of Shakespeare boasted six hundred typefaces, along with non-uniform spelling and punctuation, erratic divisions and arrangement, mispaging and irregular proofing. No two copies were identical (Johns 1998: 31).

New media geographies of readers, publisher-pirates, and interpretations emerged in a zone where the object itself—the printed book—actually created debate and conflict rather than producing a unity through technological fixity. Johns's main target in *The Nature of the Book* is Elizabeth Eisenstein's hugely influential *The Printing Press as an Agent of Change* (Eisenstein 1979). Eisenstein argued that "ancient and medieval scientific traditions were transformed by the capacity of printing to transmit records of observations without any loss of precision and in full detail" (1979: 470). As a result, new communities of experimental science emerged communicating across boundaries. For Eisenstein, standardization produced collaborative communities and experimentation. Benedict Anderson's work on nationalism (1991) takes this argument a step forward, arguing that common, imaginary print-journeys of national elites prefigured the rise of nation-states. In Johns's book, by contrast, the category of "print" is evacuated from the classic story of the serial expansion of Western modernity from Gutenberg to cosmopolitanism.

Copyright's own pasts are deeply contradictory. The late twentieth-century regime has emerged out of conflicts between authors, publishers, corporations, and states, propounding different legal philosophies that inspired statutes. The broad legal consensus is that the "origins" of copyright can be traced back to the Statute of Anne in England in 1710. This statute ended the system of royal privileges and patents that had developed in Europe in the early modern period—a moment that offers a fascinating prehistory of literary property.

Patents and the Prehistory of Copyright

Patents were privileges that were granted by states in the early modern world to forge a new relationship with artisan communities. Craft practices grouped around guilds had been initiating new models of secrecy and proprietorship around their trade (Long 2001). Patents had emerged in medieval Europe for craft protection. The first systematic general statute on patents was issued by Venice in 1447. It covered inventions and gave them protection for ten years. In return for protection against imitations, inventors were compelled to reveal details to the state, which could deploy them for its own use. Patents covered books and mechanical devices, and varied from country to country.

Patents began to be used as tools to encourage the crafts by the states and served to encourage those who held them to immigrate. Mobility was central to the model. Venice, for example, actively discouraged its inventors from taking their inventions outside its frontiers, while encouraging the inward flow of outside inventions. Thus, the early Venetian document on patents announced: "Men with most acute minds able to conceive various ingenious devices reside in this City and, thanks to its greatness and tolerance, move here every day from different countries" (cited in Biagioli 2006: 148).

Patents anticipated intellectual property in that they gave limited protection to "inventions." However, their purpose was different. Unlike modern copyright that produced a notion of authorial rights, patents set up authors and inventors as *subjects* of the state. Patents were thus gifts of the state rather than rights (Biagioli 2006: 142). Patents were granted not for originality but for possession of knowledge that would benefit the realm. It was irrelevant who had actually invented the knowledge patented. The person who sought protection simply needed to possess it. Pamela Long points out that early patents for books were not connected to authorial originality as in modern copyright. Patent was a commercial privilege granted to the author, for expenses (Long 2001: 11).

Patent holders' mobility was widespread. Inventors traveled from realm to realm, taking their invention and craft with them, and states went out of their way to attract new trades and inventions from other areas. Unlike the virtual, abstract rights of the later intellectual-property regime that moved through licensing, artisan mobility in the patent/ privilege era was physical, and a movement of persons.

At other levels, though, patent cultures of the thirteenth to the sixteenth centuries anticipated the storms of the period after the coming of intellectual property and copyright. Artisanal knowledge and the debates of alchemy and science gave a new prominence to creativity over scribal knowledge. What emerged was the figure of the artisan as author "of an extraordinarily ambitious kind—one who could transfigure, transmute, *create*" (Johns 2008: 21). This focus on discovery, practice, and creativity emerged from an "artisanal epistemology" (Long 2001) and had radical implications in future debates on authorship, creativity, and piracy.

From Patents to Copyright

England after the Civil War and the Restoration offers a useful vantage point to witness the emergence of the first copyright regime. In the last few decades of the seventeenth century, print in England was dominated by the Stationers' Company, a printer's guild that combined monopoly with censorship of prohibited works.[2] By the early eighteenth century

2. The literature on this period is vast. For lucid summaries, see Rose (1993), particularly Chapters 2 and 3, and for a comprehensive account see Johns (1998).

this monopoly was under attack and the 1710 Statute of Anne removed printed monopolies to the benefit of "authors," who were now granted rights over their work for a total period not exceeding twenty-eight years. To be sure, the rights of "authors" in a growing capitalist society meant in normal practice that writers assigned their rights as authors to publishers. At best, the statute tried to balance private monopoly with a rough notion of public purpose.

This act was followed by a long struggle in England between the idea of the author's perpetual right (i.e., that of the publishers to whom it was assigned) in common law, and the more limited right that was set up in the Statute of Anne. The matter was finally resolved in the celebrated case of Donaldson vs. Beckett in 1774, in which the statute of limitations was upheld by a majority decision of the House of Lords. Donaldson vs. Beckett was a landmark decision in early copyright law because it marked a watershed in the thinking about several issues in copyright law.

In support of their cause, the London publishers were canvassing the notion that authors had a perpetual monopoly in their works and that this right stemmed from common law. This notion of a perpetual natural right of authors in their works was an outgrowth of Enlightenment Europe's new fascination with the genius of the author (Woodmansee and Jaszi 1994). If the advocates of the perpetual common-law right focused on the author, its opponents turned their attention towards the thing (*res*)—the work. They highlighted the fundamental indeterminacy of the "property in words" that the London publishers were claiming. How could one claim property in something that was incapable of being enjoyed and harnessed exclusively?

Further, they drew analogues with patent law prevalent at the time, which granted only a limited property right to the inventor. Both sides working simultaneously, as Rose (1993) points out, led to the reification of the author-work relationship. This was to pave the way for a more extensive copyright of authors in their work, and later the representation of the "author" by media industries on a world scale.

The Nineteenth-Century Puzzle: Print, Power, Copyright

The consolidation of the hegemony of the United Kingdom in the capitalist world-economy did not mean in any sense the imposition of a global copyright regime in print that was in line with UK interests. There may be several reasons for this:

- As a cultural technology print was fragmented territorially, varying from region to region. Conflicts over print and property were typically regional, though international debates began to make themselves felt in the mid-nineteenth century.

- Legal traditions varied in mainland Europe, still dominated by romantic ideas of authorship; and in the United States the state was ambivalent about piracy.
- The United Kingdom, however, pushed versions of copyright legislation modeled on English legal principles in its colonies in Asia and Africa. Like in mainland Europe, copyright consciousness among small publishers in the colonies was slim.

One notable example of this fragmented world map of copyright enforcement was the widespread prevalence of print piracy in the United States. The Copyright Act of 1790 specifically opened the door for the piracy of materials of non-US origin by saying: "Nothing in this act shall be construed to extend to prohibit the importation or vending, reprinting, or publishing within the United States, of any map, chart, book or books, written, printed, or published by any person not a citizen of the United States, in foreign parts without the jurisdiction of the United States" (cited in Frith and Marshall 2004: 30). The spread of piracy of non-US materials derived from both its active encouragement by the state (Ben-Atar 2004) and radical republican print communities that used serialization of European texts in small publishing ventures to circulate them in mail-order form.

For over a century the United States refused to sign the Berne Convention of 1886. All this changed in the 1990s with the rise of the digital industries and the move to an information economy. Overall, copyright doctrine since the Statute of Anne has seen the confused and often conflictual coming together of three streams.

The first was the Anglo-American utilitarian legal model that modified the Lockean theory[3] of property into a system of incentives for cultural goods, setting up statutory limits on eternal property rights in print and other media to help authors and creators contribute to public good. Thus, the US Constitution argued for Congress's power to pursue the "progress of Science and Useful Arts, by securing for limited times to Authors and Inventors the exclusive Right to their respective Writings and Discoveries" (Article I, sec. 8, para. 8).[4]

The second stream was the idea of the moral rights of the author, coming from German idealist and expressivist traditions in which the idea of

---

3. Locke's "labor" theory of property argued that "everyman has a property in his person," and that man had a right to that which he mixed with their labor, converted into a "private dominion." See his *Two Treatises of Government* (2003). In this theory of appropriation, Locke argued that one may appropriate, but also should "leave enough for others." It thus followed that property was a natural right, but based on physical possession of property. Lockean theory had to be significantly amended for modern copyright doctrine, but the rhetoric of natural rights and protections has often crept into contemporary enforcement.

4. Despite this focus the United States remained ambivalent about media piracy in the nineteenth century, as discussed previously.

copyright is an expression of the personality of the author. The collusion between the idea of literary property that drew from Anglo-American utilitarianism and a nineteenth-century Romantic notion of creative authorship[5] played a significant role in the rhetorical discourse around copyright law, if not its substance (Boyle 1997; Woodmansee and Jaszi 1994).

Finally, there was the concept of an abstract authored work, which laid the grounds for immaterial control and exploitation whatever the media—print, music, image, and so on. This was summarized in the Berne Convention of 1886, which was revised many times to accommodate the spread of newer media like photography and cinema.

The rise of new forms of media, such as analog cinema, in the early twentieth century went hand in hand with the rise of the United States in the world-economy. What is significant about this transition is that for the first time since the Statute of Anne, a hegemonic power, the United States, was able to impose a dominant structure on the global media industry and set up an intellectual-property regime that was in its favor. Analog cinema and the emergence of Hollywood as an industrial form were central to this transition.

Twentieth-Century Transitions: Hollywood, Analog Power, and US Hegemony

Early cinema was dominated by French and other European producers who had pioneered the technology of celluloid. By the outbreak of the First World War in 1914, European exports dominated US film exhibition. US companies soon fought back by deploying intellectual-property rules and lobbying for limits on foreign entry into the US market.

With the transformation of film into intellectual property (Miller et al. 2005), US firms began to dominate film-stock production and the motion-picture business itself. The emergence of the film-studio system in the United States set in place a powerful industrial form, which became the driving force of cultural power in the twentieth century.

The devastation of European film industries due to the First World War placed the United States in a powerful position to obtain a dominant position in the film industry. The shift from the 1900–1914 situation was dramatic. As the authors of a book on Hollywood's global expansion point out: "Between 1915 and 1916, US exports rose from 36 million feet [of film], while imports fell from 16 million feet before the First World War to 7 million by the mid-1920s" (Miller et al. 2005: 61). The Hollywood presence expanded rapidly in Latin America, Europe, and Asia, with

---

5. Rose argues that the "the romantic elaborations of such expressions as originality, organic form, and the work of art as the expression of the unique personality of the artist was in a sense the necessary completion of the legal and economic transformation that occurred during the copyright struggle" (cited in Jaszi 1994: 31).

studios buying out local distributors, and foreign-language versions of US films expanding the reach of the industry.

With the arrival of sound, US cinema came to dominate the world-wide market. And the musical genre cemented the relationship between music and cinema. In her *Irresistible Empire: America's Advance Through Twentieth-Century Europe* (2005), Victoria de Grazia places Hollywood's success within a wider context of Americanism in European culture. This laid the framework of economy and cultural hegemony, where Hollywood increasingly played a major role.

US modernity became attractive to mass publics drawn to dream-worlds of consumption and technological power. This model was successful from the 1930s onwards as European studios like the German UFA struggled to hold their ground against the popularity of US cinema. With Europe's devastation in the Second World War and the postwar expansion under US hegemony, Hollywood's economic and cultural power over European markets was supreme, something that was also apparent in Latin America and many parts of Asia and Africa.

In the context of US hegemony on a world scale, Hollywood's cultural power was attacked by Third World intellectuals and European cultural elites. For much of the 1970s, theories of cultural imperialism were part of public discourse in many countries. The naturalization of Hollywood's cultural script and US power was addressed by many institutions, such as UNESCO in the 1970s, whose MacBride Commission investigated global cultural flows and communication networks, and came up with a call for a New Information Order.

Despite all attacks by critics and radicals, the power of US media industries on a world scale seemed unassailable for the first three decades after 1945. Not only did Hollywood dominate content, but it had near-total control over film stock and processing. US corporations ran film-exhibition chains worldwide. Represented by the powerful Motion Picture Association of America (MPAA), US media industries were able to obtain lucrative deals with relative ease despite periodic local opposition in many countries and criticisms of Hollywood "cultural imperialism."

Hollywood's power was that of an analog-media empire. By the 1930s, analog technological models were embedded in large socio-economic structures of accumulation in the West, which controlled production and distribution. Mid-twentieth-century analog structures prevented easy reproduction,[6] and required significant infrastructures of production and distribution: film stock, processing, television studios, large investment in telecommunication cables, and film theatres. Analog media in the US studio version presumed a mass public accepting streamlined cultural

---

6. This is not inherent to the technology, but an expression of its 1930s historical form. Early analog cinema had a more open-ended ownership pattern and allowed a range of audience interventions.

codes and dependent on culture industries for content. Monopoly over content was a *sine qua non* of the analog empire.

Video and the Analog Empire

The analog empire's power was premised on a stable world geography that was based on the assumption of US hegemony in the global economy. US hegemony suffered a significant setback after its military defeat in Vietnam and the collapse of the Bretton Woods system—a process of secular decline that unfolded for the following three decades. The global crisis of 1968–1973 accelerated the rise of newly industrializing countries and East Asia, as production structures shifted from the core countries of historical capitalism to new areas of stable accumulation (Arrighi 1994: 27–84).

This radical transformation of the world's economic geography and production structures fundamentally undermined the analog empire and the hegemony of US media industries. The first sign of this was the introduction of the home VHS player and video cassettes in the late 1970s, which set in motion many of the chaotic media geographies of the digital age. Video expanded globally, disrupting the stable exhibition and distribution system that Hollywood had established. Exhibitors, cinema houses, and national control were significantly destabilized as millions all over the world were drawn to the VHS experience—in private homes, in pirate-video halls, and in video clubs that evaded the copyright and censorship regime set up by national and international elites.

Writing in the Australian media journal *Continuum* in 1991, Tom O'Regan mapped out the three global sites of video: the VCR as part of the personalized home-entertainment market of the West; the extra, semi-underground TV service in eastern Europe and the post-colonial world, where national monopolies controlled television content; and a third hybrid that was part pay service and part alternative TV, as in the Persian Gulf. Piracy was identified as a major issue all over the world, with lesser effects in the West, where major studios initially moved to control distribution chains and video outlets.[7] In the event, the VCR disturbed national sovereignty and media monopolies. In the long run O'Regan forecast accurately that video would provide lucrative markets for media industries with distribution control and even more integration of media industries.[8] In the non-Western world the 1980s saw video as a mode of disassembly—of space and of audiences. The effects were diverse but equally widespread.

In Mexico, Néstor García Canclini (2001), citing a study by Deborah Holz, reported that video clubs played a significant role in disrupting

---

7. This was the age before the Internet and widespread use of digital technology.
8. See Miller et al. (2005).

the older cultural citizenship that had emerged in post-1945 Mexican society. In a report tinged with nostalgia for a disappearing age of the old cinema hall, García suggested that video took place in a "present without memory" (García Canclini 2001: 116). Old arrangements of genre were ignored in video clubs, as was information about directors, in favor of a culture of the instant.

Immediacy and the value of the instantaneous are reflected in what young videophiles sought. The numbers of images that succeeded each other by a fraction of a second were the beginning of a challenge to time that does not correspond to time (Holz, cited in García Canclini 2001: 116).

In India the early years of video saw viewers engage in a similar play against time, the rush for the latest movie, to beat the circuits of distribution, even obtaining a film before the official release. This limitless desire became a significant part of the pirate assemblage, mutating into networks that spanned global and regional temporal zones.

If the Mexican researchers perceived the emergence of video as disturbing national cultural citizenship, reports from Nigeria underlined a more democratic proliferation of video culture:

> Video rental clubs rent (pirated) videos for a very modest [price]; such businesses at the lower end are very informal affairs, run out of someone's room in a compound with no signboard to advertise their presence. There are also one-room video parlors, equipped with ordinary televisions and VCRs, which cater at low prices to a poorer clientele. Cassettes are sold out of modest shops and stalls on the street very much a part of the ubiquitous West African petty trading. Traders and market women are said to be major consumers of video films. (Haynes and Okome 1998: 117)

Video significantly blurred the relationship between the consumer and the producer of media content. As millions began using video recorders to tape home video, the US film industry recognized in the early days that this constituted a significant blow to its content monopoly and decided to pursue legal action. The most celebrated case in the 1970s was that of Sony Corporation of America vs. Universal City Studios (1984), where the media industry claimed that a "contributor infringement" had occurred in the taping of television shows by private individuals. The media industry sought to impose liabilities on Sony and makers of VCRs. In a case that went all the way to the US Supreme Court, the final judgment held that home taping, "time shifting" of programs, and private video libraries fell under the category of "non-infringing fair-use" and were not illegal.[9] The importance of this event was twofold. It exposed a new, emerging media public of user/

---

9. See http://www.law.cornell.edu/copyright/cases/464_US_U.S._417.htm (accessed April 26, 2014).

producers and highlighted the conflict around intellectual-property law of immaterial works like media.

The Return of the Empire? Enforcement and Copyright Struggles

Video exposed a new geography that threatened to disrupt US power in media property. The spread of media technologies in the post-digital era vastly expanded the potential scope of the copyright regime and the ambitions of international media industries. The Sony case was a turning point in this respect. Since the 1980s, and particularly after the early 1990s, US media industries shifted to designating defense of intellectual property in knowledge as one of the key mechanisms of global control. Since production outlets of hardware were gradually shifting to East Asia, control over the more immaterial elements of media (i.e., parts that were not "tangible") has been central to media industries. The post-video era saw a new alignment, with the US media industry (Hollywood and software giants) pushing for copyright protection and compliance on a world scale.

The older model of abstract authorship, perfected under the Trade-Related Aspects of Intellectual Property Rights agreement of the World Trade Organization (WTO) in 1994, has since moved firmly onto the global arena, with copyright and patent compliance becoming the demanded prerequisite to full membership in the world-economy. The post-WTO era has seen a new discourse of globalization emerging worldwide. Intergovernmental organizations joined advocacy and enforcement organizations for the US and regional media industries in the campaign against "piracy" and the push for "compliance."

The best-known organization is the International Intellectual Property Alliance (IIPA) formed in 1984 to represent the US copyright-based industries. [10,11] The IIPA's members include all the major US media industries—Association of American Publishers (AAP), Business Software Alliance (BSA), Entertainment Software Association (ESA), Independent Film & Television Alliance (IFTA), Motion Picture Association of America (MPAA or MPA), National Music Publishers' Association (NMPA), the Recording Industry Association of America (RIAA).

Of these MPAA, BSA, and RIAA have been the most active in the international campaign against piracy, lobbying national governments,

---

10. This umbrella organization represents the Association of American Publishers, Business Software Alliance, Entertainment Software Association, Independent Film & Television Alliance, Motion Picture Association of America, National Music Publishers' Association, and Recording Industry Association of America; www.iipa. com.

11. In addition to the IIPA's industry advocacy model, the WIPO (World Intellectual Property Organization) is a significant inter-governmental body established by the United Nations.

conducting workshops for police and judges, and leading punitive raids against "pirates." For its part the IIPA issues periodic "country" reports that detail its version of compliance with the international legal copyright regime. The reports also recommends to the US trade representative that various countries be placed on "priority watch lists" for alleged noncompliance.[12,13] For 2007, the US trade representative put Argentina, Chile, Egypt, India, Israel, Lebanon, China, Russia, Thailand, Turkey, Ukraine, and Venezuela on its priority watch list.[14] The IIPA, MPA, and BSA have all been active in India and other parts of Asia, with local offices and advocacy initiatives with local police and the local media and information industries.

The Post-Analog or a Post-Hegemonic World?

In the first decade after the emergence of the digital, a significant focus was on the emerging media industry monopolies that were seeking to take advantage of the new constellation. Notable examples were the AOL-Time Warner merger in the 1990s and the rise of software giants like Microsoft. Many argued that the digital epoch changed little. It simply provided the US media industry with an opportunity to make new profits and reconsolidate its control on the newer platforms. Media centralization in the West and the digital divide in the South were the central themes of the discourse of the 1990s.[15] What seemed almost obvious at that time was that DVDs and online platforms provided huge profits to US media companies, and Microsoft's power seemed unassailable. A decade later, the AOL-Time Warner merger was a business disaster,[16] and Microsoft faced aggressive competition from competitors using open source platforms and low-cost electronic infrastructures in the South.

---

12. For over a century the United States refused to sign the Berne Convention of 1886. All this changed in the 1990s with the rise of the information industries. In 1998 the industry-friendly Sonny Bono Copyright Term Extension Act and the Digital Millennium Copyright Act (DMCA) were passed, ushering in a new era of international enforcement and zero tolerance for any deviation, including piracy. For an extensive analysis of the DMCA see Litman (2000). For a useful survey of Hollywood's international campaigns see Miller et al. (2005).

13. The IIPA list is under four heads, the two relevant ones under its special 301 being the Priority watch list and the watch list that is used for most offenders, including India and China.

14. See http://www.iipa.com/pdf/IIPA2007PressReleaseonUSTRSpecial301decisions FINAL04302007.pdf (accessed August 7, 2014).

15. Miller et al. (2005) summarizes and even agrees with this trend.

16. The former CEO of AOL-Time Warner later apologized for the "worst deal of the century." See http://mashable.com/2010/01/04/time-warner-ceo/ (accessed August 11, 2014).

The competition came from China, not California. Many initially West-centered reactions after the 1990s tended to miss the significant material transformations on a world scale, many of which were beginning to come into view. These included the shift of many production structures to Asia and the emergence of new networks of circulation that bypassed those of property and capital. This was particularly powerful in zones outside that of the West. This changed geography allowed the United States to reflect on the problematic of power and management in a post-digital world.

Digital media and its proliferation have upset the old copyright control models pushed by studios and media corporations in the era of secure US hegemony. In the analog-studio era, both content management and media production were housed in reasonably secure models—with states, industry regulators, and censors managing content—while technological infrastructures were controlled by US corporations. The domain of the media and the domain of the social-political were separated formally, operating through different control systems. Since then, not only has corporate monopoly over media production and circulation been fundamentally disrupted, but in the 1990s the careful separation of the sphere designated as the social and the domain of the media has for all practical purposes collapsed.

Both the vast expansion of the production of world media commodities to Asia and the turbulence of the 1990s that drew millions into the cycle of money, consumption, and mediatization suggest a transformed world. Media goods were produced in China and East Asia, and low-cost infrastructures (cameras, VCRs, mobile phones, microprocessors, and computer hardware) have spread to the periphery of capital (Africa, Asia, Latin America) through circuits ranging from the bazaar to pirate networks. Older models of control have melted away, as significant urban populations (including the poor) now access low-cost, even used technological infrastructure in the digital era.

The "digital" was part of a larger destabilization of the media form beginning with video in the 1980s. Since then, more often than not, contemporary media emerged as a bad object, materializing itself in unstable assemblages that do not fit conventional accounts of media and modernity. Media piracy is an important part of this new arrangement between the old zone of the social and that of the media. Suddenly, the polarizing structures of intellectual property that were so fundamental to the capitalist world-system have been shown as fragile, and utterly incapable of responding to the recent transformations. The intellectual-property regime faces its greatest tests since the seventeenth century; it is an open question whether the current system can weather the storm.

Chapter 8

The States

by Atilio A. Boron and Paloma Nottebohm

The Development Debate

After so many years of being considered as "the lands of the future,"
a handful of Latin American nations still remain as such, lands of the
future. The literature published around 1910, during the celebrations of
the centennial of independence from Spain, is full of titles announcing
the impending maturity of countries like Argentina, Brazil, and Mexico,
destined to become as strong as the major powers of the time. Yet such
rosy anticipations proved to be wrong.

Of course, this does not mean that these countries are today in the
same position as one hundred years ago. There has been important
economic progress. All of them became significant industrial producers. Urbanization changed the national landscape. Literacy expanded
quite rapidly. And rural populations became urban dwellers and, some
of them, workers. Yet in spite of those structural changes, underdevelopment is still the mark of these countries, which continues to exhibit
its traditional features: huge pockets of poverty, indigence, and the
periodic surge of social exclusion that never completely returns to the
previous levels; extreme concentration of wealth and income; external
vulnerability; structural weakness of the state apparatus, especially to
set the rules of market exchanges; scandalously regressive taxation; and

"democracies" that are more apparent than real, in which elementary citizen rights are glaringly absent.

After so many decades of sacrifice and at times overexploitation, periodically aggravated by prolonged periods of repression and recurrent bloodbaths, capitalism has failed to be the much-proclaimed path towards development. Rather, it has been the way of perpetuating some mode or other of underdevelopment and dependency.

Why weren't these countries able to perform much better, to develop along capitalist lines and to achieve if not all at least some of the most important outcomes reached in other countries, such as those of southern Europe, to avoid a comparison with the "first comers" like the United Kingdom or the United States? Seen from a wider historical perspective, the verdict is that capitalism is a mode of production that has served as a means of development for a small group of nations—none of which were themselves "underdeveloped" in the past—but at the price of excluding such benefits to all the rest.

Some might raise the objection that in recent decades countries such as Spain, Portugal, Greece, and Ireland reached the status of developed economies. But there's a flaw in this objection. None of these were ever truly underdeveloped countries. They may have been poor or may have fallen into ruin (as Spain and Portugal did), but their situation was never remotely comparable to that which is characteristic of the majority of Third World nations.

Spain and Portugal, for example, were at one time metropolitan centers with imposing American empires, and they even made incursions into Africa and Asia. As the production from their colonial pillage began to deteriorate, they fell into ruin and remained submerged in poverty for a very long time. However, no serious economic historian would ever have considered them to be underdeveloped countries. The same might be said of Greece and Ireland, even though they were quite poor in the post-1945 era—and even before that, at the mid-nineteenth-century mark, Ireland was ravaged by famine and emigration. If these countries emerged from backwardness and poverty it was due to the fact that as a troubling periphery for an affluent Europe, they were developed "from abroad" through the policies of the European Union, just as northern Italy once developed its backward southern (*Mezzogiorno*) region.

As posed by Wallerstein and a host of Latin American theorists, underdevelopment is a relative concept that appears only at the culmination of the construction of capitalism as a world-economy. This process, which started in the sixteenth century, reached its maturity by the mid-nineteenth century and it is not accidental that Marx and Engels, in one of the most brilliant passages of the *Communist Manifesto*, observed how the bourgeoisie spread itself around the world, remaking it in its own image and character. This capitalist world-economy invariably has a commanding center, a core, which develops itself in good measure (if not exclusively) by extracting surplus value from the periphery. This is why, prior to the full constitution of a global capitalist market, the specialized literature never used the term "underdevelopment" when referring to poor or backward countries or colonies.

The reverse, then, of developed capitalism in the metropolitan centers has been stagnation or underdevelopment in the periphery. This does not deny the possibility that, on a basis of certain relationships—as, for example, those that existed between the United Kingdom and countries such as Argentina or Uruguay between 1870 and 1929—some sectors of the economy, tied to foreign trade, may have experienced significant rates of growth. One version of this thesis on development within underdevelopment, while perhaps suggested in an extreme way, can be found in the pioneering work of André Gunder Frank (1967) on Chile and Brazil, showing how the integration of world markets with certain sectors of the Chilean economy (nitrate, for example, and later, copper) and the Brazilian ones (mainly sugar and rubber) produced an initial period of sectorial growth, followed by crisis and brutal underdevelopment. It's important nevertheless to recognize that the growth in these exports, despite the fact that it may have lasted decades, did not bring about the development of the semi-peripheral economies. And this historical lesson was as valid yesterday as it is today, in contrast to that which is suggested by conventional economic thought that exalts the virtues of export-led growth.

Argentina experienced exceptional growth for nearly half a century, between 1880 and 1930. When this period was exhausted, in the middle of the rumblings of the Great Depression of 1929, its economic and social structure began to show all the signs of underdevelopment: external dependency, vulnerability to shifts in the world-economy, profound inequalities in its economic-social structure due to its "adaptation" to an international division of labor that condemned it to submission to the dictates of developed economies, weakness in industrial growth, class polarization, and social exclusion for the great majority.

The Argentine case showed with crystal clarity the radical difference that exists between economic growth and economic development. The economy grew, marvelously, for fifty years. But it did not develop. Earlier in the next century, the Argentine economy grew at "Chinese rates" from 2003 on, with only a small decline in 2009. Yet the outstanding economic performance in quantitative terms failed to produce a structural modification of the economy and the society that would assimilate Argentina to the most advanced nations of the world. Classic plagues of underdevelopment survived in full force despite the "success" of some macro-economic indicators.

No different is the history of Mexico, with its long period of "stabilizing development" between 1940 and 1982. When this "golden period" came to an end, the Mexican economy was bankrupt, social cleavages deepened, economic polarization reached hitherto-unseen levels, the country de-industrialized, and critical sectors of the economy fell into foreign hands. In other words, both Argentina and Mexico, as did Brazil and Chile, became semi-peripheral areas in the world-economy, but not developed economies.

To summarize the historical evidence: capitalist development has served to homogenize (and in most cases modernize) diverse archaic social structures, thus creating a new "civilization" in which institutions, enterprises, state forms, and patterns of consumption tended to become similar. In this regard, homogenization theorists seem to stand on some firm basis. But discontinuities both between and within countries not only persisted but were aggravated. Paradoxically, in some respects the world-economy today is much more homogeneous than ever before but, at the same time, much more unequal and heterogeneous.

A Look at Some Empirical Data

State Expenditures

This is one of the most controversial issues in contemporary policy debates. During the neoliberal tsunami the role of the state as a factor in economic development was largely disparaged as a negative interference with the smooth operation of the markets. But the fact is that capitalism needs the state, and with the passing of time capitalists became veritable addicts of state intervention (of course, on their behalf). This is a matter not only of size but especially of the quality or type of state interventions that favor capital accumulation.

Experience shows that in recent times the retreat of the state from some expenditure in areas such as health, education, and housing, for instance, went hand in hand with the inordinate expansion of many types of subsidies, tax cuts, and incentives for the rich and the megacorporations. This has been exemplified in the wake of the post-2008 economic difficulties by the huge multibillion-dollar rescue packages approved by the otherwise always exceedingly prudent and financially restrictive central bankers in Europe and the United States, who have sought to assist financial oligopolies and investment banks regarded as "too big to fail."

All these forms of state expansion have become more and more necessary to carry out the crucial process of the "socialization of losses," when they occur, and to ensure the adequate privatization of the profits and the stability of property rights in times of buoyancy. These megarescues provide sobering evidence that the neoclassical arguments of economic theory in favor of unfettered free-market dynamics are sheer ideological justifications in favor of capital, deprived of any real substantive evidence to support them.

Table 8.1 General Government Total Expenditures as a Percentage of GDP

	1870	1913	1920	1937	1946	1950	1960	1970	1980	1990	2000	2010
Argentina					24.82	29.41	22.61	20.06	29.04	30.37	33.81	
Brazil	21.09	11.02	15.96	13.55	19.25	20	24.73	22.97	32.99	38.5		
UK	9.4	12.7	26.2	30.0			32.2		43.0	39.9	36.6	47.2
Chile	5.5	14							26.4	22.4	23.8	23.5
France	12.6	17.0	27.6	29.0			34.6		46.1	49.8	51.6	56.0
Germany	10	14.8	25	42.4		35.7	32.4	38.6	48.3	44.5	45.1	48.6
Italy	11.9	11.1	22.5	24.5	25.7	30.2	28.6	32.5	40.7	52.9	46.1	51.6
Korea, Rep.									20.2	19.0	22.6	33.7
Mexico				7	6.3	9.9	12.6	24.6	41.6	26.3	21.7	
Spain	10.3	11	8.3	13.2			13.7	23.3	33.9	42.8	39.1	46.6
USA	7.3	7.5	12.1	19.7			27.0		31.4	33.3	32.8	42.2

Sources: Official statistics of each country plus other data gathered from OECD, ECLAC, and the *Economist* databases.

The figures in Table 8.1, throwing light for almost a century and a half of the evolution of governmental expenditures, speak with a clear voice.

Table 8.1 and Figure 8.1 clearly show the growth of governmental expenditures since the time of the First World War, which marked the end of the "laissez-faire" era. The case of Germany is exceptional and should be understood as a reflection of the enormous amount of war

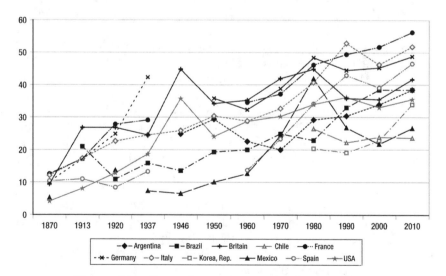

Figure 8.1 General government total expenditure as a percentage of GDP (1870–2010).

Source: Official statistics of each country and OECD, ECLAC, and the *Economist* database.

reparations mandated in the Versailles Treaty and the financial preparation for the impending Second World War.

After Germany's catastrophic defeat in the war, the economic devastation brought about a decline in governmental expenses, soon to be followed in the years of the Keynesian reconstruction by an impetuous growth that lasted until the 1990s. Then there was a small decline and, again, a recovery to the precrisis levels.

In the case of France, a country like Germany characterized by the historical presence of a strong state and a vast bureaucracy, the progression of the central government expenditures was quite rapid, superior even to that of Germany until 1920. At the beginning of the 1980s the situation of these two countries—Germany with 48.3 percent and France with 46.1 percent—was quite similar.

Yet, after that date, their paths diverged. The relative weaknesses of the German left and labor unions, as compared with the more amorphous but more militant French left (not by chance the locus of the quasi-revolutionary revolt of May 1968), caused the stagnation of German public expenditures. Thirty years later, in 2010, they still were at the same level as that of 1980, while in France the succession of socialist and Gaullist governments was unable to stop the spiraling increase of public expenses to the point that, even under the conservative government of Nicolas Sarkozy, the proportion reached an impressive 56.0 percent of the gross domestic product (GDP), a proportion that is by far the highest in Europe.

However, this figure is not the highest mark in a century-long series of data on governmental expenditures. At the peak of the welfare-state transfers in 1980, state expenditures amounted to 60.1 percent of Swedish GDP, and Sweden was able to maintain that performance for almost two decades. By 1990 the index still was quite close to the all-time high of 59.1 percent. Afterwards, several economic adjustments and financial-stabilization plans managed to reduce this proportion to 52.7 percent, still very high but tailing behind the French.

The case of Belgium is similar. Governmental expenses by 1980 were 58.6 percent of the GDP. In 2010, after two decades of neoliberal policies, the figure was still high but below the 54.0 percent of France. The other interesting case is the Netherlands, which also peaked in 1980, reaching 55.8 percent of the GDP, arriving, in 2010, at the still-high 50.0 percent mark.

The case of the United Kingdom—traditional home of anti–big government sentiments—never reached the very high proportions of the aforementioned countries. Nevertheless, by 1980 the proportion of state expenditures was close to that of the French: 43.0 percent against 46.1 percent in France. But while the latter kept increasing their governmental outlays, the brutal attack of Mrs. Margaret Thatcher against labor unions and the left in general twisted the tendency and reduced state intervention to the level of the 1960s. However, from 2000 to 2010 and in spite of the deafening neoliberal rhetoric, the UK witnessed a new surge of governmental expenses.

In the United States, a country like the United Kingdom with strong anti-big-government sentiments, the growth of governmental expenses adopted a pace even slower than that of the UK. The post-1945 expansion between 1960 and 1980 was driven, on one hand, by the new set of social policies aimed at the inclusion of the African Americans and, in general, the project of the "Great Society" launched by President Lyndon Johnson, and on the other hand by the enormous amounts of money demanded by the space race abruptly undertaken in response to the frightening progress of the Soviet Union with the launching of the two Sputniks in 1957.

During the Ronald Reagan years, in the 1980s, governmental expenses continued to grow despite the reduction in social expenditures. The engine was the extraordinary expansion of the military expenses brought about by the strategy of "Star Wars," setting the frame for the very significant increase in the governmental expenditures in the first decade of the twenty-first century, certainly fueled by the events of 9/11 and deepened by the warlike policies sponsored by George W. Bush and his successor, Barack Obama, which increased military expenses to record-high levels.

Not surprisingly, the evolution of governmental expenses in the Latin American countries considered in our analysis show the same incremental tendency but at much lower levels than that of their European or American counterparts. In the case of Argentina the demise of the first Peronista experience (1955) and the adoption of International Monetary Fund–inspired policies caused a dramatic reduction of the role of the state. With the democratic restoration of the early 1980s, public expenditures resumed their growth, notwithstanding the neoliberal policies implemented since 1987.

In Brazil, public expenditures show a big increase in the 1990s and especially in the first decade of the twenty-first century, largely due to the ambitious social programs launched by President Luiz Inacio "Lula" da Silva, which significantly altered the social landscape of the poor, especially in the Brazilian Northeast.

The most eloquent feature of the Mexican case, on the other hand, is the precipitous fall of governmental outlays after the outbreak of the foreign-debt crisis in August 1982, and the harsh dismantling of the many programs and agencies in charge of the administration of the modicum of a welfare state that the Mexican Revolution had been constructing since the 1940s.

In Chile, governmental disbursements remained basically at the same rather low level from the 1970s to 2010, showing a slight tendency downwards.

The case of South Korea, the only country of the semi-periphery that crossed the underdevelopment/development divide, poses serious challenges to the conventional wisdom. How was it possible to have produced the meaningful redistribution of incomes that took place in the 1980s and 1990s without a sizable increase in the amount of governmental disbursements? And what explains the very significant increase of state expenditures in the first decade of this century?

To conclude, as far as governmental expenses are concerned, the evidence shows a general homogenizing, upward trend for all the countries except for post-Pinochet Chile, where the figures seem to stagnate or decline. Yet a more detailed analysis should take into consideration the political and institutional structures of the states involved. This means that it is highly likely that countries with robust subnational authorities—like the states within the United States, the German *Länder*, and, to a much lesser degree, states and provinces in countries like Mexico, Brazil, and Argentina—may be in charge of the administration of some social policies that in other countries are the exclusive domain of the central government.

Another conclusion is that the extent of governmental intervention is highly correlated with the quality of democratic citizenship. Where democratic entitlements are solid and ensure the citizenry ample access to a decent standard of living, education, health care, housing, and other services, governmental expenses will be high. On the contrary, in countries in which citizens are deprived of access to those goods and services, governmental expenses are low. Governments that do not extract enough resources from the rich and powerful lack the resources to honor the citizens' rights usually exalted in their democratic constitutions. Instead of public policies, most of those governments live on charity and international cooperation, keeping their populations living in poverty and destitution.

Employment in the Public Sector

Another angle from which it is possible to examine the extent of state intervention is provided by the evolution in the numbers of public servants. If in 1960 Argentina the proportion of public employees over the total population was a little bit greater than in the United States, half a century later it was only two-thirds of the latter. Notice the brutal reduction in the proportion of public servants between 1985 and 1995, mostly under the Carlos Menem presidency, when major neoliberal reforms were carried out, a diminution much sharper than the one experienced in the United States during the Reagan years. Brazil, Mexico, and Chile show a moderate tendency towards increase in this index, while Germany and Italy show a modest decline in the first decade of the twenty-first century and Spain a slight movement in the other direction.

As mentioned in the previous section, South Korea again is a striking exception because it has a surprisingly small proportion of public

Table 8.2 Public Servants as a Percentage of the Total Population

	1960	1970	1980	1985	1990	1995	2000	2005	2010
Argentina	6.7	5.7	5.4	5.5	5	3.3	3.5	4.1	4
Brazil				3.5	5	5.2	4.6	4.6	
Chile		2.9	3	2.5		3	3.6	3.4	3.8
Germany			7.7	5.4	5.4	6.6	7.8	6.8	6.9
Italy				6.3	6.5	6.3	6.3	6.1	5.8
Korea, Rep.				1.6	1.8	2	1.8		
Mexico	0.38	0.89	2.14	2.7	2.47	2.39	2.35	2.32	
Spain				4.6	5.3	5.5	6.1	6.7	6.6
US	6.6	7.8	8.09	7.87	7.05	7.08	7.31	6.48	6.29

Source: Official statistics of each country and OECD, ILO, and World Bank (WB) databases.

employees despite the very important extent of governmental intervention in the economy and the significant increase in public expenditures during the last decade of the twentieth century.

Finally, the United States, the ideological champion of neoliberalism and the attack on "big government," reduced the proportion of public employees but the proportion still remained at very high levels, well above those of the countries of the semi-periphery or the periphery. It should be noticed that the major factor pushing up the US index has been the expansion of local and state bureaucracies, something that is certainly related to the processes of administrative decentralization that took place in the United States starting in 1980. While civilian federal employees decreased their numbers, the contrary happened at the level of the states. Between 1972 and 2010 the number of federal employees remained quite stable, around 2.8 million, while public servants at state and local levels jumped from some 11 to 17 million during the same period.[1]

Taxation

Finally, let us have a quick glance to the trends in the evolution of the extractive capacities of the states, as measured by the proportion of the GDP collected as tax revenues (see Table 8.3 and Figure 8.2).

The inspection of this almost half-century period allows us to distinguish two main periods: one from the mid-1960s to 1990, and the second from 1990 to 2010. In the first period tax revenues increased almost everywhere, with the sole exceptions of Germany between 1980 and 1990 and Brazil between 1970 and 1980. In the second period, while all the countries of the semi-periphery continued to improve their extractive capacities, the picture in the core zone was rather different. Between

---

1. See http://www.census.gov/prod/2/gov/gc92-3/gc923-2.pdf (accessed April 26, 2014).

Table 8.3   Total Tax Revenue as a Percentage of GDP

| | Years | | | | | |
	1965	1970	1980	1990	2000	2009
Argentina			17.4	16.2	21.49	31.5
Brazil	19.7	25.9	24.4	27.9	32.7	34.9
Chile				15.7	18.0	18.2
France	34.1	34.1	40.1	42.0	44.4	41.9
Germany	31.6	31.5	36.4	34.8	37.2	37.0
Italy	25.5	25.7	29.7	37.8	42.2	43.5
Korea, Rep.			17.1	19.5	22.6	25.6
Mexico			14.8	15.8	16.9	17.5
Spain	14.7	15.9	22.6	32.5	34.2	30.7
UK	30.4	36.7	34.8	35.5	36.4	34.3
United States	24.7	27.0	26.4	27.4	29.5	24.0

Sources: Official statistics of each country and the OECD database

2000 and 2009, France, Spain, the United Kingdom, and the United States reduced the proportion of tax revenues as a percentage of GDP, in the case of the United States in a precipitate manner. In Germany there was almost no reduction and in Italy the index kept growing.

Summing up, the general picture provided by these indicators proves that along these dimensions the capitalist world-economy has become more homogeneous. Of course, we did not include in our analysis

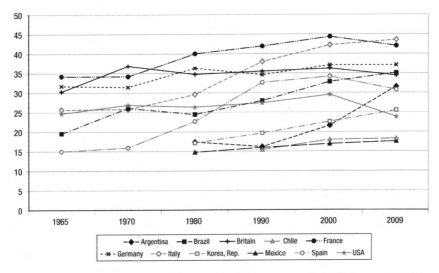

Figure 8.2   Total tax revenue as a percentage of GDP (1965–2009).

Source: Official statistics of each country and OECD database.

countries located in the periphery of the system, in which, presumably, the trends could be rather different.

The fact that these trends seem to be intractable explains the persistent complaints of right-wing experts and publicists, who have never stopped criticizing the inability, even of conservative governments, to bring the state back to "reasonable" dimensions without ever saying, of course, what those dimensions are and how to measure the "reasonableness" of state size.

What they complain of is that, in spite of the neoliberal restructuring following the exhaustion of the Keynesian cycle, the proportion of the state expenditures over the GDP never ceased to grow. What really happened was that the pace of growth of state expenses slowed down, but state size did not radically shrink as a result of the neoliberal policies (Thompson 1997). The rhythm of growth of public expenditures certainly diminished, especially when compared with the very high figures of the post-1945 years, but this slowing down did not entail a diminution of the state's size.

Despite the inflamed neoliberal rhetoric, the governmental record of Margaret Thatcher and John Major shows that the "downsizing" of British public expenditures that occurred in those years was far from irreversible, and the resilience of state expenses projected them, in 2010, to an unprecedented level in British history. This confirms that in consolidated democracies there are severe and quite insurmountable limits to any attempt to roll back the public expenditures to pre-Keynesian levels.

The reason for this inflexibility is easy to understand. The popular advances in terms of social rights and effective provision of public goods put into practice in the Keynesian state in the post-1945 period became fundamental, nonnegotiable chapters in the new social contract of advanced capitalist nations, which no change in the always-unstable electoral correlation of forces could unmake.

The comparative figures on state expenditures strongly support John Williamson's contention that "Washington does not always practice what it preaches" (Williamson 1990: 17). Not only Washington! Not in Bonn, Rome, Paris, or Tokyo did so-called state reform (a euphemism for massive layoffs of public employees and wild budgetary cuts) command as a policy the genuine respect of governmental circles in the core zone.

Two different reports of the *Economist* confirmed the strength and persistence of these trends. The first one, published in 1997, had as its title "The Visible Hand," and one of its main conclusions was that "big government is still in charge." Despite the "neoliberal reforms" between 1980—when orthodox economic policies of austerity and fiscal equilibrium were established—and 1996, the public expenditure of the fourteen most advanced nations in the Organisation for Economic Co-operation and Development (OECD) climbed from 43.3 percent of the GNP to 47.1 percent (Crook 1997: 8). The author of the special report, Clive Crook, regretfully concluded: "The growth of the governments of the advanced economies in the last forty years has been persistent, universal and counterproductive ... the progress towards a smaller government has been more apparent than real" (Crook 1997: 48).

In March 2011, another report, this time written by John Micklethwait, reached similar conclusions urging the politicians and governments to "tame the Leviathan."

> Nobody should expect that to be easy. The vested interests opposing change are huge: the state's growth has been encouraged by the right as well as the left, by favor-seeking companies as well as public-sector unions, by voters as well as bureaucrats. Indeed, given the pressures for ever larger government, many reformers feel they will have to work hard just to keep it at its present size. (p. 4)

Looking at this problem from the semi-periphery, the resilience of state expenditures is not only associated with full citizenship rights, aging populations, and so on. In countries of the Third World it is also linked to the fact that historical evidence shows there is no route to development, capitalist or otherwise, that does not require a strong state as a prerequisite.

By "strong" we are not referring to what the right has always emphasized—an authoritarian or despotic government always ready to repress the popular classes, disband unions, shut down parliaments, and suppress liberties. By "strong" we mean rather the development of the state's capacities necessary to guarantee the governance of societies sharply divided across class lines and to discipline the markets and the economic agents. A state of this sort requires a solid democratic legitimacy, without which its strength would be inexorably undermined (Weiss 1997: 15–17; 1998).

We are talking of a state "strong" enough, for instance, to provide safe water to the 1.5 billion people that in the Third World lack it, and whose chances to get it through the operation of market forces is nil. Who would invest money to carry safe water to the poorest of the poor living at the sheer subsistence level, housed in shacks in occupied public lands, without any kind of property title, ID, or street address, chronically unemployed, and suffering from an incredible educational deficit that made them unemployable in the current economy? It is not the market but the democratic state that is the institution suitable to face and eventually solve this problem.

Some Preliminary Conclusions

The gravitation of the states, measured by the governmental expenditures, the number of public employees, and taxation seems to lend support to the "convergence" theorists. Yet if other data are brought into consideration, such as the growing distance between rich and poor nations, or between rich and poor people within each nation, or the radical asymmetries along the digital divide, or in research and development, the image that the world-economy projects today is that of a highly polarized and divergent collection of countries.

Polarization has become blatant in two critical areas of the modern world-economy and the so-called "information society"—access to the Internet and research and development. In both indicators the gap between core and periphery is both enormous and growing, especially in the critical area of filing and granting of patents. The resulting quasi-monopolies guarantee the continuing polarization of the world-system.

Chapter 9

Citizenship

by Oleksandr Fisun and Volodymyr Golovko

The Concept of Citizens

The traditional mechanism of inclusion/exclusion was based on a system of estates or orders into which people were placed by family descent. In the modern world-system, this arrangement was replaced by one that proclaimed that all people were equal and therefore in principle were entitled to equal rights of inclusion. These people were called citizens. Citizens were citizens of a state.

There have been two major ways of deciding who were the citizens of a state. One is called *jus soli,* a system that defines citizenship in territorial terms, usually place of birth. The other is called *jus sanguinis,* a system that defines citizens in terms of descent from people of a certain "ethnic" group, supposedly the group that has rights within a given state. But whichever the mode of definition, all citizens were presumably to have equal rights.

Since equality of rights seemed to pose an inherent threat to privileged minorities within the population, a system of distinction was evolved that effectively limited the rights of citizens to a minority of the group, leading to the reinstallation of a mechanism of inclusion/exclusion within a system that in theory did not permit it.

The mechanism to effectuate this distinction was the creation of dual categories of citizens—those with so-called active rights and those with so-called passive rights. While the latter had under the laws the rights to equal treatment with all other citizens, only the former had the right to participate in making decisions about the laws. Historically, this revolved primarily around the right to suffrage and to hold public office. Initially, access to suffrage and holding public office were restricted to male citizens of a certain minimum age with a certain level of property holdings, and often additionally belonging to certain religious/ethnic/racial groups.

The struggle over access to these rights left a major footprint on the development of the capitalist world-system and became the immediate demand in a number of revolutions—from the Springtime of Nations of 1848 to the anticolonial uprisings, principally after 1945.

The discussion of citizenship in the second half of the twentieth century resulted in a great deal of work on theoretical conceptualizations of citizenship as an institution, as well as on analysis of major trends in the development of citizenship.

One of the most influential theorizations is to be found in the 1950 book of Thomas Humphrey Marshall. Marshall proposed a typology of three major types of rights, which he said constituted a sequence. The first is *civil rights*—those that secure an individual's equality before the law and adequate protection of his/her freedoms. The second is *political rights*—particularly the right to elect and to be elected. The third is *social (or socio-economic) rights*—those that guarantee equal access to quality education and to retirement and healthcare benefits. These three fundamental rights allow one to talk of three kinds of citizenship—civil citizenship, political citizenship, and social citizenship.

Immanuel Wallerstein (2003) argues that the binary opposition that had been proclaimed between active and passive citizens is crucial for understanding the dynamics of citizenship as a tool of inclusion/exclusion within the capitalist world-system. In fact, passive citizens enjoyed Marshall's civil rights while active citizens enjoyed both civil and political rights. He outlines the ways in which, historically, women, Blacks (and other ethnic/racial "minorities"), and the working class were deprived of political rights for quite awhile.

Our empirical analysis will trace the evolution of these rights, using certain historical turning points that permitted both new interpretations of citizenship and the assertion of new dimensions of rights. We believe that these turning points are the French Revolution, the revolutions of 1848–1849 in Europe, the Bolshevik Revolution in Russia, and the events of the 1960s.

Periodization of the Historical Dynamics of Citizenship

The historical development of citizenship can be considered to have three main stages.

The first stage is the period beginning with the French Revolution, which is the principal source of the concept of citizenship as it has come to be understood in the modern world-system, through the end of the nineteenth century. It includes the adoption of the Declaration of the Rights of Man and of the Citizen, the rise and fall of Napoleon's empire, the Bourbon Restoration, the revolutions of the Springtime of Nations, and the United States Civil War, and ends with the creation of the first European grassroots political parties. The focus of this period was political citizenship—the right to elect and to be elected, attempting to overcome the unequal access to the rights of suffrage for certain groups.

The second stage of the history of citizenship we take to be the period from the Bolshevik Revolution through the end of the Cold War in 1989/1991. The period includes both world wars, the disintegration of the colonial empires, the political rise of the working class, and much increased trans-state migration. During this period the final extensions of political citizenship took place, which in turn highlighted the issues of social citizenship: retirement and healthcare benefits, social insurance, and education.

The disintegration of colonial empires spawned a large number of independent states in the peripheral and semi-peripheral zones and accounted in large part for the dramatic growth of migration worldwide. The relevance of regulating in-migration issues in the core zones became the basis for the widespread development and transformation of naturalization practices. Limitations of social citizenship provisions and new naturalization laws became the tools of the reproduction of inequality in the second half of the twentieth century.

The third stage—from the 1990s through 2010—was characterized by the transformation of citizenship as a result of globalization processes and the creation of supranational institutions. In this period global transnational citizenship came to be discussed. During the age of globalization, citizenship became the mechanism of hierarchical differentiation of states within the capitalist world-system, leading to the creation of several clusters in its structure.

Evolution of Citizenship in the Nineteenth Century: The French Revolution and the Springtime of Nations

The Treaty of Westphalia in 1648 is often considered the founding moment of the modern interstate system. But it was also crucial in the development of the concept of the nation-state. By making the religious preferences of the rulers the official religion of the states, the states were supposed to become relatively homogeneous national communities in practice. They began to incarnate the so-called imagined communities of which Benedict Anderson has written (1991).

The ideology of "civil nationalism" was needed to undergird the creation of "political nations." The project was implemented as a sort of joint product of the French Revolution and the American Revolutionary War in the concept of political citizenship and the institutionalization of political rights as inalienable rights of a citizen. What had earlier been a privilege of some urban denizens now became an attribute of each member of the political nation. The French Revolution abolished the archaic estates system of the *ancien régime* and balanced the distribution of political and civil privileges and statuses throughout all the three estates of the French society (Brubaker 1989).

The key ideological principles of political citizenship were anchored in the text of the 1789 Declaration of the Rights of Man and of the Citizen, which laid the foundation of the political system of the French Republic and expanded the limits of the self-governing community from a city to a nation-state. The basis of the liberal concept of citizenship was established along with that declaration. This became the tool for creation of modern nation-states and the development of parliamentary institutions in the core zones of the capitalist world-system—western Europe, Great Britain, and North America. The existence of an active political citizenship—participation of individuals in electoral procedures—is a key element of the liberal concept.

Nonetheless, as Wallerstein (2003) points out, this liberal interpretation of citizenship contained hidden mechanisms for the reproduction of inequality by introducing various qualifying criteria for the vote, criteria that eliminated more than two-thirds of the population. The concept of citizenship was functioning as a mechanism of both inclusion and exclusion at the same time, integrating certain groups into the political realm while excluding others.

This is clearly illustrated in the works of Adam Przeworski (2009a; 2009b), who studied the development of electoral practices and involvement of the population in the political life from 1791 through 2000. On the one hand, between 1791 and the end of the nineteenth century, rights of suffrage spread throughout most of the states of the core zones and to some semi-peripheral states—notably France, Great Britain, the United States, Greece, Spain, Belgium, the Netherlands, Norway, Portugal, Luxembourg, Mexico, Liberia, and Austria-Hungary. By 1900 there were forty-three countries that had significantly extended male suffrage.

On the other hand, it wasn't until 1893 that women in the European countries began to have rights of suffrage, with the exception of some landowners in Austria-Hungary. Literacy tests or property qualifications were standard. Only Greece, Mexico, and El Salvador granted active political citizenship to all male citizens. In addition, strict national borders began to be set in place, and the states introduced multiple restrictions on foreigners and often on "minority" ethnicities—for example, Czechs, Croats, and Hungarians in the patchwork Habsburg Empire.

Exclusion from political participation was of course much wider in the peripheral zones. In colonized countries, European and US rulers deprived the indigenous population of these lands of the whole set of civil rights that were being granted at that time to the people in the home countries of the colonial powers.

The limitations of political access in the core zones and their total denial in colonial territories resulted in continuing social tensions, creating the preconditions for enduring struggles for active political citizenship.

The first extensive episode was the 1848 revolutionary struggles in Europe—what Wallerstein has called the first world-revolution of the modern world-system (2003). He calls it this not only because of the large geographic scale of these events and their contribution to the rise of national identity in some regions, but also because the pivotal motive was the struggle to overcome the continuing exclusions from active political citizenship.

In analyzing the events of 1848–1849, Wallerstein distinguished two different forms of this struggle. The first was the struggle both to widen citizenship within the framework of one country (such as occurred in France from February to June 1848) and the achievement of greater equality in distribution. This was a class struggle within the state, a social revolution. The second form was that of multiple nationalist revolutions, what the historians came to call collectively the Springtime of Nations. Some of these revolutions sought unifications (Germany, Italy). Some sought separations (Poland, Hungary). In both cases, the revolutionaries were seeking fuller rights for "ethnic" groups that had been or who felt they had been excluded from active self-fulfilling participation in the political process.

Both the social revolution (in France) and the various nationalist revolutions failed in their immediate political objectives. The movements suffered various kinds of repression afterwards. But the longer-run consequence was to permit the emergence of social movements and political parties that would continue these struggles in the later decades of the nineteenth century. Socialists, social democrats, and anarchists played a significant role in these later attempts to create mass political parties, and these parties became the leading political force of the struggles for active political citizenship in Europe.

One can argue, in summary, that there were in this period contradictory trends in the development of citizenship. Whenever there was more inclusion, there seemed to be "compensatory" exclusions. On the other hand, the counteraction of those excluded led to new forms of organizing, which would bear fruit in the first quarter of the twentieth century.

Dynamics of Citizenship in the Twentieth Century: Social Citizenship and Disintegration of the Colonial System

The basic reason why the struggle for citizenship changed in the twentieth century was the incongruity between aggressive colonial expansion and policy on one hand and steady albeit slow extension of active political rights and growth of well-being in the core zones on the other hand.

The shift of emphasis in development of the citizenship was a result of the final granting of active political citizenship to all strata of population in the core zone. By the end of the twentieth century, there was practically no country with electoral procedures that had formal restrictions on participation in electoral process. Eventually, active political citizenship extended beyond the limits of the core zones of the world-system to peripheral and semi-peripheral zones. Figures 9.1 through 9.3 are based on statistical data for the period 1850–2000 and provide a picture of the dynamics of suffrage extension.

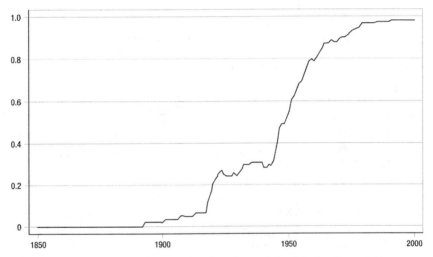

Figure 9.1 Percentage of countries with universal suffrage.

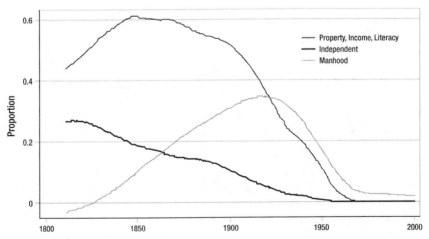

Figure 9.2 Dynamics of electoral qualifications for different forms of male suffrage.

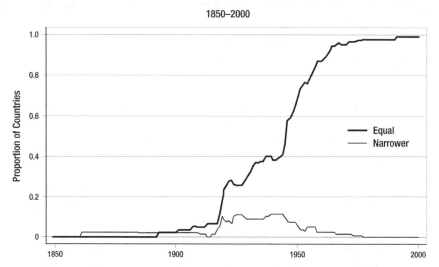

1850–2000

Figure 9.3 **Proportion of countries with female suffrage relative to countries with any kind of suffrage.**

The more successful the struggle for extension of suffrage rights became, the bigger was the role of political parties and trade unions. These represented the interests of the working classes, seeking improvement of conditions in hazardous jobs, securing decent retirement benefits and insurance, increasing advancement of health care, etc.

The idea of social citizenship evolved into a central concept in the 1950s. The principal objective of social citizenship was a progressive integration of the working classes into society and a "softening" of the classical liberal market economy's impact on broad layers of the population via redistribution of benefits. Its practical implementation in postwar Europe led to the creation of "welfare states," helping to rebuild destroyed economies and to overcome the demographic crisis caused by the mass deaths of civil populations during the Second World War. With the onset of economic difficulties in the 1980s, a process of gradual dismantlement of broad welfare programs began in the leading states of the core zone of the capitalist world-system: Great Britain (under Margaret Thatcher) and the United States (under Ronald Reagan).

Meanwhile, citizenship took on a slightly different character with the spread of ideas of individual social rights. A key element of this new emphasis was the restriction of access to social benefits to certain strata of the dominant indigenous population while denying access to social benefits to migrants and refugees.

Currently, provision of broad social rights in some states in the semi-peripheral and peripheral zones is used as a substitute for political and civil rights. Such a widening of social citizenship, while narrowing civil and political rights, is typical of neo-patrimonial regimes in the former Soviet republics (e.g., Turkmenistan and Belarus) as well as in some Latin American and African countries.

Accelerated industrialization and the demise of colonial empires—such as the British and French empires—led to a large-scale influx of a cheap labor force to Europe, Australia, and North America in the second half of the twentieth century. The newly independent states of Asia and Africa found it difficult to provide minimum life and security standards for their citizens who thereupon began to seek a better life in the countries of the former colonial powers. The significant increase of migration flows resulted in ethnic tensions in the countries that were importers of a labor force. Particularly as the world-economy slowed down, new restrictions on the variety of rights of migrants were instituted and additional barriers to their entry were put in place.

The structural reproduction of inequality through the institution of citizenship may be easily traced by comparing naturalization practices. Currently there are three groups of states in the core zones that, to a certain extent, have been importing a significant part of their labor force. The first group consists of the former colonial powers—Great Britain, France, Portugal, the Netherlands, and Spain. The second consists of countries that did not have colonies (at least as of 1945): Germany, Poland, Ireland, and Japan. The third group is made of so-called settler countries that were founded by European immigrants: the United States, Canada, Australia, and New Zealand. Each group has different naturalization practices, and their mechanisms of inclusion/exclusion have different features.

The former colonial powers tried to establish different restrictions for arriving immigrants in order to guarantee their maximal assimilation as the price of full citizenship. Inclusion/exclusion practices sometimes were instituted by providing unequal naturalization rights for the citizens of certain countries. For example, in the second half of the 1960s France recognized the right of Algerians to come to metropolitan France and to claim French citizenship, while people from other French colonies were denied this option. This had to do with the fact that Algeria had been considered juridically part of metropolitan France until the Algerians won independence in 1962. This provision allowed those who had helped the French fight Algerian revolutionaries to maintain their former status as full French citizens.

In the Portuguese colonies, there had been special "assimilation" rules, allowing a limited number of people of non-Portuguese ethnicity to obtain access to the rights of Portuguese citizens. In theory, to be an *assimilado* was based on the presumption that one had demonstrated acceptance of certain basic Portuguese values and therefore could be said to have been assimilated into Portuguese culture. Only this rather tiny group could claim Portuguese citizenship. Belgium had a similar tiny group, called *évolués*, in its colonies.

Immigrants arriving in countries that had no colonies (at least as of 1945) were usually not granted active political citizenship. They did, however, have opportunities for wide social rights. Usually only descendants of these immigrants in the second or third generation had the right to claim active citizenship.

The settler states granted the most extensive naturalization opportunities for immigrants. One can find confirmation in an extensive practice of the principle of *jus soli* in the United States and Canada. Thomas Janoski (2010) reports that in the period 1975–2000 the number of naturalized people per 100,000 resident foreigners was as high as 14,692 in Canada and as low as 313 in Germany. The settler states—Australia, Canada, and the United States—are the leaders in terms of the numbers of naturalized people, while Japan and Germany have the lowest rates of naturalization, and the former colonial powers—France, Great Britain, and Portugal—are in-between.

The surge in a national state of multiple ethnic minorities without anything in common with the dominant majority presented many challenges. In order to deal with these challenges, attempts were made to adjust the citizenship institution via the assertion of a program/theory of multiculturalism. This program/theory was based on the principle of the vulnerability of small ethnic groups and the need to protect their identity by providing them with a number of group rights. Currently, the most popular approach consists of providing legal immigrants with extensive socio-economic rights while narrowing their active political participation (right of suffrage).

During the age of globalization, new forms of citizenship are appearing, and transnational and dual citizenship are the most significant among them. One good example is the European Union and its complicated immigration policy, which allows immigrants to have multiple levels of identity yet maintain a strong connection with their homeland. According to Riva Kastoryano (2005), dual citizenship is a key element in a huge number of transnational communities and networks, formal and informal. Some of them are based on identity, others on interests, or often both as in the case of immigrants—i.e., residents or legal citizens of one member state according to the legislation on citizenship but claiming the recognition of a different collective identity. Therefore, immigrants foster primordial solidarity networks that cross national borders on the basis of a so-called identity of origin linking the home country to the country of residence and to the broader European space.

A good instance of dual citizenship may be found in Germany, where the Turkish community claims dual citizenship status. Having both Turkish and German citizenship, they can build a transnational network, distinguishing political, economic, and social rights. For instance, they can use their suffrage rights in parliamentary and even local elections in Turkey, and simultaneously continue to secure social rights from German authorities. Therefore, such transnational communities are increasing the mobility of immigrants between their home and host countries, and have become a way of expressing political and economic participation in both spaces.

Supplements

Supplement 1

As a first supplement to the research of the retrospective dynamics of citizenship, a comparative analysis was made among states representing different clusters of the current world-system. The research was focused on suffrage citizenship, granting of right of suffrage to noncitizens, as well as on acquiring citizenship and naturalization practices. The results are presented in three tables (Table 9.1, 9.2, and 9.3).

The outcomes of the research may illustrate the following regularities. First and most importantly, the naturalization process is well developed mainly in the countries of core and semi-peripheral zones. It is less widespread in the peripheral zones. It shows that naturalization laws and regulations in the core and semi-peripheral zones are based on the "inclusion" principle and focused on the integration of new members into national community.

In addition, we may state that *jus soli* is widely used in the core and semi-peripheral zones. This fact may be explained by the settlement descent of the countries of Latin America and by the imperial past of major countries of the core as well as rapid economic development and the necessity to regulate migration processes.

Supplement 2

The second supplement is devoted to the explanation of Figures 9.1 through 9.3. These were originally made by Adam Przezworski and they illustrate different aspects of citizenship historical development.

Figure 9.1 demonstrates the dynamics of suffrage extension in the world-system. In 1900 only seventeen countries had suffrage rights, and those were only for men; nevertheless, in the first half of the twentieth century universal suffrage became a kind of self-evident norm. Moreover, according to the chart we may assume that the newly emerging countries (like former national outskirts of European empires or post-colonial countries) tended to grant suffrage rights immediately after independence and to all citizens.

Figure 9.2 shows the development of suffrage qualifications during the period after the French Revolution. Przezworski defines the three main groups of criteria for suffrage.

Table 9.1   The Representatives of the Core Zone: The United States and Germany

	Suffrage Citizenship	*Suffrage Rights for Noncitizens*	*Acquisition of Citizenship*
United States	Extension of suffrage rights was a gradual process. The Fifteenth Amendment of 1870 extended the suffrage rights to African Americans. However, some states (mostly in the South) preserved discriminatory restrictions for Black people—level of income, literacy, etc. Ultimately, those barriers were removed in 1964–1965. The Nineteenth Amendment of 1920 established suffrage rights for women. However, D.C. residents cannot vote for congressional representation, while Puerto Rico residents do not have full US suffrage rights.	Beginning in 1968 foreigners under certain conditions could vote in local elections in twenty US states and territories. However, they cannot vote in presidential and congressional elections.	A child born on US soil is a US citizen regardless of parents' nationality, even if they are illegally on US soil. Naturalization requirement: a person must have legally resided on US soil for no less than five years, be at least eighteen years of age, be a "person of good moral character," speak English fluently, be familiar with the US Constitution, and respect American culture. A marriage with a US citizen allows claiming US citizenship after three years of living together.
Germany	From the moment of creation of the German Empire in 1871 through the time of the Nuremberg Laws in the 1930s, suffrage rights were established for all men voting in national elections, while there were certain restrictions for some local elections.	In 1989 Schleswig-Holstein granted voting rights in local elections for citizens of Denmark, Ireland, Norway, the Netherlands, Sweden, and Switzerland. At the same time Hamburg granted voting rights in local elections for foreigners who uninterruptedly resided in Germany for at least eight years. Both decisions were revoked by the German Federal	*Jus soli* was introduced in Germany only in 2000. As a result a child born on German territory after 2000 is entitled to German citizenship, provided that one parent has lived in Germany uninterruptedly for at least eight years. The same right exists for a child born out of wedlock on condition that the father is an *apatride,* and the mother is

Table 9.1 *(continued)*

Suffrage Citizenship	Suffrage Rights for Noncitizens	Acquisition of Citizenship
	Constitutional Court in 1990. However, in the period between 1995 and 1999 the relevancy of granting voting rights to EU nationals permanently residing in Germany was recognized.	German, or a child born out of wedlock with a foreign mother and a German father, if the father recognizes his child. Naturalization requirement: uninterrupted residency in Germany for at least eight years.

The first one was manhood—a person had to be older than eighteen or twenty-one years. It also included certain residence requirements (a person had to live in a particular territory for a specific period—for instance, a minimum of five years). Nevertheless, according to Przeworski (2009a: 296–297), in the middle of the nineteenth century, "manhood" had a more compound meaning than it possesses now. It was more similar to the term *"vecino,"* which was introduced in Latin American countries and meant "someone who was a good member of a local community." Only being a *"vecino"* allowed person to participate in elections. The second criterion consisted of such requirements as income, literacy, or property (a person had to be literate, possess a particular amount of property, or sufficient monthly income). The third criterion was independence (slaves were not eligible to vote). As a result, only three countries—Greece, Mexico, and El Salvador—had universal suffrage in the middle of the nineteenth century. Subsequently, universal suffrage was extended to the majority of the countries of the world-system, but suffrage qualifications were the most powerful instrument for exclusion before 1945.

Figure 9.3 is devoted to female suffrage and its ratio to male suffrage. Females were practically excluded from the political space throughout the nineteenth century and only in 1893 did New Zealand extend suffrage to them. In the core zones women acquired suffrage only after the First and in some cases the Second World War. After 1945, universal suffrage for men and women was established in most of the countries of the world.

Table 9.2 The Representatives of the Semi-Peripheral Zone: India and Brazil

	Suffrage Citizenship	Suffrage Rights for Noncitizens	Acquisition of Citizenship
India	The universal right of suffrage was introduced in 1950 for all Indian citizens.	None	A child born on Indian soil is an Indian citizen regardless of the parents' nationality. The procedure for becoming a citizen takes place at eighteen years of age. If the father is Indian, the child becomes Indian regardless of place of birth. If the mother is Indian, the child becomes Indian only if the mother and child continue residing in India.
Brazil	The right of suffrage was introduced in 1891. Women, priests, military, illiterates, and the homeless had no right to vote. The universal right of suffrage was introduced in 1932. Brazilian electoral citizenship has particular features: * Age restriction—only people of the age group eighteen to seventy can vote (voluntarily one can start voting at the age of sixteen). * Regular soldiers cannot vote.	The Friendship Treaty between Brazil and Portugal provides that Portuguese citizens permanently residing in Brazil for more than three years, who speak Portuguese, and who have active political citizenship in Portugal, may apply to the Brazilian Justice Ministry for suffrage rights.	A person becomes a Brazilian citizen if he/she is one of the following: * A child born in Brazil regardless of parents' nationality * A child born outside of Brazilian territory, if one parent is a Brazilian citizen Marriage to a Brazilian citizen does not lead to Brazilian citizenship but facilitates residence in Brazil. Naturalization requirement: no less than five years of residency in Brazil.

Table 9.3 The Representatives of the Peripheral Zone: Ghana and Morocco

	Suffrage Citizenship	Suffrage Rights for Noncitizens	Acquisition of Citizenship
Ghana	Universal right of suffrage for everyone over eighteen years.	None	A person born within Ghana's borders does not automatically become a citizen. A child whose parents or grandparents are citizens of Ghana may automatically obtain Ghanaian citizenship. Acquisition of Ghanaian citizenship by marriage is considerably complicated: a person married to a Ghanaian citizen may apply for citizenship. In case of divorce, citizenship will be revoked immediately. Moreover, a registered Ghanaian citizen may be asked to prove that the marriage was based on a good faith. Naturalization requirement: Ghana does not encourage naturalization for people who don't have blood or marital ties with the country.
Morocco	The universal right of suffrage was introduced in 1963. Before that only men had suffrage rights.	Naturalized Moroccan citizens have no suffrage rights for a five-year period.	A child born on Moroccan territory has no rights to Moroccan citizenship. A child whose father is Moroccan—regardless of place of birth—is a citizen. A woman married to a Moroccan citizen becomes a Moroccan citizen after two years of cohabitation. Naturalization requirement: people who have reached eighteen years of age and resided in Morocco no less than five years can be naturalized.

Chapter 10

Women's Spaces and a Patriarchal System

by Linda Christiansen-Ruffman

This analysis focuses on the global social change from the perspective of women, gender, and the changing patriarchal system that helped to shape the world-system in the last millennium. It is based on an inductive and empirically based approach to macrohistorical and comparative research. This chapter addresses the book's key question about polarization, in this case of women and men, and discusses related analytic issues.

We also name a new historical form and process of patriarchy that developed in Europe starting around 1000 CE, when its core interrelated values of violence, inequality, and greed (VIG) were legitimized by the Catholic Church. Europeans exported the values of EuroPatriarchy, or what might also be called VIG-Patriarchy, through colonization, resource extraction, and its so-called civilizing mission beginning around 1500 and continuing through imperialism, international financial institutions, and neoliberal globalization. These processes closed spaces that women had previously occupied and excluded them from new spaces being created, thereby increasing the polarization between men and women. The resulting social, cultural, economic, and political institutions during this era were all built on patriarchal assumptions that were exploitative, competitive, and masculine at their core. Values, including respect for the natural world and each other, caring and gifting (see Miles 2013; Starhawk 2002; Vaughan 2007), once appreciated and shared by both genders, became in real danger of being lost within a further polarized EuroPatriarchal culture still based on legitimized violence, greed, individualism, and hierarchies. Two possible futures are suggested in this chapter's conclusion.

This analysis is informed by thousands of texts from all scholarly disciplines and from other scholarly based sources, including radio broadcasts from Canada's CBC1 Radio, field experiences, conversations with colleagues, and oral histories. It builds on feminist analysis with multileveled relationships, a focus on social process, and the use of sociological principles of grounded theory (usually associated with microlevel ethnography) such as the constant comparative method, theoretic sampling, and inductive theorizing (Glaser and Strauss 1967). In addition to the usual challenges of comparative historical research,[1] the research for this analysis also faced challenges from the patriarchal nature of scholarship: the underrepresentation of women in history; the relative absence of feminist scholarship and especially the lack of autonomous feminist theorizing; the fact that women's presence and contributions have been made invisible by a myth of historical linearity (most often considered progress from patriarchy to women's equality);[2] the active suppression of women's contributions, both at the time and in retrospect;[3] and the pure

---

1. Overgeneralization is common. Studies often fail to fully recognize the diversity of differences over time and space within medieval Europe. For example, after becoming acquainted with the scholarship, it became possible for us as researchers to predict the inclusion criteria (in time and space), based on the purported description and specific characterization of "medieval Europe" by paying attention to the *de facto* theoretic sampling being used.

2. This "progress assumption" was often implicit but followed a common pattern—namely, that if a particular achievement of a women's right were gained *by* a particular year, then the earlier presence or absence of that right and/or activities related to that right did not require empirical investigation and was assumed not to exist. The concept of "progress" has tended to lock peasants and family forms into timeless patriarchal characterizations and assumptions. At least Abu-Lughod (1989), in one of her two passages related to women, makes it explicit that she is quoting a nineteenth-to-early-twentieth-century description of Chinese family silkworm production because she could not find one from the Middle Ages. An overwhelming majority of the scholarly literature simply seems to assume a patriarchal family model and a never-changing peasant family remarkably similar to a modern nuclear family. To avoid this bias and following the advice of Smith, Wallerstein, and Evers (1984), much of our research focused on households, not families, as the best unit for comparative research and analytic understanding.

3. For example, Macy (2008) provides solid data and analysis of how a change in the definition of ordination during the eleventh and twelfth centuries excluded women from the ministry, and he also analyzes how male "reformers" eliminated traces of women's previous ordination.

fabrication and invention of images and artifacts as well as stories.[4] These problems are compounded—by post-modern influences that consider the constructed story, argument, or clever point to be more important than evidence; by recent scholarly trends to ignore history, especially in the long term; by the failure to consider the importance of history's contributions to the future;[5] and, not surprisingly, by the lack of sociological analytic skills by those in other disciplines whose invaluable empirically based work related to material realities of time, culture, structure, and/or space is too often inadequately or misleadingly theorized.[6] Partly because of these methodological challenges, this analysis focuses narrowly on the most macro levels of patriarchal systems, especially as related to gender hierarchies, women's spaces, and the growth of the world-system.

Inductive research led from the initial focus on women, personhood,[7] and gender to include a more systemic and macro focus on changing patriarchal systems and the ways in which the related historical processes of developing systems of militarism, capitalism, colonialism, and hierarchical social relations created and constituted the modern world-system. It did so by excluding, subordinating, and exploiting women and the environment. Using a broadened, refined, systemic, and macro concept of patriarchy, it focuses on major macro shifts in the breadth, density, and depth of patriarchy and the types of women's spaces of relative autonomy that each system supports, permits, restrains, or suppresses. Women's space is defined as a conceptual and methodological device used to explore and understand the gendered political possibilities for women's actions in differing historical times and geographic locations within a changing

---

4. For example, Bennett (2006) points to fraudulent chastity belts said to be from this period.

5. See Bennett (2006) for startling data on the retreat from women's history in the academic literature, comparing 1975–1978 with 2001–2004.

6. The scholarly debates, even those such as polarization versus progress, sometimes lead to problematic assumptions and presentations, even among those whose historical work has been specific and systematic and who do share a feminist analysis that includes patriarchy. For example, while Bennett (2006) is pointing to problematic assumptions, particularly characteristic of the literature on household economies and equality, she criticizes the literature on the relative equality of the times by quoting from the late part of this period when patriarchal utterances were at their strongest. Our analytic framing, and indeed parts of Bennett's own analysis (e.g., Bennett 2006: 80), would suggest that a different interpretation is needed.

7. Personhood is a concept developed in 1978. It built from a 1929 legal appeal, initiated by five Canadian women to the Privy Council of Great Britain, which overruled Canada's Supreme Court. The decision agreed that Canadian women should be considered as persons under law and allowed to be Canadian senators. Our definition was developed to conceive of the autonomy and power of women and their organizations in southern Labrador coastal communities and their ability to define a priority and achieve the desired community-based outcome (Christiansen-Ruffman 1980).

patriarchal system.[8] Personhood would allow for the full expression and participation of the whole female person without limits set by patriarchy and related forms of exclusion, suppression, and exploitation.

Patriarchy is often defined as rule by the father, fathers, or older men, conveying the notion of male power with a specific focus on forms and/ or functions of the gendered "relations of ruling."[9] Sylvia Walby theorizes patriarchy as gendered structural relations (1990). Allen (1985; 1997b) also focuses specifically on male/female gender (in)equalities, specifically on polarity, unity, and complementarity.[10] Our views are closer to those of Maria Mies (1986) and Claudia von Werlhof (1984; 2007). Like them, we extend the concept of patriarchy to include broad, layered, and exploitative systemic features as well as their historically specific framing. More explicitly than all of these authors, however, we treat what we call embedded patriarchy, the institutionalized consequences of structures established under historically constructed systems of patriarchal social relations, institutions, and paradigmatic knowledge. The concept of patriarchy in this essay therefore calls attention to the social structural and cultural consequences for women and men of the gendered historical outputs of a male-dominated system and paradigm, including both those focused explicitly on gender and the outputs that do not appear to be about gender but that derive from centuries of male-standpoint theorizing or patricentrism (Christiansen-Ruffman 1989). These long-term consequences from multileveled and changing relations of ruling harm women more than men by limiting women's spaces, but they also entrap men in sets of social relations that are outdated in contemporary society. This institutionalized patricentric legacy in scholarship and political discourse includes ideas celebrated as intellectual breakthroughs in history, such as dichotomous thinking, abstracted universalisms, individuality, hierarchies, (in)equality, "rational man," "technological fixes," and conquering nature. This obsolete paradigm still perpetuates assumptions and ideas

---

8. Women's space is also a concept used by feminist community-based groups and academics to identify, theorize, and create women-friendly social realities. The concept has had a territorial dimension, such as described by Virginia Woolf in *A Room of One's Own* (1929) and by McFadden (2007), as well as a socio-political and cultural feature that includes women's values such as active peace and their visions and imagined futures.

9. We have borrowed the concept from Dorothy Smith (1987), who once pointed out that her named methodology, institutional ethnography, was giving a name to the grounded feminist research being practiced in Canada at that time. Her associated concept, relations of ruling, has enabled others to incorporate political economy and world-systems analyses into feminist analyses of patriarchal relations.

10. See also Bennett (2006), especially Chapter 4. Bennett, however, does not include such extensions in her three definitions although they are implicitly present in her footnote 23 on debates around patriarchy. Like us and Sylvia Walby (personal communication, Sweden, 2010), she considers patriarchy to be a necessary component of feminist analysis although our concept of patriarchy differs.

of "social order" that not only exclude women but also make no sense for continuing life on the planet. It is detrimental to local, national, and global relations in the twenty-first century.

One useful way in which feminists think about oppression or patriarchy is with the analogy of a bird in a cage (Frye 1983). If you look at each wire, the relationship of the wires is not clear. Even if you cut one of the wires, the others continue to contain the bird. Assembling the wires in the cage and connecting them conveys the development of patriarchy as a system and its density, but not the depth and breadth of its interrelated systems. For an analogy that better fits more complex embedded patriarchies, picture the bird trapped in a series of cages of different sizes and shapes or interlocking systems. Both the development (or mesh) of each system and the depth and breadth of this second band of a layer or layers of patriarchy is experienced as a loss or gain of women's space within patriarchy[11]—or, in the language of this book, as an increase or decrease in polarization.

Our concept of EuroPatriarchy is more fluid than this analogy conveys. Contrary to conventional wisdom, in the year 1000 diverse women (whether living as peasants, rulers, church women, or townsfolk) took on a wide variety of important social activities. At that time, the system of EuroPatriarchy had only a few wires constraining women, such as a patrilineal ruling preference in some territories, but even that seemed open to negotiations. As more patriarchal wires were put into place, there were often still open windows, doors, spaces between the wires related to exceptions. Indeed, the ways around and through the emergent system, as Erickson (2005) describes in her analysis of coverature and her associated analytic insight that finding institutionally legitimate ways around coverature and such apparently constraining laws, helped foster capitalism in England.

Methodology and Initial Findings Related to the Starting Date

Initially research on women's spaces and patriarchy began at 1500 in those parts of Europe that would become the core zone of the emerging world-system. Our extensive reading of secondary sources around 1500 found little analysis of gender but hints of changing times. The isolated glimpses of women all seemed to indicate an active social process of increasing polarization between men and women that needed analysis. The active suppression of women, the closing down of their spaces as

---

11. Note the direct relationship here that is part of the logic of power in EuroPatriarchy—power of men over women, conceived as control. The binary logic of computers has trouble designating equals and seeing the whole. Other paradigms imagine "power to" and "power with" rather than "power over," and inclusive rather than exclusive approaches.

individuals and communities, and the increasing misogyny and exclusion between 1400 and 1500 included Christine de Pisan's (1364–1430) writing on increasing misogyny, especially in cities;[12] the taking over by men of guilds that women helped create; "enclosure" of women's religious communities by the institutional church (Brennan 1985); the development of elaborate architectural drawings on how to prevent women's escape from the cloister; instruction by the pope to women heads of abbeys to stop hearing confessions; harassment of rural women healers and wise women, who were accused as witches and burned; and formal sanction by the pope of the torture of women. The search for a more appropriate starting date confirmed that more political and social spaces for women could be found, as analytic focus was gradually taken back in time, first in approximately fifty-year and then one-hundred-year periods from 1500 to 1000. The date 1000 was selected by the ongoing secondary research, suggestions from classical and medieval scholarly experts, and, initially, simplicity. Later, upon further reflection and discovery of confirmatory scholarly sources, it seemed like an excellent choice. It is clear that far more space was available for women to act as women without constraints and to negotiate successfully with a full range of competing interests in 1000–1250 than in 1250–1500. The macro trend continued up until the present as a broader, deeper, and more intrusive version of EuroPatriarchy developed and became embedded as taken-for-granted practices.

Methodologies and Initial Findings on the Colonization Experiences

The larger temporal scope of the study, uncertainties about validity of secondary sources, and wonder about paradigm shifts—or what Ceceña (2008, ch. 2) calls two coexisting but contradictory civilizational magmas—led towards a more restricted comparative approach focusing on initial contact between Europeans and different types of indigenous communities in the Americas and Africa.[13] We selected the indigenous peoples of east-coast

12. See Joan Kelly (1982; 1984), who identified de Pisan as an early feminist theorist and the originator of the *Querelle des Femmes*, 1400–1789. The association between the city and an abstracted male-created culture is also described by Colin Starnes (2012, especially Chapter 1).

13. Research from Asia, especially Japan, is not explicitly included in this chapter but has informed its analysis. Initially, Nova Scotia was selected as the contrast to the better-known colonial history of other parts of North and South America. Later I began to use theoretic sampling of indigenous societies. I also was drawn to this quote by French (2002: 123) who suggests that everywhere the Europeans went, "their guns, their greed, and their diseases left behind devastation and converts to power-worship." Were men or women more likely to be converts? Did the society being colonized make any difference? What about patterns of protocontact, "contact" and coloniality?

Canada, the Mi'kmaw,[14] initially because of local scholarly sources and to contrast with the Latin American experience described by Ceceña. The Mi'kmaw had helped the first Nova Scotian settlers in 1605 by teaching survival skills with sophisticated indigenous technologies like snowshoes and birchbark canoes after half the settlers had not survived the first winter in New Brunswick. As Reid (2009a; 2009b) points out, the first 140 years of contact with settlers, especially with the (French) Acadiens who settled on land not used by the Mi'kmaw, were very different from relations after the English settled Halifax in 1749 (and expelled many of the Acadiens from Nova Scotia within the decade). Theoretic sampling was used to select other comparable communities, including the matriarchal six-nation confederacy Haudenosaunee (Mann and Fields 1997) and its respected wise women, Gantowisas (Johansen and Mann 2000), and the considerably more recent contact in Northwest Canada. Friesen (2013: 53) applied world-systems theory explicitly and used archaeological research to describe different stages of incorporation (autonomous contact periphery [1800–1889], marginal periphery [1889–1907], and dependent periphery [1907–]), a pattern very different from the east coast. Our work is not complete, but we have found that in spite of many socio-economic and cultural differences as well as different contact years, patterns, relations, and circumstances, remarkably similar gendered polarization and colonialized relations resulted at the macro levels. We are still exploring the suggestions of Canadian scholar John Ralston Saul (2008) who contrasted Europe and the United States with Canada because of the Canadian tradition of compromise learned in relations with aboriginal peoples.

Initial Findings and Implications of the Myth of Progress

As mentioned previously, most scholarly texts and chronologies that consider women, either implicitly or explicitly, are constructed to support a history of the increasing progress of women.[15] In fact, this myth of increasing unilinear progress for women in a world that began as patriarchal produced a methodological problem and interfered with our empirical project (see footnote 1). An earlier empirical study of women and personhood comparing communities in two areas of Atlantic Canada

---

14. The Eastern Woodland Mi'kmaw (Knockwood 2001) are also known as Micmac (Davis 1992; Gonzalez 1981; McGee 1974, 1983), Micmaq, or Mi'kmaq (Paul 2000; Schmidt and Marshall 1995, Walls 2010), and live in Mi'kma'ki (Reid 2009).

15. For example, Boles and Hoeveler (2006) begin their chronology in 1405, with Christine de Pizan, who is the only entry before 1501 when *The Book of Margery Kempe* appears. See Allen (1985) and Hufton (1995). Their current examples seem to be drawn from US newspapers, with the word "first" in many places.

identified a need to reconsider this assumption of unilinearity,[16] but it became apparent in our research that this is a minority view even among feminists. Scholars such as Walby (2009) who rely on statistical data from the relatively recent past to point to women's progress in areas such as politics, education, and employment feed the contemporary unilinear-progress myth by not addressing the historic losses in each of these areas within the last millennium.

The blinding nature of the myth of progress has led us to reassess the importance of the academic literature on the history and/or origins of patriarchy. See thinkers such as Biaggi (2005), Boulding (1976), Eisler (1987), Hamilton (1978), Lerner (1986), Mies (1986), and von Werlhof (2007), including archaeologists such as Marija Gimbutas (see Keller 1996). These scholars differ in their analysis and in the time period, but all of them put the origins of patriarchy before the Christian Era and posit a more equalitarian society before patriarchy. Goettner-Abendroth (2009), the founder of modern matriarchal studies, argues that societies were matriarchal before patriarchy, characterized by a lack of a hierarchy and the presence of peace rather than violence and conflict. We argue that the historically constructed EuroPatriarchy was being created and formed from 1000 to the end of Braudel's "long sixteenth century" (c.1450–c.1640). This system and its sets of social relations and orientations had a significant effect on the shape of the world-system at the time of its expansion to the Americas and Africa circa 1500, as described previously.

In EuroPatriarchy's Macro Polarizing Frame—Short-Term Changes

The macro-level methodology of this study and its limited time frame along with a related attempt to narrow its scope led us not to focus on patriarchy's frequent short-term fluctuations. The tentative conclusion, which we believe has some empirical confirmation, is that for the inhabitants of almost every particular era of this millennium within the world-system, within a thirty-year period an inhabitant would be more likely than not to witness some noticeable gendered change or changes. This level of patriarchal change tends to be related sometimes to sexuality, sometimes to changing religious and/or secular ideals, sometimes to misogyny, and other times to specific historical circumstances and interactions. There are also gendered fluctuations between competing gendered dichotomous societal ideals (e.g., equality and difference, a

---

16. Chritiansen-Ruffman (1980) found the opposite, that women in small communities of Labrador at the periphery in the 1970s had more ability to define their realities from their standpoints as women in their community groups than did women in the regional center, linked to the core. They were able to advocate successfully for the social needs that they considered to be most important, hence demonstrating more personhood than women in the regional core.

saint and a whore, moral superiority and moral inferiority, spiritual brilliance or spiritual incapacity, and intellectual talent or inferiority). Many of these historical fluctuations are documented in historical overviews such as those by Anderson and Zinsser (2000), Boulding (1976), French (2002; 2003), Hughes and Hughes (1997), and Smith (2004; 2005), although not necessarily identified as such.

Women's Spaces and the Foundations of EuroPatriarchy

While a few world-history scholars mention Christianity's women-friendly face in its first four centuries, almost no scholar except Elise Boulding even hinted at any pattern related to women and the church around the millennium.

Boulding (1976: 415, 423) describes the dawning of the millennium in Europe and Byzantium as "peaceful enough," a time of new beginnings because of some success in controlling rampant violence, greed, and inequality, with the help of women who were experiencing relative equality. In the last months before 1000, she writes, "women and men had been bringing wagon loads of possessions, parcels of land deeds, valuable jewels, and manuscripts, to the monasteries and churches of Christendom ... to be ready and in good standing on Judgement Day." She describes an "orgy of church-building all over Europe,"[17] and the return of the "old prophecy tradition."[18]

A number of priests who subsequently became saints were known for envisioning Mary during this period. In this largely peasant society with relative peace, where everyone's subsistence depended on agriculture and the cycles of the seasons, the reverence for Mary, nature, and what we would now in the twenty-first century see as more feminine elements of the church had a resurgence.[19] In European churches, some of the more patriarchal imagery as well as Mary's singular symbolic function as mother of baby came later. During the twelfth century, Mary, also Stella Maris, was considered as the loving protector on both land

---

17. Further research is needed on its implications for women at that time and long-term consequences for gendered relations inside and outside of the church, as well as the historical impact of this windfall wealth.

18. Boulding (1976: 423) continues: "The charismatic face of the church could smile on the woman visionary even while the bureaucratic face was trying to clamp down on women's initiatives."

19. Mary was important in recruiting pagan communities to Christianity in the early Christian Church, in early missionary work by St. Patrick in Ireland, and later, after contact with the Americas. The image of Mary is reported as appealing to peoples who lived in harmony and praised "Mother Earth" for providing their necessities of life. Mary had a special appeal to some seventeenth-century Algonquian women in Canada (Green-Devins, 1992).

and sea. Davis (1971) reminds us that the philosopher Albertus Magnus (1193/1206–1280) called Mary the "Goddess."[20]

Clearly the Catholic Church was more women-friendly in the eleventh and twelfth centuries than at other times during this millennium. Religious communities of women and men effectively had parallel institutions. Women and men who headed abbeys were running comparable institutions with similar authority and many of the same privileges and obligations, including the giving of advice to both sacred and secular authorities and hearing confessions from members and those from nearby communities.[21] The church provided space for women's intellectual debates and knowledge creation as well as for women to take social, intellectual, political, and religious initiatives as illustrated in the lives of Herrad of Landesberg (1130–1198) and Hildegard von Bingen (1098–1179). Both headed their own women's abbeys and were poets, illustrators, religious philosophers, and thinkers who participated in debates with male scholars within the church. Herrad is best known for capturing the knowledge of her times in words and pictures in the women's encyclopedia *Hortus Deliciarum* or *Garden of Delights*. Also, like her predecessor, Rilinda (who started the encyclopedia), Herrad could be called a social entrepreneur. She became abbess in 1176, asked for land to construct a priory and chapel in 1178, and in 1180 "bought and founded a second monastery, larger than the first. It included—in addition to the church and convent—a farm, a hospital for the poor, and a hospice for pilgrims" (Allen 1985: 317). Hildegard, a German feminist visionary,[22] known as "the Sibyl of the Rhine," was confirmed by an ecclesiastical commission as "a divinely inspired prophet" (Olsen 1994: 43). Hildegard composed music, and Allen (1985) describes her highly sophisticated philosophical analyses of gender complementarity that included both the female and the male as full human beings. Her philosophy was holistic, "integrating the rational, material and spiritual aspects of human nature into a unified whole" (Allen 1985: 408). She was a sophisticated political advisor, skilled at working with the top ranks of men in both the sacred and secular domains (Olsen 1994). Clancy-Smith (2004: 117) emphasizes her

---

20. As Boulding (1976: 424), citing Henry Adams, suggests, it may be seen as "revenge that a society deprived since pagan days of significant female leadership took on the Christian Church" or a sign of respect for women thinkers and leaders at that time—philosophers, abbesses, humanitarians, and encyclopedists such as Herrad of Landesberg (1130–1195). Arguably Hildegard von Bingen (1098–1179) and Eleanor of Aquitaine (1122/1124–1204), the latter who was queen of both France and England, were prominent, well-rounded, enlightened Renaissance people despite their genders.

21. Subsequently, church officials tried to stop this practice by women, with increasing success in the fifteenth century (see also Brennan 1985).

22. For example, Clancy-Smith (2004) notes that Hildegard depicted her visions with specifically female spiritual symbols such as the egg.

conflict with the ecclesiastical establishment, "which opposed Hildegard's claims that God spoke directly through her."[23]

Our analysis identified isolated hints of a major women-friendly period at the dawn of the new millennium, followed by a massive and systematic attempt at patriarchal restructuring. Gary Macy (2008) sheds confirmatory light on our analysis in three ways. (1) His careful scholarship provides convincing and "overwhelming" historical evidence that women were ordained in the early years of the church and into the early centuries of the millennium, helping us to explain both the pattern and individual incidents reported by scholars, such as women's administration of churches and dioceses and hearing confessions that were inconsistent with the patriarchal church that most scholars described. He also acknowledges his debt to earlier feminist scholars. (2) Macy also explains how women were able to be excluded when the church radically redefined the concept of ordination "from a ceremony that celebrated the move to a new ministry in a particular community" to a "ceremony that granted power and a new spiritual status to a particular individual" (pp. 109–110). At the same time, the church limited ordination to only one ministry (the priesthood) and only one power (to consecrate bread and wine at the altar). Under these new definitions, women could no longer be ordained nor even considered to have been ordained. (3) Macy explains that "rarely has ritual practice and understanding changed so rapidly and so completely" (p. 109). He gives this hypothetical example: "In the 1130s Abelard could still staunchly defend the *ordo* of deaconess as divinely instituted, as truly ordained, and as still functioning in the guise of abbesses, one of whom was his own wife, Heloise. By 1230, such a defense would have been most unlikely, if not, in fact, unthinkable" (p. 109). This hypothetical example may well be true because this ritual practice and understanding were under the control of the increasingly institutionalized hierarchy of the Catholic Church. It may have been the beginning but not the end of the paradigm shift from a balanced world that included women and assumed both love and intellect to be part of human nature (see Ruether and McLaughlin 1998), to the patriarchal worldview that began to dominate the lives of Christian women in the early fifteenth century.[24]

---

23. Indeed, subsequent women and men with such ideas were burned as heretics. Later they were called witches and brought before the inquisition, and still later called Protestants. History might be very different if such women and their ideas had not been ignored, rejected, or suppressed by what Allen (1985; 1997a; 1997b) calls the Aristotelian Revolution.

24. See Ruether and McLaughlin (1998) for an example of paradigmatic continuity that is exemplified in the Christian lives of three church women: Saint Lioba (eighth century), Christina of Markyate (eleventh century), and Saint Catherine of Siena (fourteenth century). Catherine tried to illustrate alternatives by insisting that the church become the Mother she is called to be rather than a rapacious robber so that pope and church are worthy of obedience. Ruether and McLaughlin argue that both men and women in 1500 saw the church to include what the twenty-first century calls the "feminine."

As part of his analysis, Macy provides us with a caution about the misleading assumption that decrees from popes and councils were always implemented. He points out, in fact, that the program of reforms from Merovingian bishops and the Carolingians about imposing celibacy and/or continence on the clergy and trying to deter abbesses and deaconesses from (their then-traditional) ritual roles was not heeded, but the massive collection of these documents by the reformers of the eleventh and twelfth centuries' church "gave the impression of unity and uniformity, as indeed they were meant to do. Once so gathered, the wish lists of disparate councils and popes were understood as descriptions of how the past once was and now, once again, ought to be" (p. 87). These reforms clearly were of great consequence for the church, for women, and for the world-system.

Boulding describes the church in changing times (1976: 415):

> Underneath the mantle, battles raged between popes, kings, and emperors competing for legitimacy and power, but the respite was, in a sense, real. . . . The church was strong enough to declare and enforce the Truce of God, spelling out when and where fighting could take place.[25] . . . The war-control measures[26] contributed substantially to the conditions in which agricultural and craft productivity and trade could develop. New agricultural land was cleared, and new towns sprang up on old and new trade routes. Merchant guilds formed, and their spin-offs, craft guilds, multiplied. New monasteries opened to absorb

---

25. The Crusades (see Claster 2009 for dating them as 1095–1396) were effective in directing fighting to other places and in legitimizing violence and fighting as a basis for the developing European patriarchal system. Claster also mentions that in the First Crusade men needed their wives' permission before they left on a crusade, a requirement that changed in the thirteenth century.

26. The "war-control measures" took on a number of forms over time and place, with some feudal contracts specifying forty days per year of military service, with the expectation that a battle would cease once the limit had been reached. Boulding (1976: 416, quoting the last part of this note from Nicherson) mentions that "the church was strong enough to declare and enforce the Truce of God," which specified that war was permitted only on three days and two nights per week (Monday through Wednesday) and not at all during Lent, Advent, or "the great feasts of Our Lady, the feasts of the Apostles, and certain other saints." This pacifist face of the church was soon in contradiction with the Crusades, designed by the pope. In the two world wars of the twentieth century, this war-control measure was reduced to a locally negotiated Christmas truce in only a few places. Indeed, throughout the millennium, the emphasis of the exponents of EuroPatriarchy was on building nations with military might rather than on building sustainable human communities. In the contemporary world, the concepts of patriarchy have informed the story lines of video games, enforcing imagery of conquest and male violence against women. Peace has been conceived mainly as the absence of war, despite a United Nations decade, and with increasing capitalism, humans and nations increasingly have become resources to be controlled and exploited.

surplus populations. What had been miserable towns in 1000 were flourishing cities by 1350.

In the church's attempts to "civilize" both violence and greed during this period, women were sometimes enlisted. While the church ostentatiously displayed wealth, both institutionally with the new cathedrals and other church buildings and often by persons of high institutional clerical ranks, it also enlisted women to help it preach against greed. For example, in 1215–1216, when the Catholic Church was trying to increase its ranks of (male) priests and establish authorized procedures, Thomas Chobham's *Manual for Confessors*, as quoted by Rubin (1998: 39), points out:

> In imposing penance, it should always be enjoined upon women to be preachers ("praedicatrices") to their husbands, because no priest is able to soften the heart of a man the way his wife can. . . . Even in the bedroom, in the midst of their embraces, a wife should speak alluringly to her husband, and if he is hard and unmerciful, and an oppressor of the poor, she should invite him to be merciful; if he is a plunderer, she should denounce plundering. . . . For it is permissible for a woman to expend much of her husband's property, without his knowing, in ways beneficial to him and for pious causes.[27]

While some in the church enlisted women to help "civilize" men and assist the church's aggrandizement, giving advice that would later feed misogynous criticism of women's spending habits, others were in the process of trying to "decivilize" women and exclude them from church authority so that the church could define itself as a patriarchal institution with an official structure of hierarchy (one male God, male pope, male cardinals, male bishops, male priests). Hierarchical rule at the time, however, was not fully institutionalized within the church, as exemplified by the fact that two men claimed to be the rightful pope at one time, and there is popular debate about whether there was a pope (Joan) who was female. Abbeys at this time were not only religious communities but fulfilled intellectual functions of knowledge generation, spirituality, learning from experience, maintaining knowledge, and visionary thinking. Abbeys were both coed and single gender, especially in the Benedictine monasteries, and were largely self-sufficient communities. They usually not only created their own provisioning of basic needs but also cultivated the arts of poetry, literature, music, and song while providing the historical memory of former civilizations by copying old texts, compiling encyclopedias of knowledge, and maintaining

---

27. See Rubin (note 14) for citations to source, translator, and a related source of interest. Further research and many books could be written using this quote as a baseline for the patriarchal social reformation that followed.

oral-history traditions. The relatively high gender equality of the times was reflected in instances of clearly egalitarian and collaborative coed learning environments, in the spiritual equivalency of Mary and Jesus within Christianity, and in the parallel structures of gendered abbeys.

Higher Education and Access to the Professions

Education in the first two centuries of the millennium was mainly through "on the job" training and apprenticeships. By contemporary standards, there was neither "childhood" nor schooling for almost anyone. However, nobility hired tutors to educate their children. Schools in cathedrals were established to train priests, and some cathedral schools trained not only men but women, especially of the nobility.[28] In this period, Hildegard von Bingen both practiced medicine and wrote about the cure of disease. When the first medical school was developed outside the monastic tradition in Salerno, Italy, women were present there and in five other Italian medical schools, as faculty and students who were given licenses to practice medicine, although many had to work hard against much resistance to do so.[29]

---

28. See Allen (1985, especially ch. 5). She also argues that Aristotelian works were "only partially integrated into Christian institutionalized education" before 1200 and the formation of the University of Paris, which was based on texts and secular ideas that excluded women philosophers (pp. 413–415). She also points, at least implicitly, to alternative theories for the exclusion of women—that they are based on cathedral schools designed to increase the numbers of priests (the most common explanation) or that the university was modeled on military conceptions of knighthood. Allen (1997a: 416) refers to Hastings Rashdall's notion of "an intellectual knighthood" and says that the queen regent of France, Blanche of Castile, could have intervened around 1231 during her battle on another issue with the University of Paris. She perhaps underestimated the generalized and growing attempts to impose patriarchal principles in the situations she describes. For example, she describes the discussions between individuals among the four "nations" of France, England (later Germany), the Normans, and the Picards that became the constitutive basis for the Faculty of Arts and Letters in 1231 and the related Bull of Gregory IX in that year, the negotiations between what she calls the "secular bishops" and the ecclesiastics (associated more institutionally with the church as students, masters, and therefore men). Allen mentions but does not single out the power of Catholic Church ascetic traditions and its impact on women and their exclusion from Western science, as does Noble (1993), who seems unaware of Allen's work (1985).

29. Allen (1997a: 431) quotes the official decree and rationale upon graduation of Francesca, wife of Merreo de Romana, with a doctorate in surgery: "Whereas the laws permit women to practice medicine, and whereas, from the viewpoint of good morals, women are best adapted to the treatment of their own sex, we, after having received the oath of fidelity, permit the said Francesca to practice the said art of healing, etc." Whether this gender-specific decree may point to a "special daughter of famous father" pattern of what might be called gender exceptionalism, as may be

The relative gender equality in the rudiments of education was ruptured by decisions made that excluded the intellectual work in philosophy and medicine of Hildegard von Bingen from the curriculum of the University of Paris and that explicitly excluded all women as students and masters from this newly created university. This total exclusion of women from the start in universities in France and Germany, as well as in England, where Oxford and Cambridge were being established,[30] also had the result that women were excluded from knowledge.

The exclusion of women had an effect on what was considered knowledge. A good portion of the gendered knowledge and of the holistic perspective that had been conceived by Hildegard von Bingen and others became invisible. The exclusive masculine gaze or patricentrism shaped the emerging notions of knowledge, of "reason," and of science and technology. They became focused on order, control, dichotomies, abstractions, and rational man rather than on relationships, living well, and the common good. Selfishness, violence, fear (of death), and greed trumped concerns for each other and living together as well as love and life. The patriarchal institutions of what became the modern world were built apart from life, based on men's abilities to think abstractly as individuals. The world was seen as patriarchally ordered and controlled, one in which men's technologies and abilities made it possible to conquer the natural world. In this world, women were shaped and exploited to serve the abstracted and hierarchical "progress" system, a system built apart from life while also attempting to transform the world, first through inventions, alchemy, and exploration, then through science, engineering, and new technologies, and now through creating artificial intelligence, military drones, biotechnologies, and "man-made" living beings.

The exclusion of women also had an effect on each of the new areas of learning and professional knowledge. Law and medicine became, by definition, new secular professions that, like the clergy, would be restricted to men. Medicine is a particularly interesting case because it appears to have been an area that had long been in the sphere of women. Some women were certainly known at that time to be healers. Within a century, women doctors such as Jacqueline Félicie, who had been practicing medicine and who were leaders of the healing professions, were being tried and convicted for practicing without a diploma or degree

---

the case, or the general ability of women to access medical licenses in Italy, it does point to women's presence in healing institutions at the beginning of the millennium and to their continued presence as midwives and healers under the radar of the restricted and exclusionary rules being imposed against women at various periods. It was only in the late twentieth and early twenty-first centuries that midwives gained recognition in some Canadian provinces.

30. This contrasts with Italian universities in Salerno, Bologna, Padua, Pavia, Rome, and Naples. See almost any chronology or encyclopedia of famous women that covers this early period.

from the University of Paris, despite positive patient endorsements of women's medical knowledge and skills. The crime was not incompetence but being a woman healer.

The deliberate exclusion of women from universities had significant and increasing consequences on women's inequality in most institutional and professional sectors. It also served as a rationale to exclude women from desirable positions in the labor force, both as individuals and as a category. There are examples of women being expelled or not being accepted in guilds around that time because of their gender, and most guilds became more male over time. The long-term decrease of women in a job or occupation such as brewers (from the beginning of this period when almost all were women, up to the seventeenth century when almost none were women) has been carefully studied by Alice Clark (1919) and Judith Bennett (2006).[31] French (2002) cites a 1356 German law that barred women from inheriting[32] and from several jobs they previously held—levying troops, holding courts of justice, coining money, and participating in legal assemblies. It would be interesting to find out more about the women money-changers that Abu-Lughod (1989: 92) mentions, citing Raymond de Roover as claiming this to be "apparently one of the few professions where there was no discrimination against women . . . in Western Europe. . . . No less than six women appear in a list of eleven money-changers . . . doing business . . . in 1368 at Frankfurt-on-the-Main." These examples of the strong presence, constrictions, and absence of women's labor-force participation often took different paths throughout the diverse and growing jurisdictional forms that would govern the peoples of Europe. As well, sometimes, when needed, women were called to new jobs and to jobs that had previously been forbidden to them and from which they had withdrawn, such as those of body removers, doctors, and hospital heads during the plague. In this example, women acted more like the "reserve army of labor" that has characterized women's work patterns also in more contemporary times.

It was 650 years before women began to gain entrance to some parts of the university in the middle of the nineteenth century. They were

---

31. While Clark focuses on transformation and Bennett more on continuities, Bennett (2006: 73) quotes Clark's "classic study of the negative effects of industrialism and capitalism on women's status" as follows: "With the growth of capitalism and the establishment of a monopoly for 'Common Brewers,' women were virtually excluded from their old trade of brewing." Bennett, in her study of this process from 1300 to 1600, was struck by what she called a "patriarchal equilibrium," a term suggested by Bennett (2006). While she uses that term to point to the importance of a continually changing but constant patriarchy, our analysis points to an increase in patriarchal misogyny, the suppression of women, and gendered polarization during this period and beyond.

32. Erickson (2005) argues that inventing legal loopholes to get around inheritance and property laws in England was one of the major reasons that capitalism developed first in England.

only gradually and hesitantly admitted, and only if they fit in. Those who suggested changes in ways of knowing were often made invisible or expelled, and the scholarly "fathers" continued to theorize in ways that undermined women's autonomy and priorities. Most knowledge and structures within universities and outside were still fundamentally oriented to domination, violence, competition, and control rather than fostering life, creativity, cooperative engagements, and personhood.

Thus, in the thousand years since 1000 CE, the structures of male/female education went from relatively parallel institutions to total female exclusion, to women's incorporation into male-created systems within increasingly institutionalized larger and deeper patriarchal structures. In addition to the systemic patriarchal exclusion of women, the hierarchical structures imposed on the university during the medieval period, as Allen (1985) has demonstrated, and the imposed structures of Western science (Merchant 1989; Noble 1993) still have consequences in the twenty-first century for nonintegrated, exploitative, and segmented ways of thinking in disciplines, faculties, and bureaucratic departments. Furthermore, the dichotomous, binary logic on which both scholarly "arguments" and computers are based continues to reinforce simplistic, "opposite-sided," and nonintegrated arguments rather than more complex, holistic, multileveled, and consensus-based ideas, approaches, and solutions to living together. Moreover, the institutionalization of education during this period, as French (2002) has pointed out, tended to impose rigid uniformity of knowledge, with regulated curricula, measured accomplishments by exams, and abstract language with which to manipulate "reality" within narrowly defined dichotomous logic and topics aimed to control the natural and social world rather than to learn from it and from human experiences. Instead, as Allen, French, and many others have pointed out, women's abilities were also devalued, associated with beasts or lesser human beings than men. This intellectual tradition that subordinated women provided the rationale for writing women out of history in many different ways.[33] The rapid growth of literacy from less than 1 percent of the population of women and men in the western Europe of the mid-eleventh century to 40 percent male literacy in Florence at the end of the fourteenth century and 50 percent of English males by the end of the fifteenth century led to a steadily growing gender gap in literacy that helped to embed gendered social-power differentials, both interpersonally and in the new culture, society, occupations, and institutions of Europe.

---

33. See Rogers (1966) for the different forms misogyny took in describing what was considered appropriate in successive historic periods, such as the shrewish wife in the Middle Ages, the "Court Wanton, the Bossy Bourgeoise, ... the Insatiable Strumpet," and the whore in the Renaissance, the unfeminine women in the nineteenth century, and the devouring mother in the twentieth century.

Consolidation of EuroPatriachy: Inventing "Civilization,"
Misogyny, and the Subordination and Suppression of Women

Greed, violence, hierarchy, exploitation, and active suppression of women were major themes in the years around 1250 through 1500 after the beginning of what Allen (1985) calls the Aristotelian Revolution. Philosophers such as Albertus Magnus and his student, St. Thomas Aquinus, were actively advocating the suppression of women, citing written sources (both sacred and secular) from previous "civilizations" of Greece and Rome, such as Aristotle's idea that women were imperfect and unformed men, incapable of thought and thus clearly subordinate.[34] Biblical interpretations about Adam and Eve, including those of previous misogynous theologians such as St. Augustine (354–430), were prevalent and pointed to women's sinful, evil, and tempting qualities and the dangers women posed to men. These ideas became more widespread with the development of the printing press, especially in the fifteenth and sixteenth centuries. These times were characterized by inquisitions and witch hunts by church and state, with mainly women being accused as witches.[35] Poor women, independent women, and wise women were particularly vulnerable, and immense fortunes changed hands as land rights and the bodies and possessions of witches became the property of the state and/or subordinated to its authority and its unnatural beliefs. Foundations of professions, such as medicine (Ehrenreich and English 1973), law (Mies 1986), and various money schemes grew around this phenomenon. Papal authority legitimized the torture of women, and new inventions and approaches abounded; in that vein, the book *Malleus Maleficarum (The Witches' Hammer)* was essentially a guidebook to witch trials that specified roles and procedures for doctors, lawyers, and judges. It ensured that the accused were stripped, completely shaved, and dragged backwards into the court so as to protect the judge from their spells. Published in 1486, this book was written by Jacob Sprenger and Heinrich Kraemer, two Dominican inquisitors. Like others writing about witchcraft but contrary to the non-misogyny of creative writers at the time, they asserted that witchcraft existed, especially among women, and that it was heresy not to believe

---

34. Allen (1985: 362–364) credits the work of these two philosophers for the final adoption of the sex polarity theory of Aristotle while pointing out that Albertus Magnus was mainly "a transmitter of ideas in the field." She does credit him with an interesting theory of Mary as having perfect knowledge compared to man but man being superior on all relevant dimensions compared to women.

35. There is an immense literature on the witch hunts or later witch craze, which seems to follow a pattern. Many recent books say that it took place over two hundred years, but which two hundred years varies by more than five hundred years. Older studies seem to suggest a longer period (four hundred years) over an even wider range of dates (e.g., from 1100). The dates specified seem to depend on definitions.

in witches.[36] Protestants also participated in misogynous attacks against women, although they did think that women could and should communicate directly with God and hence needed literacy to read the Bible. They also tended to quote the patriarchal misogyny of St. Paul (Rogers 1966). The Protestant theologian John Knox blasted women politicians, but perhaps the most significant and underrecognized conceptual symbolic advance for EuroPatriarchy was the Protestant (and Puritan-led) focus on the subordination of the wife—namely, that in marriage a woman should obey her husband and recognize her faults. This rhetoric around the time of the Reformation and Counter-Reformation was particularly misogynist and implicitly bestowed privilege on every man. The image of the family had become a hierarchy, like both church and state, with the father as the head, symbolic leader—God-like and in control of His family. Nevertheless, the history of Quakers and especially of Quaker women in the Boston States indicates that these patriarchal visions were contested in the European core zones and emerging US peripheral zones. Both the consistencies and reshapings in Quaker history of peace and women's equality also implicitly document both the power and more micro-level changes of EuroPatriachy over time.

Women's Spaces and Polarization: A Summary View

The concepts of personhood, patriarchy, and women's spaces introduced in this chapter were found to be both conceptually and empirically useful in our focus on macro-gendered structures. The clear finding is that personhood and women's spaces were larger and patriarchy clearly smaller in the year 1000 than in 2000, thus supporting a finding of polarization. In the first 650 to 850 or 1000 years, these shifts resulted in the establishment of an increasingly systemic and more polarized gendered hierarchy in the spaces of religion, economics, politicism, and family. They reduced women's political spaces and power to take significant actions to achieve their priorities. The changing shape, form, extent, and depth of patriarchy during this period directly increased women's exclusion and undermined women's autonomy and dignity. Both religious and secular thinkers borrowed from classical texts, considering women inferior and associated with evil. Misogyny and women's exclusion were encouraged by church and state. This paradigm strengthened and deepened in the remainder of the millennium, spurred by patricentric ideals, concepts, and priorities. Patriarchal institutions became more embedded and increasingly interlocked in institutional patriarchal frameworks of inequalities,

---

36. It was endorsed as well by the theology faculty at the University of Cologne and published with many additions and translations over time. See Rogers (1966: 148) for details about the charges of witchcraft and issues of correct translation.

both with and without gendered intent. This secondary embedding of patriarchy further reduced women's spaces and increased the effective disadvantages faced by women in comparison to men as well as reducing women's and men's autonomous spaces within what have been called public and private spheres.[37]

As part of our historical and material feminist analysis, we also named EuroPatriarchy, a set of social relations developed historically in Europe and spread through colonialisms and their exploitative and totalizing world institutions of legitimized inequality, violence, and greed in increasing interaction with one another.

The grounded-theory finding is that a EuroPatriarchal system began with an unexpected economic windfall for the Catholic Church that was left by the devout before the predicted judgement day at the end of the first millennium (1000). The sudden wealth put growing strains on the institutional church and led immediately to new buildings, plans, infighting, and expansion. Within the century, the idea of indulgences was invented and added to tithing. With the Domesday Book, ideas of taxation soon followed as heads of the church, manors, abbeys, and political entities established and expanded unequal patterns of wealth transfer from the bottom or periphery to the top or core zones of power. The heads of church and state both competed and supported one another in achieving new forms of economic returns from their hierarchic inferiors, deals for power and authority, and, later, the domination of women and the environment. The legitimization and embeddedness of violence, greed, and inequality helps us to understand the violent history of our past and present and the exploitative rather than people- and community-based system enshrined in our nations and national priorities, cultures, and social relations.

Greed, as well as violence and inequality, the bases of EuroPatriarchy, are gendered in the year 1000. Lady Godiva became a folkloric symbol for her successful attempt to counter the greed of her husband in support of those on their manor paying lower taxes. Two centuries later, women were described as protesting to the visiting queen the unfairness of the abbot's insistence that they use and pay for his new technology of a furling mill to make cloth rather than use their traditional ways. At about that same time, a fictional character (Peeping Tom) was added to the Lady Godiva story, which added a new moral, obedience to authority, to the mitigation of greed in the folktale.

In addition to the legitimating of exploitative greed and inequality at this period, violence was also legitimized and, to some extent, controlled by the church (in the ways described in this chapter) that regularized and moderated it in the daily lives of Europeans. Violence was also legitimated by the church in its garnering of support for the Crusades

---

37. This politicized dichotomy includes men as producers and women as reproducers, omitting all other possibilities.

and the pope's declaration of a just war that would also support the total salvation of its participants.

Thus, in concert with the conditions of the times, violence, exploitative greed, and inequality were beginning to be legitimated and institutionalized in church and state as a character of institutional social relations. They have remained governing values of the modern world-system, despite continued avowals of the early church values of peace, love, and equality that were also valued by women during the last millennium and a *de facto* part of many indigenous paradigms.

Many global and local feminists (see Miles 2013), feminist networks—e.g., Feminists for a Gift Economy, DAWN (Development Alternatives with Women for a New Era), and the International Feminist University Network—and scholarly trajectories (e.g., ecofeminism and modern matriarchal studies) have informed global women's movements. They overlap with other social movements, such as environmental movements worried about climate change, the Arab Spring, Occupy, and the indigenous-women-initiated Idle No More. Together they advocate for a fundamental paradigm shift that ends inequalities and embedded injustices and the legitimized hierarchies of what we have called EuroPatriarchy. They criticize contemporary top-down relationships and governmental forms of anti-participatory democracy with its "fast tracks," its "logic" that institutions are too big to fail, and its creation of institutions such as the World Trade Organization (WTO).[38] Only time will tell if the patriarchal WTO develops hierarchical dominance as did the newly monied Catholic Church at the dawn of the last century, but our guess is that it contains, already, too many contradictions and no redemptive qualities. A life-based paradigm and new ages of reason and enlightenment, this one including everyone, may be our only hope for collective survival, giving a new meaning to progress, such as living well.

---

38. It was effectively an economic coup d'etat (overtaking of the state) in 1995 when elected governments gave away their authority to act in the interests of their peoples. With secretive negotiations, without parliamentary knowledge or public debate, the WTO was given power to enforce trade rules over governments' and peoples' interests as well as to destroy life and nature. With misguided, arrogant omnipotence, current leaders are acting like gods on Earth in their patriarchal alchemist tradition, this time believing that they can create progress and even new life forms as they work with failed assumptions to deliver the powers of economic fundamentalism and try to embed the world with that antiquated dichotomous, contained logic. Many of the elite men making these decisions, unaware of their embedded patriarchal logics, likely do not comprehend how this unbalanced focus contains a death logic that in fact could well destroy life on Earth.

Chapter 11

Deviance

*by Ari Sitas, Sumangala Damodaran,
Wiebke Keim, and Nicos Trimikliniotis*

Don Quixote tilted at windmills. He was considered to be "deviant," but this was the opinion of the bewildered mill-owners.

Our study begins in the 1600s and continues through to the present time. We are concerned with showing briefly how modernity steered human effort, and how people were clustered in unique ways to achieve goals. We start from a historical moment when a number of foraging states redefined world relations. Starting from the seventeenth century enables us to bring Latin America, Africa, and Asia within the narrative of modernity.

It also avoids the silliness of concepts like "traditional society" and "mechanical solidarity" and the outrageous binaries of evolutionary sociology. There was nothing traditional about the world in 1650 and there were very few places untouched by the robust exchanges of an emerging capitalist modernity.

A Typology of Deviance

It is hardly unusual to define the alterity of individuals or groups as "deviant." Although the word has suffered from a century of overuse, it is nevertheless a pragmatic concept that can be used to describe something disquieting to the upholders of dominant norms in a given society. Similarly, it is not strange to have bouts of panic about deviance or deviants, about the conditions that produce such phenomena or people, or about the perceived failure of the institutions that were supposed to eliminate, control, or shape deviance.

Modern institutions have tried to cluster people in certain ways to achieve both long-term and contingent goals. The particularity of each institution usually has to do with the manner in which it clusters people and the modalities through which it does so. The familiar list of institutions includes the factory, the mine, the plantation, the corporation, the state or local bureaucracy, the army, the police, the prison, the concentration camp, the gulag, the school, the hospital, the madhouse, and so on. Be they "closed" or "total" (Goffman 1974) or more open and permeable in their design, their social architecture is filled with commonalities and resemblances. There is a rhythm to their story punctuated by property and possession, by fences and boundaries.

We shall deal with four forms of perceived deviance, whose importance and frequency waxes and wanes throughout key turning points in modern history, but which never disappear entirely:

- Behavioral deviance: when the behavior of an individual, a group, or a social ensemble is deemed to be deviant. Different strategies are followed for its containment, depending on whether it is seen as "reformable" or not.
- Articulatory deviance: when an individual or a group articulates or signifies something in word, sign, or symbolic performance that is deemed to be deviant. This might be a religious tract, a document, or a public statement.
- Existential deviance: when a national, ethnic, racial, or religious group of people or an individual belonging to such a group is classified as "other" or "deviant" sui generis. The social majority may eliminate such a group in whole or in part, or may dispossess it of its demarcated territories.
- Miasmic deviance: when a group or an individual belonging to a group is seen as a polluted carrier of impure substances, such as bad spirits or viruses.

There are two possible criticisms of this pragmatic four-way split of the concept of deviance—that the "existential" mode is rather unorthodox, and that the distinction between "behavioral" and "articulatory" is rather forced.

It is, however, not true that the "existential" mode is unorthodox. Two pieces of legislation passed in Nazi Germany in 1936 resulted in a classification of Jews and non-Jews that was existential and, in the long term, lethal. Both the Law of the Reich Citizen and the Law for the Protection of German Blood and German Honor involved classification and codification of existential deviance and its contrasting normality. Such work was common from the seventeenth century onwards. Social groups all too often were classified as other, foreign, excludable, or exterminable because of who they were rather than what they did.

As for the second criticism, we know from theories of social agency and communication that a speech act can have illocutive or perlocutive effects—that is, the saying of something turns into the doing of something (Habermas 1981: 388–390). In this sense, the threshold between articulatory and behavioral becomes permeable, often blurred, and subject to interpretation. Some jurisdictions and institutions have been particularly sensitive to this and tended to define an expressed belief as a concrete subversive action, thus turning articulatory into behavioral deviance. We felt it was necessary to distinguish between the two because, on many occasions, men and women of socially faultless manners and behavior went to the rack because of what they said, wrote, or drew. This is particularly relevant to struggles relating to freedom of expression, scientific freedom, and censorship.

So how can these four types of deviance be utilized in our analysis? Before we can study forms of deviance over the last five centuries, we need more refinement and focus.

Clearing the Undergrowth

The story starts with absolutist states in interaction. There were patterns of expansion and contraction. Boundaries shifted and borders became permeable. People were clustered by states. We shall speak metaphorically of foragers and of fence-builders. The foragers set boundaries and borders, and the fence-builders defined them and clustered human effort.

The foragers engaged in wealth creation. They had to be innovators and model-builders in the process of colonizing the planet. Models that were successful resulted in expansion and assimilation, and were often ruthless. Models that succeeded include the seventeenth-century United Provinces (Dutch), England, France, Russia, and the embryonic United States. Models that failed resulted in contraction and collapse—the Mughals or the Spanish Crown. Case studies of comparative modernity or of the comparative paths to it tend to miss these entanglements and interrelationships.

Boundary-setting and -keeping was the preserve of well-organized armed ensembles of men. Good foragers created long-distance capacities, better logistics, and more effective long-term boundary-keeping forces. They also had capacities that allowed them to contract boundaries without losing much advantage.

Foraging states also played a major role in clustering people in new ways. And this leads to our second metaphor. The fence-builders (literal and metaphorical) ensured that the private appropriation and owner-ship of the planet's land surface grew from the original hypothetical 3 percent to a guesstimated 51 percent of the contemporary period. The commons and collective, state, conservation, and faith-based surfaces shrank accordingly over time. The emergence of an "absolute property right" involved "the right to use and manage it; to derive income by let-ting others use it; to transfer it to another by gift or bequest; to capture the value [of it] by sale; to claim immunity against expropriation of the property" (Weaver 2006: 49). These modern institutions have all prided themselves on their efficiency and effectiveness, their rationality, their "purposiveness" (Weber 1991: 244). It is a powerful ideology of success and of human improvement that defines, however violent and inhuman it is, our contemporary humanity.

Between the foragers and the fence-builders exists a complex dia-lectic of clustering human effort. Perhaps Jean-Baptiste Colbert's *Code Noir* of 1685 was the ultimate turning point in the fate of the modern. Alongside the criminal and civil codes of the 1670s, also pioneered by Colbert, France created norm-setting institutions that defined the spirit of capitalism as did the very early norm-setting institutions of Spain and the subsequent ones of the United Provinces.

Two Hypotheses

We largely agree with Michel Foucault (2004: 52) that deviance is "pro-ductive." Part of the impetus behind an impressive record of innovation and organization laws involved the attempted elimination, control, and management of deviance. It was, at the same time, as Foucault so aptly described, a process of confining and segregating deviant populations into dedicated institutions for the purposes of work, service, punishment, treatment, or care. The evidence we have garnered across four centuries has led us to the development of two interrelated hypotheses.

1. A focus on nonteleological thinking, deviance, and institutions brings Michel Foucault center stage. We share with Foucault a concern that, instead of more freedom or progress, we see dif-ferent forms of control and domination replacing each other over time. In his words, we witness "the endlessly repeated play of dominations" (Foucault 1984a: 85). But Foucault tells only one part of the story. The modern world has not been only about the shift from one form of domination to another. There has also been the ratcheting and cascading effect of deviant struggles towards more freedoms and autonomy. We observe "progress" when the struggle by the deviants succeeds in winning space and societal recogni-tion. Many forms of deviance came to be integral components of

popular-cultural formation, and some of them have remained so in story and song—the rebel, the bandit, the pirate, the rebellious peasant, the slave. However much we agree with Immanuel Wallerstein's work and world-systems analysis (1974), we have to stand the theory of economic cycles on its head—the up-phases of the world-economy are contingent on the ways deviance and alterity have been dealt with by those powerful enough to do so. In that way, new paths for accumulation and growth became possible.

2. The central and perhaps the most important point in our work is our contention that there are anomalic phases and cycles of deviance that are fascinating to study in their own rights. They tell us something about the societies we live in at present.

Cycles of Deviance

A key pivot for our work is that there are cycles of deviance that are very much like the cycles of boom and bust in the capitalist system, cycles that enable creative destruction and innovation.

We believe that cycles of deviance have accompanied the development of capitalist modernity, discrediting simplistic accounts of linear human progress. Some periods were defined by an increasing public shrillness about the proliferation of deviance. Stanley Cohen (1972) defined these shrill episodes of perceived or real deviance as "moral panics"—an amplified and angry reaction to individuals or groups who were deemed to be a threat to values, resulting in escalating demands for greater social control. The cycles have proceeded in this way: There is a real or perceived proliferation of deviancy, and a growing perception of social disorganization and normlessness, reaching levels of moral panic. This brings about efforts to define and classify the "problem" as well as debates about such definitions. There is then a process of classifying the deviance and codifying it into rule, norm, or law. At that point starts the process of reorganization, institutional reform, violence, reclustering, and the creation of new institutions. This launches a new up-phase.

Failures in each historical period cut right through a powerful ideology of success and improvement that defined, however violent and inhuman it has been, contemporary humanity. And panic was at its shrillest because the new attempt was perceived as the "best way"—the most advanced, technically sound, and rational. We are trying to turn "cycle theory" on its head—the fixers, through their innovations and repression, through the reconfigurations they bring with them, create conditions for a new sustained A-phase of accumulation. Without that, any system would have spun out of control.

We postulate that such a cycle becomes what we term an "anomalic phase" when it coincides with two other cyclical processes—an economic

B-phase and a cycle of increasing subaltern resistance. The B-phase throws many more people into unemployment, landlessness, and vulnerability, and more often than not it increases actions that are deemed by societal elites to be antisocial. The coincidence of a B-phase with a proliferation of deviance has been common, but so has been the coincidence of the two with the rise of movements challenging the class or social order of a society. There is always dissonance in any social system, and this often turns into alterity—an understanding by those below that there is an "us" and a "them." This may or may not lead to resistance. But when it does, and when this coincides with an economic B-phase and when deviance is on the increase, it translates into an anomalic phase—a period of social polarization.

On the basis of our research (Sitas et al. 2014), we could present detailed accounts of cycles of deviance in each century. However, the scope of this paper does not permit that. We shall offer only a very brief summary of some examples.

Deviance during the Seventeenth Century

The first period of the seventeenth century was primarily concerned with behavioral deviance, even though articulatory, miasmic, and existential deviance were strongly present.

In the early seventeenth century, a spread of moral panic was evident in many places. Because this largely coincided with an economic downswing and the rise of challenges to existing forms of authority, we may call it an anomalic phase. There was panic about "masterless men" roaming the countryside and invading cities, the proliferation of beggars and vagabonds in all the major towns of the West, fleeing serfs and slaves in the Russian domain, Brahmin defiance in the interstices of the Mughal Empire, slave rebellions in the Americas, recalcitrant lords resisting Manchu rule, pirates everywhere, and a general restlessness in "frontier" encounters from China and Russia to Ireland, the Americas, India, and West Africa.

At one level, the story is simple. There was a worldwide crisis in the first part of the seventeenth century. Many millions died during the Thirty Years' War, the Manchu conquest of China, the continuing destruction of indigenous peoples in North America, the mass slaughter of Jews by Cossacks in Poland, Aurangzeb's campaigns on the Indian subcontinent, and the escalation of the slave trade. The ascending strata reorganized repressive apparatuses and introduced new rules of conduct and behavior, enabling the "inhaling" of a new economic phase. The period after 1650 should be understood as a period of methodical organization of the means of destruction by absolutist states. It also strengthened the claim of the state to monopolize the means of violence.

The most vital work, though, was to create the preconditions for a dynamic new phase of accumulation. In the process deviants were confined, transported, or killed. The world at the end of the century had been "normalized"—the new laws or tropes of power pointed to new indices of domination that were more effective than ever before. Yet in this shift some strata won more spaces than others, and more nascent rights were negotiated. Property rights were the most enduring of these.

Existential, articulatory forms of deviance were in ample supply in this century, but behavioral deviance troubled authorities the most. Peasant and slave rebellions and "idleness" were paradigmatic in the "Iron Century" (Kamen 1971). Such rebellions were common through Russia, Hungary, and the southern parts of the Germanic zone. They took acute forms in France after a plague that ravaged the countryside between 1627 and 1630 and a deflation of agricultural prices in the 1630s (LeRoy Ladurie 1975: 386). Slavery provided new images of Black deviance (Fouchard 1981)—an uncontrollable and savage figure of animal sensuality and sexuality, murderous and cannibalistic, irrational and utterly destructive. It has remained a persistent latent basis of White feelings of otherness and danger ever since (Sala-Molins 1987).

If the behavior of peasants and slaves ranked high as a deviance, idleness was close by as a perceived social malady. A commission established by the king of France in 1630 recommended prosecuting beggars and vagabonds, as well as "all those who live in idleness and will not work for reasonable wages or who spend what they have in taverns" (Foucault 1984a: 131–132).

The behavioral deviants were part and parcel of the cultural formations of the working masses in both rural and urban locales. What was deviance for those in power was the normal stuff of people's lives. Such deviants stood at the point of tension of the system. The slave whose ears were cut off after flight would make other slaves shudder, but the empathy would never be with the cutters of ears, nor would it de-legitimize "flight" as a survival strategy. And so it was with the criminals against private property, the cutters of fences, the poachers, and the indigent poor. It is from these groups that ships were crewed, armies constituted, and settlers served.

As for articulatory deviance, apostasy was everywhere (Blackwell 2006; Embree 1991; Sumner 1986). All governments in Europe responded to the rise of printing by establishing controls and censorship. If the printed word and a radical outlook made people deviant, the performance of those recently colonized or enslaved made authorities shrill. Sedition, blaspheming, Godless thinking, apostasy, and slander kept institutions hard-pressed to respond, but as the century moved on and absolutist states gained in confidence, the apparatus of rule was refined.

During the seventeenth century, a "knowledge interest" emerged. Its rationalism was embryonic, but it was there (Sumner 1986). It was encouraged by factors such as travel, new discoveries by the likes of Kepler and Copernicus, and revolutions in cartography, philology, and medicine. Much of it was conducted through the networks of the Reformation and the Counter-Reformation (Hill 1991: 287ff.). It was also a time of religious ferment in Hinduism and Islam (Chand 1979; Embree 1991). In Ethiopia, the Arabs controlled the coast and the Ottomans the north. The route to the Christian spiritual homeland of Alexandria was blocked. The Portuguese offered a new way: silver, arquebuses, and cannon (Sumner 1986).

One of the most distinguishing features of absolutism was its military organization, creating powerful repressive apparatuses that could defend and extend its rule. This, as Wallerstein (1974a) argued, went together with bureaucratization—a powerful tool in the organization of society. It aided the power of the throne against grumbling and resistant overlords, but at the same time it limited the despot's personal power.

New institutions emerged at this time. The core innovations in the West though were the chartered companies—the Dutch East India Company, the British East India Company, and the French East India Company, as well as the slave factories that processed people for trans-Atlantic passage.

Since each state furthermore existed within a web of interstate relations, the development of military strategy, tactics, and logistics made each one believe that the balance of forces could lie in its hands. As expected, the foragers were the most active in managing, controlling, and attempting to eradicate deviance. Then, on the basis of miasmic forms of deviance and the panics that followed plague outbreaks and diseases in the slave factories, the beginnings of comprehensive medical institutions were inaugurated in western Europe and its new possessions, with parallel achievements in Mughal India. The zeal with which behavioral, articulatory, miasmic, and existential deviance was addressed was unprecedented. The social tensions brought about in the first half of the century demanded swift solutions by emerging social strata.

Underlying many of the new institutional arrangements was a determined effort at classification and codification. It is important to distinguish between the two. Classification was the domain of new and rising intellectual elites in Europe, the Mandarins in China, religious scholars in the papacy and Islam, and of the growing scientific spirit. Foraging provided the motivation for taxonomies and orders. Codification, on the other hand, was the process of defining and refining categories of discipline and categories of people. Through the latter, people become existential deviants.

The latter part of the seventeenth century involved the classification of races, which was to become a fundamental prop for all foraging states. Although the taxonomies and definitions of biology were to take off only in the next century, its framework was created in the seventeenth century.

Two people in particular should be mentioned here. François Bernier was the first definer of "race" (Bernier 1864; 1981; Lach 1993). Bernier's work led to Carl Linnaeus's binomial classification of plants, animals, and humans seven decades later. Then there was the great Jean-Baptiste Colbert. He led the work on the impressive Civil Law Ordinance of 1667 and the Criminal Ordinance of 1670, which stand out as remarkable works of rationalization. Colbert and his aides thought hard about the world of races. The Black Code (*Code Noir*) of 1685 (*Édit du Roi* 1687) was the formidably decisive result (Sala-Molins 1987).

The *Édit du Roi* of 1685 set out several important ground rules about slavery. Slaves had to be baptized in the Roman Catholic Church and all slave masters had to be Catholic. Slaves were the economic domain of their masters but they were at the same time a property of the state's domain (community property) and therefore protected by the domain. Masters could beat their slaves but not kill or torture them. Slaves belonging to different masters were prohibited from gathering together. Slaves could not carry weapons. Fugitive slaves would have their ears cut off if away for up to one month, their hamstrings cut if they were away for up to two months, and they would be executed if their absence was longer. But then the code turned to areas of freedom from slavery. Slaves could be freed and would then be considered to be legal subjects of the French domain.

This period, despite its short-term normalization, left behind dissonance and alterity. John Locke, for example, declared that hereditary powers were not absolute but accountable through a social contract. This created a new terrain of struggle. For the "laboring poor"—wage-earners, serfs, peasants, slaves, and the indentured—there was a growing sense that authority was not a divine right.

Deviance in the Eighteenth and Nineteenth Centuries

It could be said that by the eighteenth century, although behavioral deviance was not in decline, the intensity of articulatory forms was at a crescendo—for example, the literary pogroms in China (Brook 2007) and the large numbers of Levellers in Europe. Existential forms of deviance were also on the rise, as indigenous people in the great land rush of the century were defined, classified, and rendered surplus to the emerging forms of possession.

During the first half of the eighteenth century, the emerging powers in Europe and the settlers they unleashed through their forage points were gravely concerned because indigenous peoples did not cede land willingly but rather fought against incursions with some ferocity. This shaped a European conception of savagery, which was used to justify the fierceness of the "savages'" suppression by settler militia and by troops.

This existential deviance had two dimensions—their relation to nature and to land as pastoralists and/or hunter-gatherers, and their heathenism. Indigenous people were inassimilable others who had to be cleared off the land—the surplus people of a shifting frontier. Key here was the Lockean idea of private property (Thompson 1977).

Levelling ideas were also on the rise. The critique of arbitrary authority was part of widely distributed provocative publications like Voltaire's essays on toleration and Rousseau's *Social Contract*. Voltaire asserted the equality of all people and their right to religious freedom. Couched in deist argument, he preached tolerance even if the other was patently wrong. Rousseau wrote about the necessary accountability of rule to those ruled. In addition, the voicing of egalitarian ideas in bourgeois and artisan circles in London were direct challenges to the social order. The critique of Manchu rule was more veiled, but the establishment of literary Inquisitions located and killed off the dissenters.

The foraging and settlement frontiers had their rough and ready definitions of the existential deviants. Back in Europe, however, there was a broader taxonomic zeal. Much of the foraging brought with it an enormous amount of information about creatures, human or animal. Systematic investigation in Europe reached amazing levels of cooperation and peer respect. The Levelling tradition led to polarization and social, political, and national revolution. In most cases "deviants" won the day. At the same time, the foragers prohibited Black subjects from becoming citizens. The former tradition became the heart of antislavery sentiment; the latter legitimated subordination and, in the longer term, colonialism.

In short, in the eighteenth century the intensities and polarizations were expressed as existential and articulatory deviance. Of course, there were expanding boundaries as armed men took possession of larger tracts of land. This in itself created tensions, which brought about exclusions and violence. For European societies the conquest of the Americas was the last step in the development of a global market. This was the period of specific forms of deviance that threatened the functioning of the market—the pirates by sea and the bandits on land (Cordingly 1999; Haude 2010; Linebaugh and Rediker 2000).

By contrast the nineteenth century was shrill in three domains: first, the enormous behavioral and articulatory deviances industrial capitalism found in its working classes and emerging nationalisms in their demos; second, the enormous behavioral, existential, and miasmic forms of deviance that the subcontinent of India threw in the face of colonizing Britain; third, the emergence of sharp distinctions in the African continent between insiders and outsiders in centralizing states that were based on slavery and the raids of slaves before and after its de jure abolition.

The most significant aspect of the late nineteenth and early twentieth centuries was the explosion of existential deviance and how quickly interimperial rivalry made such definitions, classifications, and forms of control similar. But it also provided the backdrop for the emergence of the Holocaust and racial deviance (Keim 2014).

Deviance in the Twentieth Century

The post–Second World War period was defined by a bold attempt to create a transnational system of rules of engagement and create norms that made the horrors of the Holocaust nonreplicable. Due to space limitations we have to assume that the reader is conversant with the conditions of growth and social development and the forms of interstate relation in the bipolar world after 1945.

In the contemporary period beginning in the 1970s, articulatory and existential forms of deviance have decreased but behavioral forms have gained new momentum.

The anomalic phase in the twentieth century combined an economic B-phase, a cycle of increased deviance, and a new cycle of resistances. The decline of the old movements of collective action has not ended alterity and conflict, but it has animated new forms of resistance, not least through new technologies and networks. The very same technologies, however, also enable better systems of control, discipline, and surveillance. Acting together, these produce serious tensions.

It is apparent that we now live in a "world which is lurching from crisis to crisis" (Krugman 2008: 184). Unlike previous B-phases and anomalic phases, this one is in a quagmire. In the West, the restructuring of the welfare state, a new market orthodoxy, and monetarism preceded the development of a new ideology of institutional change, neoliberalism. In the Far East, too, a new phase was ushered in, which within a decade moved the economy away from self-reliance. The unprecedented growth of capitalist production had as much to do with the former as with the latter.

The down-phase has had polarizing effects at many levels. The rupture of 1989—the crumbling of the Warsaw Pact, the dissolution of the Soviet Union, and the annexation of the former German Democratic Republic by the Federal Republic of Germany—marked the defeat of so-called communism in the bipolar confrontation between East and West and was said to demonstrate the worldwide victory of capitalism. With China and India joining the global accumulation game, the attempt to create a market-driven world is today global. A large number of the deviants of the colonial phase were co-opted and sanitized. The new deviants were those who worked against the consensus on national development and the priority of increasing output and undertaking land reforms. These approaches reached points of rupture by the late 1960s and early 1970s, when the inability of large parts of the developing world to address fundamentally livelihood, poverty, and consumption became clear. Since then, the dismantling of welfare-state structures and neoliberal structural adjustment has led to the decline of the middle strata. This has had a profound polarizing effect between the powerful rich and the powerless poor.

As for intensities, we argue that we can see a dramatic increase in moral panics about behavioral deviance—economic, social, and political—even though existential and articulatory deviance might be said to have declined. Existential deviance is no longer defensible as an idea, and racial superiority and gender discrimination no longer expressible within the paradigm of modernity. The granting of gender, ethnic, and racial rights has meant that it is no longer possible to define any group as a category to be eliminated or disciplined. Furthermore, it is no longer possible to condemn modes of expression and their dissemination by entire groups of people. In other words, multiracial, multiethnic contexts are upheld as the framework of rational capitalist modernity.

Democratic freedoms exist in perhaps half of the world's countries today. Formal reciprocity (Sitas 2004: 104–113) favors the legitimacy and necessity of coexisting divergent views and positions, and therefore articulatory deviance is on the decline. Nevertheless, some recent cases—like those of Salman Rushdie's *Satanic Verses* or the Mohammed cartoons—have stretched the limits of intercultural relations. There are tensions concerning the explosion of pornography. There are modes of dress and appearance that define deviant prototypes at custom control points and in the streets. Nevertheless, in comparison to other periods, the post-1970s have been more tolerant to the world of signification.

There is a stupendous number of poor people on the land, whose income is often supplemented by remittances from migrations. Two types of deviance have emerged—where rural cultivators have turned to the mass cropping of coca, hashish, opium, and marijuana and where they seek the assistance of armed bands. Their relatives in the urban areas are also proving to be troublesome: vigilante slum-defenders, enforcers, gang recruits, and coastline pirates.

There has also been a breakdown of the distinction between categories of deviance. The melding of behavioral, articulatory, and existential deviance is not new, but it has taken on a particular form that is seriously animating social dynamics. The perceived deviant behavior of (illegalized) migrants, drug dealers, religious fundamentalists, or terrorists turns into existential deviance of certain supposedly recognizable groups. Given the deeply rooted historical underpinning to the connection between *subaltern groups* (such as race, ethnic minorities, migrants, and working-class persons) and *crime*, inevitably these groups have been targeted.

There are important colonial linkages to the current "era of migration" (Castles and Miller 2003). Modern migration can be traced back to colonial time via its historical antecedents (chattel slavery, transmigration, indentured labor). The current migratory systems are products of the colonial division of the world. This migration of people from the former colonies to the more "developed" world has created a multicultural setting within the North that is redefining the world. Nation-states have been under severe pressure by social reactions to a perceived social insecurity about such others.

Existential profiling of racial, cultural, and gender types is on the increase again. This melds with articulatory deviance into a dangerous mix. At the core of anti-immigrant politics is the discourse and political praxis of combating "illegal immigration," a subject intimately connected to social phenomena such as racist populism in debates regarding social citizenship. Illegal migrants and economic and political refugees may easily give rise to moral panics about xenophobia, and could lead to genocide.

Articulatory deviance has often been seen as behavioral deviance insofar as the expression of a belief in visible or audible signs is considered to represent a concrete and serious threat to the established order. Generic panics about dangerous spaces and places are increasingly being racialized, to the extent that it is almost impossible to dissociate race, space, and deviance in dominant discourses of power. Categories of people are assumed to be dangerous *in potentio*—dangerous seas and trading routes, the habitations of dangerous classes. However, as urban social exclusion increased and darker strangers came to be nudged to live in those urban slums, an inherent lawlessness and normlessness became attached to their existence.

Finally, there are countries whose people in general have been identified as deviance-bearing or potentially deviance-bearing. These threatening states are to be found mostly in Africa and in ungovernable urban locales. The existence of such states of being, and the need for a balance between direct and indirect interventions, refines and constantly transforms the forms of governance necessary to decrease the threats.

To pull together what is being presented here, this "melding process" has three dimensions: first, an ontologizing tendency made up of a range of commonsense tautologies about others; second, the creation of three sites of deviance that need direct or indirect intervention; and third, a metadiscourse of the need to manage crises by defining the period as a state of exception. It has turned politics and political competition into the politics of unease, and has opened up the space for the media to valorize fear.

Many contemporary institutions were developed to deal decisively with the fallout of a previous cycle—for example, the economic depression of the 1930s, the rise of fascism, the Holocaust. The multilateral, regional, national, and local institutions that were created faced a serious crisis by the late 1960s. There was a growing consensus that the welfare and developmental states that emerged were seen to be a hindrance to profitability and growth.

There is currently a series of institutions that have come to be seen as incapable of dealing with deviance and with deviants, which has exacerbated moral panics. Key here has been the nation-state as the boundary-keeper and norm-enforcer (Castells 1999; Sassen 2005). The denationalization of activities—be they criminal, economic, military, or political—has increased the calls for a planetary carapace of rules and norms. However, the international regimes formed to create such rules and norms faltered at implementation.

As a result, it has become as essential as ever for the nation-state to define, control, and discipline the new behavioral deviants, not least through the erection and expansion of infrastructure for surveillance, imprisonment, and punishment. Even as rights have been granted and safeguards against existential deviance institutionalized, discrimination against those who stretched limits was allowed.

The privatization of policing and technological control of whole populations has exacerbated the problem on the institutional side that defines, administers, and manages the deviants. At the same time, organized violence—such as networked terrorist associations; mafia-like structures in drug, weapons, and human trafficking; and violent criminal behavior by former soldiers (the three kinds often being interrelated or combined)—has increased. The transfer of policing functions to civil society has not necessarily led to increasing "success" and more democracy. It has made communities more resolute in their frustration with the state and more ready to take on a vigilante role.

Nevertheless, the state has not caved in. Three patterns have been forming through the interaction of states in the contemporary period. First, the "war on terror" has brought about an intelligence and surveillance system coordinated by the United States that is unaccountable to national legislatures or the United Nations. Second, there is an executive-led commitment to regionalism as a new form of multilateral interstate relationship, whose exemplar is the European Union. Third, we see a reformed national administration that fiscally is larger than ever before and whose *raison d'etre* has brought about new allocative priorities, creating the preconditions necessary for the easier movement of global flows in goods, information, communication, financial transactions, and, to a lesser extent, people. Neither the new surveillance systems nor an enhanced regionalism has seemed to lessen the moral panics about institutional failure.

The Search for a New Don Quixote

Thousands gathered to witness the stoning of an adulterer, and news crews sent televised images of it to the world. Tens of millions watched the last moments of Saddam Hussein with a rope around his neck, thanks to a cell phone's video function. Knives were used to commandeer airplanes and fly them into the World Trade Center. Stones, twine, and knives, the oldest means of violence, interfaced with the latest technologies to bring performances of violence and deviance into our intimate spaces.

The moral panic is perhaps shriller in present times due to the contradictory duality outlined so far. On one hand, there is progress in terms of recognition of rights as a result of historic struggles. On the other, there is the expansion of disciplinary surveillance and the law-and-order institutions to control society.

The evidence we have garnered points in two directions. First, there are cycles in which, instead of more freedom or progress, we see more control and domination. In Foucault's words (1984b: 85), we witness "the endlessly repeated play of dominations" or how "humanity installs each of its violences in a system of rules and thus proceeds from domination to domination." Some periods are defined as polarizing, as a threat to the socio-economic system, as signs of imminent collapse, followed by decisive action, change, and resteering. Yes, there are cycles that involve the perceived proliferation of deviance (anomalic phases), which point to institutional failures. These cycles not only generate concern but bring with them improvisation, innovation, and institutional reconfiguration. Nevertheless, we also observe a cascading "progress" when the deviants struggle hard enough to win space or societal recognition. Not all deviants did so effectively, but the many that did have countersteered the system to more equality and more freedom. So for the current period the correct question is, "What are the polarizations embedded in current forms of deviance, and can this anomalic phase be fixed?"

No matter how sophisticated the technologies of surveillance and control might have become since the digital and the genetic revolutions, and how much the 226 nation-states that constitute the map of the present invest in them, the bubbles of panic continue in a very long B-phase. We can sketch the anomalic phase but cannot as yet grasp the ascending fixers and moral entrepreneurs. Technology has made deviance theatrical and immediate, but the world is in no way "normalized." So virus carriers, foreign migrants, terrorists, traffickers, and rogues keep the media working, the panic sustained, and the world on tenterhooks as it searches for a new Don Quixote.

Chapter 12

Conclusion

by Immanuel Wallerstein

As seemed evident from the outset, the distinction between homogenizing and heterogenizing (or between converging and polarizing) trends in the history of the modern world-system is not at all a simple one. Obviously both thrusts have been inherent in the operation of the system. The question is not there.

Those who have upheld the case for the inevitability of a progressive convergence of the entire planet have argued that whatever divergences continue to exist or even have been brought into existence are anomalies. And that such anomalies are bound sooner or later to be overcome or overwhelmed by the operations of a rationality that drives us all towards the sounder choices of modernity. The extreme version of this argument has been the one put forth by neoliberal expositions of the necessary primacy of the market in all individual and collective decision making. Or, as Mrs. Thatcher famously put it, there is no alternative.

What we have been exploring in this book is the degree to which this vision of reality is false in three senses.

1. Despite the many ways in which there has been convergence, there has been simultaneous and strong polarization, often hidden from direct view. Much of this polarization can be observed only if we look at the world-system as a single interacting entity rather than

a series of self-contained "national" units. Only this way are we able to observe that form of polarization that separates different regions of the world.

2. Unlike the thesis of inevitable convergence, which assumes an eternal linearity of social existence, we believe that historical systems, like all systems, have lives. They come into existence; they pursue their lives according to the rules of the system; and at some point they enter into structural crisis and therefore go out of existence, to be replaced by another system or systems.

3. We believe that historical systems that are oppressive breed their own resistance, which never disappears and which comes to play a crucial role during such structural crises. This then opens the way to analyzing the degrees of freedom we all have at the present moment in constructing the future.

What have we learned that gives credence to these three premises? The first premise is the crucial one in the sense that if it doesn't hold, there is no sense arguing the second and third premises.

Premise 1: The Existence of Significant Polarization

Chapter 3, on economic inequality, shows two things. First of all, the picture of polarization looks very different if we deal only or primarily with what occurs within relatively wealthy states or if we deal with what occurs within the world-system as a whole. If we take the latter viewpoint, we discover that, by the twentieth century, the degree of interstate inequality (however measured) had become greater than the degree of internal inequality within states.

But then we learn a second thing. This statement begins to be true only in the nineteenth century, and therefore the process is one that has been widening over time. This is reinforced by a finding in Chapter 5, on peasantries, where we learn that if the difference in real income between wealthier and less wealthy rural zones in the world was 1:4 in 1950, it had risen to 1:20 by 2000.

This picture of somewhat hidden polarization is strongly reinforced by Chapter 4, on cities. The growing urbanization of the world, an unquestionable phenomenon that all of us perceive, has long been a basic pillar of the case for linear convergence. Today we find that, in the period 1950–2000, what are termed periphery-making city growth processes exceed core-making growth processes, and this is occurring for the first time since 1500. This, therefore, seems to demonstrate "convergence" in that there is now remarkable growth in the size of peripheral cities. But on closer observation, we discover that the outcome of this growth is quite different from the growth of core-making cities since it is essentially creating cities of megaslums peopled by the global dispossessed, increasingly located in urban zones.

And if we turn again to Chapter 5, on peasantries, we discover that, yes, it is true that there is de-agrarianization, de-ruralization, and de-peasantization in the world-system everywhere, as both the thesis of convergence and our analysis shows for three radically different zones of the world. However, it is not true that the peasantry has simply disappeared, or is simply disappearing. It turns out that the uneven incorporation of rural zones leads recurrently to the creation of new frontier zones. What seems at the macro level to be homogenization turns out at the micro level to be heterogenization, as rural producers find niches in which to survive, even when the classic role of village communities as informal credit networks has been replaced by dominant individualism in which landowning oligarchies have taken over control of poor relief.

Similarly, when we look at the construction of state bureaucracies and their roles, we find that the states have indeed been expanding their role (despite all the loud antistate rhetoric), and they are doing this across the world. But the outcomes in different parts of the world-system are not the same. There is surface similarity but aggravated inequalities and radical asymmetrics. And when we look at Chapter 9, on citizenship, we discover that while citizenship seems to be a mode of expanding inclusion in the social framework, the inclusions are constantly matched by new modes of exclusion.

Finally, Chapter 10, on women's spaces and patriarchal systems, goes against the grain of most writing, even feminist writing, about what has been happening. The argument is that if one starts the picture in the European world in 1000 rather than circa 1500 as is usually done, the pattern is revealed as moving steadily from a much more gender-equal world to one that is far less so. We may speak of the creation of what we may term EuroPatriarchy, a set of largely hidden institutionalized value premises that have increasingly reduced women's spaces of relative autonomy. It is argued that this reduction of women's spaces has not been significantly ameliorated by recent legislative changes such as women's suffrage.

Premise 2: Structural Crisis of the Modern World-System

The primary object of our analysis was to argue the case for Premise 1. Most chapters did not focus directly on Premise 2. Still, many observations of the various chapters discuss, implicitly or explicitly, Premise 2. Chapter 2, on ecology, is the one that makes the case most clearly. It recounts the "huge scales of production-appropriation-objectivation" that have been "disproportionate" and amounted to an "ecological overshoot." It argues that this has led to a fatal disaster in which the very scientific advances that permitted this overshoot have moved the planetary structures beyond science's own abilities to ensure the "perdurability of life and of the planet."

Chapter 11, on deviance, concludes by saying the evidence points in two directions. On the one hand, there has existed a cyclical pattern of types and strengths of deviance in a "play of dominations" throughout the history of the world-system. But on the other hand, the correct question for the current period is, what are the polarizations embedded in current forms of deviance, and can this anomalic phase be fixed? What are called "the bubbles of panic" are continuing today in a very long B-phase. One may therefore ask, is this the phase of "structural crisis"?

Rereading each of the arguments made in support of Premise 1, we see that all of them seem to emphasize a steady escalation of the inequalities. One has to wonder, therefore, whether this escalation can continue indefinitely or whether there aren't other "overshoots" comparable to the "ecological overshoot."

We then have to think also about "resistances." Again Chapter 2, on ecology, balances the gloomy picture of an overshoot about which science itself can do little or nothing with the subsistence of "an underground heterogeneous magma" of resistance that has "limited the destructive power of the system." True, "these incipient potential systemic alternatives carry the contradictions of modernity in which they have been forged." But it is "modernity, and not only capitalism," that is being criticized.

Chapter 4, on cities, argues that if the agents of change can no longer be located in the urban proletariat or in the peripheral peasantry, they may now be replaced in this role by the "global urban dispossessed." But agents of change there are, if not the ones that seemed so prominent in the nineteenth and early twentieth centuries. Chapter 8, on states, finds the loci of resistance in the relatively more "democratic" states, which are the wealthier ones, since it is more difficult there politically to reduce the advantages of the Keynesian welfare state. More difficult may not mean impossible, however, as "the bubble of panic" grows stronger.

Premise 3: Ergo, What?

Unless one is obdurate, it is patently clear that one cannot avoid the political implications of alternative ways of framing the issues. Those who start with a premise of eternal linear progress must necessarily believe that any difficulties in which the world finds itself are essentially transitory and momentary. Sooner or later, the difficulties will be overcome by the logic and the pressures of the system. In our present situation, there are two major variants of this expression of certainty about the future.

One group believes that as long as we maximize the priority of the so-called free market, the seeming difficulties of the moment will be overcome and further economic growth will ensue, to everyone's mutual benefit. A second group believes that as long as we defend and expand a social-democratic "welfare state," the seeming difficulties of the moment will be overcome and further economic growth will ensue, to everyone's mutual benefit.

However, if one believes that there has been increasing polarization and that systems have finite lives, and therefore that we may now be in our system's structural crisis, then neither of these optimistic scenarios has much plausibility. Quite the contrary! It would follow from the thesis of increasing polarization that no "solution" to our current difficulties looms on the horizon. There exists neither a neoliberal nor a social-democratic way out of the structural crisis.

We would then have to look elsewhere for obtaining the outcome we desire. We would have to turn to what we know about structural crises, how they operate, and what we can do within them. What happens in a structural crisis is that the system bifurcates, which means essentially that there emerge two alternative ways of ending the structural crisis, in which "we" (but who exactly is this "we"?) "choose" collectively one of the alternatives.

The principal characteristic of a structural crisis is a series of chaotic and wild fluctuations of everything—the markets, the geopolitical alliances, the stability of state boundaries, employment, debts, taxes, and the groups we blame for the crisis. Uncertainty, even in the short run, becomes chronic. And uncertainty tends to freeze economic decision-making, which of course makes things worse, primarily by reducing levels of real income for the vast majority of the world's populations.

Here are some of the things we may expect in the middle run of the next decade or two. Most states are facing, and are going to continue to face, a squeeze between reduced income and increased expenditures. Most states have been reducing expenditures in two ways. One has been to cut into (even eliminate) a great many of the safety nets that have been constructed in the past to help ordinary people deal with the multiple contingencies they face. But there is a second way as well. Most states are cutting the money transfers to subordinate state entities—federated structures if the sovereign state is a federation, and local governments. This simply transfers the squeeze to these subordinate units, who in turn can either reduce expenditures or raise taxes. If the lower-level structures find this impossible, they can go bankrupt, which thereupon eliminates other parts of the safety nets (most notably pensions).

This has an immediate impact on the states. On one hand, it weakens them, as more and more units seek to secede from their states if they think it is economically advantageous, at least in the short run. But on the other hand the states turn out to be more important than ever, as the populations more and more seek refuge in state protectionist policies—keep our jobs, at the expense of the jobs of others. State boundaries have always been changing. But the structural crisis creates pressures to push such redefinition of boundaries more frequently now. At the same time, new regional structures linking together existing states (or their subunits)—such as the European Union (EU) and the new South American structure (UNASUR)—will continue to flourish and play an increasingly important geopolitical role.

The juggling between the multiple loci of geopolitical power will also become ever more unstable in a situation in which none of these loci will be in a position to dictate the interstate rules. The United States is today no longer hegemonic. It has become an erstwhile hegemonic power with feet of clay. However, it still remains powerful enough to be able to wreak damage by missteps.

China today seems to have the strongest emerging economic position, but it is probably less strong than both it and others think. It seems unlikely that China can maintain the level of annual growth of the first decade of the twenty-first century.

The degree to which western Europe and Russia will draw closer is still an open question, and is very much on the agenda of both sides. How India will play its cards is undecided by India. What this means for civil wars is that outside interveners tend to cancel each other out and internal conflicts become ever more organized around fratricidal identity groups.

Obviously, these wild oscillations and increased short-term uncertainties do not offer happy outcomes for most people. World unemployment can be expected to rise, not fall. And ordinary people will feel the pinch very severely. They have already shown that they are ready to fight back in multiple forms, and this popular resistance will grow. We shall find ourselves in the midst of a vast political battle to determine the world's future.

Those who have wealth and privilege today will not sit idly by. However, it will become increasingly clear to them that they cannot secure their future through the existing capitalist system. They will seek to bring into existence some other system, one based not on a central role of the market but rather on a combination of brute force and deception. The primary objective would be to ensure that the new system guaranteed the continuation of three key features of the present system—hierarchy, exploitation, and polarization.

On the other side will be popular forces across the world, which will also seek to create a new kind of historical system, one that is based on relative democracy and relative equality. Such a system has never yet existed. What this would mean in terms of the institutions the world will create is almost impossible to foresee. We shall learn what they look like in the building of this system in the decades to come.

Who will win out in this battle? No one can predict. It will be the result of an infinity of nano-actions by an infinity of nano-actors at an infinity of nano-moments. At some point the cumulated actions of every-one as they lend their support to one or the other of the two alternative solutions will tilt definitively in favor of one side or the other. There is no way of predicting the outcome. But this uncertainty is precisely what gives us hope. It turns out that what each of us does at each moment about each immediate issue really matters. Some people call it the "butterfly effect." The fluttering of a butterfly's wings actually affects the climate at the other end of the world. In that sense, we are all little butterflies today. This is more than a metaphor. It is rather an operative reality, if one impossible to calculate (and therefore to predict).

We have tried in this book to outline an alternative vision of social reality. We hope we have made a case that is sufficiently plausible that its premises may be discussed publicly and seriously by scholars, by political actors, and by ordinary persons affected by all these realities. No doubt an enormous amount of serious research still needs to be done. And the world needs an enormous amount of debate about political strategy. Whatever we have contributed here is offered only as a beginning. We welcome, therefore, not only critique of our arguments but all efforts to go beyond where we have gone. This is an intellectual task, a moral obligation, and a political effort.

Bibliography

Abu-Lughod, Janet. 1989. *Before European Hegemony: The World System A.D. 1250–1350.* New York: Oxford Univ. Press.

Achard, Frédéric et al. 2002. "Determination of Deforestation Rates of the World's Humid Tropical Forests," *Science* 297, no. 5583 (August 9), 999–1002.

Ahn, Christine, and Kavita Ramdas. 2011. "The IMF: Violating Women Since 1945." Issues/Global Governance, *Foreign Policy in Focus* (Washington, DC: FPIF @ips-dc .org), http://www.ips-dc.org/FPIF, May 19. Reproduced in Common Dreams: http://www.commondreams.org/view/2011/05/20-3. Accessed Aug. 11, 2014.

Allen, Ann Taylor. 1999. "Feminism, Social Science, and the Meanings of Modernity: The Debates on the Origin of the Family in Europe and the United States, 1860–1914," *American Historical Review* CIV, no. 4 (October), 1085–1113.

Allen, Sister Prudence. 1985. *The Concept of Woman: The Aristotelian Revolution, 750 BC–AD 1250.* Montreal: Eden Press.

———. 1997a. *The Concept of Woman: The Aristotelian Revolution, 750 B.C.–A.D. 1250,* vol. I. Grand Rapids, MI: William B. Eerdmans Publishing.

———. 1997b. *The Concept of Woman: The Early Humanist Reformation, 1250–1500.* Grand Rapids, MI: William B. Eerdmans Publishing.

Allen, Robert C. 2009. *The British Industrial Revolution in Global Perspective.* Cambridge, UK: Cambridge Univ. Press.

Alva Ixtlilxóchitl, Fernando de. 1989. "De la venida de los españoles y principios de la ley evangélica," in Miguel León-Portilla, *La visión de los vencidos.* México: UNAM, Biblioteca del Estudiante Universitario.

Amnesty International. 2007. *The Reality of Trade Unionism in Colombia.* London: Amnesty International Publications.

Anderson, Benedict R. 1991. *Imagined Communities: Reflections on the Origin and Spread of Nationalism,* 2nd ed. London: Verso.

Anderson, Bonnie S. 2000. *Joyous Greetings: The First International Women's Movement, 1830–1860.* New York: Oxford Univ. Press.

Anderson, Bonnie S., and Judith P. Zinsser. 2000. *A History of Their Own: Women in Europe from Prehistory to the Present,* rev. ed., 2 vols. New York: Oxford Univ. Press.

Andreff, Wladimir, and Olivier Pastré. 1981. "La genèse des banques multinationales et l'expansion du capital financier international," in *Internationalisation des banques et des groupes financiers*. Paris: Centre National de la Recherche Scientifique, 51–103.

Andrien, Kenneth J. 2001. *Andean Worlds: Indigenous History, Culture, and Consciousness under Spanish Rule, 1532–1825*, Albuquerque: Univ. of New Mexico Press.

Antrobus, Peggy. 2004. *The Global Women's Movement: Origins, Issues and Strategies*. London: Zed Books.

Arrighi, Giovanni. 1994. *The Long Twentieth Century: Money, Power and the Origins of Our Times*. London: Verso.

Assadourian, Carlos Sempat. 1982. *El Sistema de la economía colonial: Mercado interno, regiones, y espacio económico*. Lima: Instituto de Estudios Peruanos.

Atwell, William S. 1982. "International Bullion Flows and the Chinese Economy, circa 1530–1650," *Past and Present* 95 (May), 68–90.

Ayala Mora, Enrique, coord. gen. 1999. *Historia de América Andina*. vol. 2: Manuel Braga, ed., *Formación y apogeo del sistema colonial*; vol. 3: Margarita Garrido, ed., *El sistema colonial tardío*. Quito: Univ. Andina Simón Bolívar.

Aylwin, José. 2002. *El acceso de los indígenas a la tierra en los ordenamientos jurídicos de America Latina: Un estudio de casos*. 2 vols. Serie Desarrollo Productivo, no. 128. Santiago: CEPAL.

Backer, Dorothy Anne Liat. 1974. *Precious Women: A Feminist Phenomenon in the Age of Louis XIV*. New York: Basic Books.

Bacon, Margaret Hope. 1986. *Mothers of Feminism: The Story of Quaker Women in America*. San Francisco: Harper and Row.

Bailey, Michael D. 2009. *The A to Z of Witchcraft*. Lanham, MD: Scarecrow Press.

Belich, James. 2009. *Replenishing the Earth: the Settler Revolution and the Rise of the Anglo-World, 1783–1939*. Oxford: Oxford Univ. Press.

Ben-Atar, Doron. 2004. *Intellectual Piracy and the Origins of American Power*. New Haven, CT: Yale Univ. Press.

Benjamin, Walter. 2008. *Tésis sobre la historia y otros fragmentos*. México: ITACA.

Bennett, Judith M. 2006. *History Matters: Patriarchy and the Challenge of Feminism*. Philadelphia: Temple Univ. Press.

Berberoglu, Berch. 1987. *The Internationalization of Capital. Imperialism and Capitalist Development on a World Scale*. New York: Praeger.

Berkeley Earth. 2011. *Cooling the Warming Debate*. http://static.berkeleyearth.org/pdf /berkeley-earth-announcement-oct-20-11.pdf. Accessed Aug. 11, 2014.

Bernier, François. 1864. "A New Division of the Earth," originally in the *Journal des Savants*, April 24, 1684, trans. T. Bendyphe in "Memoirs Read before the Anthroplogical Society of London" I, 360–364.

———. 1981 [1670]. *Voyage dans les états du Grand Mogol,* with an introduction by France Bhattacharya. Paris: Fayard.

Bernstein, Henry. 2010. *Class Dynamics of Agrarian Change*. Halifax, Canada: Fernwood Publishing and Kumarian Press.

Biaggi, Christina. 2005. *The Rule of Mars: Readings on the Origins, History and Impact of Patriarchy*. Manchester: Knowledge, Ideas and Trends (KIT).

Biagioli, Mario. 2006. "From Print to Patents: Living on Instruments in Early Modern Europe," *History of Science* XLIV, 139–186.

Black, Edwin. 2001. *IBM y el holocausto*. Buenos Aires: Atlántida.

Blackwell, Richard J. 2006. *Behind the Scenes at Galileo's Trial*. Notre Dame, IN: Notre Dame Univ. Press.

Boles, Judith K., Diane Long Hoeveler. 2006. *The A to Z of Feminism*. New York: Scarecrow Press.

Bonilla, Heraclio. 2007. "Los Andes: La metamorfosis y los particularismos de una región," in *Congreso en conmemoración de 50 años de FLACSO, 29–31 octubre 2007.* Quito: FLACSO.

Bosch, Alfred. 2007. *El Atlas fúrtivo.* México City: Editorial Planeta.

Boulding, Elise. 1976. *The Underside of History: A View of Women through Time.* New York: Halsted.

Boyle, James. 1997. *Shamans, Software, and Spleens: Law and the Construction of the Information Society.* Cambridge, MA: Harvard Univ. Press.

Brading, D.A. 1990. "La España de los Bórbones y su imperio americano," in L. Bethell, ed., *Historia de América Latina.* Barcelona: Crítica.

Brakeman, Lynne, and Susan Gall. 1997. *Chronology of Women Worldwide: People, Places and Events That Shaped Women's History.* Detroit: Gale Research.

Braudel, Fernand. 1979. *La civilization matérielle.* Paris: Lib. Armand Colin.

——. 1981. *The Structures of Everyday Life.* New York: Harper and Row.

——. 1982. *The Wheels of Commerce.* New York: Harper and Row.

——. 1984. *The Perspective of the World.* New York: Harper and Row.

Brennan, Margaret. 1985. "Enclosure: Institutionalizing the Invisibility of Women in Ecclesiastical Communities," in E.S. Fiorenza and M. Collins, eds., *Women—Invisible in Theology and Church.* Concilium 192, no. 6 (December) and Edinburgh: T and T Clark.

Bridenthal, Renate, and Claudia Koonz. 1977. *Becoming Visible: Women in European History.* Boston: Houghton Mifflin.

Brinkhoff, Thomas. 2007. "The Principal Agglomerations of the World," *City Population.* Accessed December 11, 2007. http://www.citypopulation.de. Accessed Aug. 11, 2014.

Brook, Timothy. 2007. *Vermeer's Hat.* London: Bloomsbury.

Brown, Mark. 2003. "Ethnology and Colonial Administration in Nineteenth-Century British India: The Question of Native Crime and Criminality," *British Journal for the History of Science* XXXVI, no. 2 (June), 201–219.

Brubaker, Rogers W. 1989. "The French Revolution and the Invention of Citizenship," *French Politics and Society* VII, no. 3, 30–49.

Brugmann, Jeb. 2009. *Welcome to the Urban Revolution.* New York: Bloomsbury.

Bryceson, Deborah Fahy. 1999. *African Rural Labour, Income Diversification and Livelihood Approaches: A Long-Term Development Perspective.* Leiden: African Studies Center.

Bryceson, Deborah Fahy et al., eds. 2000. *Disappearing Peasantries? Rural Labour in Africa, Asia and Latin America.* London: Intermediate Technology Publications.

Bulmer-Thomas, Victor et al., eds. 2006. *Cambridge Economic History of Latin America,* vol. I: *The Colonial Era and the Short Nineteenth Century;* vol. II: *The Long Twentieth Century.* Cambridge, UK: Cambridge Univ. Press.

Bustelo, Pablo. 2010. *Chindia: Asia a la conquista del siglo XXI.* Madrid: Tecnos.

Carmagnani, Marcello, Alicia Hernández Chávez, and Ruggiero Romano. 1999. *Para una historia de América,* vol. 1: *Los nudos.* México: Colegio de México, Fideicomiso Historia de las Américas.

Carpentier, Alejo. 2001. *El siglo de las luces.* La Habana: Instituto Cubano del Libro.

——. 2009. *El reino de este mundo.* España: Alianza Editorial.

Carter, Michael R. et al. 1996. "An Empirical Analysis of the Induced Institutional Change in Post-Reform Rural China." Mimeo, Department of Agricultural and Applied Economics, Univ. of Wisconsin-Madison.

Castells, Manuel. 1996. *The Rise of the Network Society.* Oxford: Blackwell.

——. 1999. *End of Millennium.* Oxford: Blackwell.

Castles, Stephen. 2005. "Hierarchical Citizenship in a World of Unequal Nation-States," *PS: Political Science and Politics* XXXVIII, no. 4, 689–692.

Castles, Stephen, and Mark J. Miller. 2003 [1983]. *The Age of Migration: International Population Movements in the Modern World*, 3rd rev. ed. Basingstoke, UK: Palgrave Macmillan and Guilford Books.

Castro, Guillermo. 1994. *Los trabajos de ajuste y combate. Naturaleza y sociedad en la historia de América Latina.* Havana: Casa de las Américas.

———. *Transformaciones de la Tierra. Una Antología Mínima de la Tierra.* Montevideo: Donald Worster.

Caton, Hiram. 1988. *The Politics of Progress.* Gainsville: Univ. of Florida Press.

Ceceña, Ana Esther. 2008. *Derivas del mundo en el que caben todos los mundos.* México: Siglo XXI–CLACSO.

Centro Peruano de Estudios Sociales (CEPES). 1998. *Regional Report on South America.* Rome: International Land Coalition (ILC).

Chand, Tara. 1979. "Indian Thought and the Sufis," in Idries Shah, ed., *The World of the Sufi: An Anthology of Writings about Sufis and Their Work.* London: Octagon Press.

Chandler, Tertius. 1987. *Four Thousand Years of Urban Growth: A Historical Census.* Lewiston, ME: Edwin Mellen.

Chang, Ha-Joon. 2004. *Kicking Away the Ladder: Development Strategy in Historical Perspective.* London: Anthem Press.

Chao, Kang. 2006. *Land Distribution in Traditional Rural China (Zhongguo Chuantong Nongcun de Diquan Feipei).* Beijing: New Star Press.

Christiansen-Ruffman, Linda. 1980. "Women as Persons in Atlantic Canadian Communities," in *Resources for Feminist Research*, Special Publication, no. 8, 55–57.

———. 1989. "Inherited Biases within Feminism: The 'Patricentric Syndrome' and the 'Either/Or Syndrome' in Sociology," in A. Miles and G. Finn, eds., *Feminism: From Pressure to Politics.* Montreal: Black Rose Books.

———. 1998. "Developing Feminist Sociological Knowledge: Processes of Discovery," in L. Christiansen-Ruffman, ed., *Feminist Perspectives: The Global Feminist Enlightenment: Women and Social Knowledge.* Madrid: International Sociological Association, 13–36.

Clancy-Smith, Julia A. 2004. "Exemplary Women and Sacred Journeys: Women and Gender in Judaism, Christianity, and Islam from Late Antiquity to the Eve of Modernity," in Bonnie G. Smith, ed. *Women's History in Global Perspective,* vol. I. Urbana: Univ. of Illinois Press, 92–144.

Clark, Alice. 1919. *Working Life of Women in the Seventeenth Century.* New York: E. P. Dutton.

Claster, Jill N. 2009. *Sacred Violence: The European Crusades to the Middle East, 1095–1396.* Toronto: Univ. of Toronto Press.

Cohen, Stanley. 1972. *Folk Devils and Moral Panics,* new ed. Oxford: Martin Robertson.

Cohn, Carol. 1996. "Sex and Death in the Rational World of Defense Intellectuals," in B. Laslett et al., *Gender and Scientific Authority.* Chicago: Univ. of Chicago Press, 183–214 [reprinted from *Signs,* 1987].

Collier, George A., Renato I. Resaldo, and John D. Wirth, eds. 1982. *Inca and Aztec States, 1400–1800: Anthropology and History.* New York: Academic Press.

Colón, Cristóbal. 1493. "Cartas," in Francisco Morales Padrón 1990, *Primeras cartas sobre América (1493–1503).* Seville: Univ. de Sevilla.

Convenio sobre la Diversidad Biológica (CDB). 2010. *Perspectiva mundial sobre la biodiversidad 3.* Geneva: United Nations Office.

Cordingly, David. 1999. *Unter schwarzer Flagge. Legende und Wirklichkeit des Piratenlebens.* Zurich: Sanssouci.

Cortés, Hernán. 1970. *Cartas de Relación.* México: Porrúa.

Crook, Clive. 1997. "The Future of the State," in *Economist,* September 18. http://www
.economist.com/node/850929. Accessed Aug. 11, 2014.

Crosby, Alfred W. 1993. *Ecological Imperialism: The Biological Expansion of Europe,
900–1900.* Cambridge, UK: Cambridge Univ. Press.

Davis, Clarence B., and Kenneth E. Wilburne. 1991. *Railway Imperialism.* New York:
Greenwood Press.

Davis, Elizabeth Gould. 1971. *The First Sex.* New York: G. P. Putnam.

Davis, Mike. 2006. *Planet of Slums.* London: Verso

Davis, Stephen A. 1992. *Micmac,* 2nd ed., part of series *Peoples of the Maritimes.* Tan-
tallon, NS: Four East Publications.

De Ayala, Felipe Guaman Poma. 2009. *The First Chronicle and Good Government: On
the History of the World and the Incas Up to 1615.* Houston: Texas Univ. Press.

de Ferranti, David, Guillermo E. Perry, Francisco H.G. Ferreira, and Michael Walton. 2004.
Inequality in Latin America: Breaking with History? Washington, DC: The World Bank.

de Gramont, Sanche. 1975. *El Dios Indómito. La Historia del Río Níger.* México-Madrid:
Turner-FCE.

de Grazia, Victoria. 2005. *Irresistible Empire: America's Advance through Twentieth-Century
Europe.* Cambridge, MA: Harvard Univ. Press.

de la Court, Pieter. 1972 [1662]. *The True Interests and Political Maxims of the Republic
of Holland.* New York: Arno.

de Pizan, Christine. 1982 [1374]. *The Book of the City of Ladies,* trans. Earl Jeffrey Rich-
ards. New York: Persea Books.

de Vries, Jan. 1984. *European Urbanization, 1500–1800.* London: Methuen.

de Vries, Jan, and Ad van der Woude. 1987. *The First Modern Economy: Success, Failure,
and Perseverance of the Dutch Economy, 1500–1815.* Cambridge, UK: Cambridge
Univ. Press.

Deacon, Desley. 1996. "Political Arithmetic: The Nineteenth-Century Australian Census and the Construction of the Dependent Woman," in B. Laslett et al., *Gender
and Scientific Authority.* Chicago: Univ. of Chicago Press, 103–123 [reprinted from
Signs, 1985].

Debord, Guy. 1994. *The Society of the Spectacle.* Brooklyn: Zone Books.

Deegan, Mary Jo. 1991. *Women in Sociology: A Bio-Bibliographical Soucebook.* New York:
Greenwood.

Diamond, Jared. 1999. *Guns, Germs, and Steel: The Fates of Human Society.* New York:
Norton.

du Boff, Richard B. 1989. *Accumulation and Power. An Economic History of the United
States.* New York: M.E. Sharpe,

Dunning, John H., and Sarianna M. Lundan. 2008. *Multinational Enterprises and the
Global Economy,* 2nd ed. Northampton, MA: Edward Elgar.

Durkheim, Emile. 1952 [1897]. *Suicide, a Study in Sociology.* London: Routledge and
Kegan Paul.

Dussel, Enrique. 1993. *Von der Erfindung Amerikas zur Entdeckung des Anderen. Ein
Projekt der Transmoderne.* Düsseldorf: Patmos.

Dyer, Christopher. 2005. *An Age of Transition? Economy and Society in Late Medieval
England.* Oxford: Oxford Univ. Press.

Earth Policy Institute (EPI) from U.S. Department of Agriculture. n.d. *Production,
Supply, and Distribution.* Electronic database at www.fas.usda.gov/psdonline,
updated July 9, 2010. Accessed Aug. 11, 2014.

Édit du Roi. 1687. *Touchant la Police des Isles de l'Amérique Française.* Paris.

Ehrenreich, Barbara, and Deirdre English. 1973. *For Her Own Good: 150 Years of the
Experts' Advice to Women.* Garden City, NY: Anchor Books.

Eisenstein, Elizabeth L. 1979. The Printing Press as an Agent of Change. Cambridge, UK: Cambridge Univ. Press.

Eisler, Riane. 1987. The Chalice and the Blade: Our History, Our Future. San Francisco: Harper One.

Elias, Norbert. 1996 [1984]. Du temps. Paris: Fayard.

Elliot, John H. 1990a. "La conquista española y las colonias de América," in L. Bethell, ed., Historia de América Latina. América Latina Colonial: La América precolombina y la conquista. Barcelona: Crítica

———. 1990b. "España y América en los siglos XVI y XVII," in L. Bethell, ed., Historia de América Latina. América Latina colonial: Europa y América en los siglos XVI, XVII, XVIII. Barcelona: Crítica.

Embree, Ainslie T., ed. 1991 [1958]. Sources of Indian Tradition, 3rd ed. New Delhi: Penguin Books.

Engels, Friedrich. 1896. "The Part Played by Labour in the Transition from Ape to Man," Die Neue Zeit.

Erickson, Amy Louise. 2005. "Coverture and Capitalism," History Workshop Journal 59, Spring, 1–16.

Fagan, Brian. 2000. The Little Ice Age. How Climate Made History. New York: Basic Books.

Fan, Jinmin. 2008. National Economy and People's Livelihood, Socioeconomic Studies of Ming and Qing (Guoji Mingsheng, MingQing Shehui Jingji Yanjiu). Fuzhou: Fujian People's Press.

Fan, Shuzhi. 2005. Jiangnan Towns: Tradition and Transition (Jiangnan Shizhen: Chuantong yu Bianqian). Shanghai: Fudan Univ. Press.

Feng, Xianliang. 2002. Environmental Change and Social Control in Jiangnan during Ming-Qing Period (MingQing Jiangnan Diqu de Huanjing Biandong yu Shehui Kongzhi). Shanghai: Shanghai People's Press.

Ferguson, Kathy E. 1984. The Feminist Case Against Bureaucracy. Philadelphia: Temple Univ. Press.

Flynn, Dennis O., and Arturo Giráldez. 1995. "Born with a 'Silver Spoon': The Origin of World Trade in 1571," Journal of World History VI, no. 2 (Fall), 201–221.

Fonseca, Jorge. 1992. Especialización productiva dentro de la economía mundial. Industrialización y desindustrialización en Argentina. Madrid: Editorial de la Univ. Complutense de Madrid.

———. 1993. "The Restructuring of Production, Global Markets and Critical Economics," in J. Torras et al., The Spaces of the Market. Valencia: Centre d'Estudis d'Història Local, 301–346.

———. 2008. "Corporaciones transnacionales y tendencias en la inversión extranjera en la globalización," Ekonomiaz 68: 310–353.

Fonseca, Jorge, and Martínez Gz.-Tablas. 2008. "Economía política de la globalización y sus crisis," in La globalización en el siglo XXI: retos y dilemas. Vitoria: Federación de Cajas de Ahorros Vasco-Navarras, 33–54.

Forbath, Peter. 1977. The River Congo: The Discovery, Exploration, and Exploitation of the World's Most Dramatic River. New York: Harper and Row/Mariner Books.

Forbes. 2011. Global 2000. www.forbes.com.

Fortune. 2007. Global 500. New York: Time.

Foster, John Bellamy. 2000. Marx's Ecology: Materialism and Nature. New York: Monthly Review Press.

———. 2009. The Ecological Revolution: Making Peace with the Planet. New York: Monthly Review Press.

Foucault, Michel. 1974 [1971]. The Order of Things. London: Routledge.

———. 1977. Discipline and Punish: the Birth of the Prison. Harmondsworth, UK: Penguin.

———. 1984a [1961]. "The Great Confinement," in Paul Rabinow, ed., *The Foucault Reader.* Hammondsworth, UK: Penguin, 124–140.

———. 1984b [1971]. "Nietzsche, Genealogy, History," in Paul Rabinow, ed., *The Foucault Reader.* Hammondsworth, UK: Penguin, 76–100.

———. 2004. *Abnormal: Lectures at the College de France, 1974–1975.* London: Picador.

Fouchard, Jean. 1981. *The Haitian Maroons: Liberty or Death.* New York: Edward W. Blyden Press.

Frank, Andre Gunder. 1967. *"Capitalism and Underdevelopment" in Latin America. Historical Studies of Chile and Brazil.* New York: Monthly Review Press.

———. 1969. *Latin America: Underdevelopment or Revolution.* New York: Monthly Review Press.

Franklin, Ursula M. 2006. *The Ursula Franklin Reader: Pacifism as a Map.* Toronto: Between the Lines.

Fredrickson, George M. 1982 [1981]. *White Supremacy: A Comparative Study in American and South African History.* New York: Oxford Univ. Press.

French, Marilyn. 2002. *From Eve to Dawn: A History of Women,* vol. 2: *The Masculine Mystique.* Toronto: McArthur and Co.

———. 2003. *From Eve to Dawn: A History of Women,* vol. 3: *Infernos and Paradises.* Toronto: McArthur and Co.

French, William E. 1991. "In the Path of Progress: Railroads and Moral Reform in Porfirian Mexico," in C.B. Davis et al., *Railway Imperialism.* Westport CT: Greenwood Press.

Frith, Simon, and Lee Marshall. 2004. *Music and Copyright.* Edinburgh: Edinburgh Univ. Press.

Frye, Marilyn. 1983. *The Politics of Reality: Essays in Feminist Theory.* Freedom, CA: Crossing Press.

Fuma, Susumu. 2005. *A Study of Benevolent Societies and Benevolent Halls in China (Zhongguo Shanhui Shantangshi Yangjiu).* Beijing: Commercial Press.

Fundación TIERRA. 2003. *Collana: Conflicto por la tierra en el altiplano.* La Paz: Plural Editores.

Gaines, Jane. 2006. "Early Cinema's Heyday of Copying," *Cultural Studies* XX, no. 2–3, 227–244.

Gao, Wangling. 2005. *New Discussion on the Tenancy Relationship: Landlords, Peasants and Rents (Zudian Guanxi Xinlun: Dizhu, Nongmin he Dizu).* Shanghai: Shanghai Bookstore Publishing House.

Garavaglia, Juan Carlos. 1983. *Mercado interno y economía colonial.* México: Grijalbo.

García Canclini, Néstor. 2001. *Consumers and Citizens: Globalization and Multicultural Conflicts.* Minneapolis: Univ. of Minnesota Press.

Garner, Richard L. 1988. "Long-Term Silver Mining Trends in Spanish America: A Comparative Analysis of Peru and Mexico," *American Historical Review* XCIII, no. 4 (October), 898–935.

Garrido, Margarita, ed. 2001. *Historia de América Andina,* vol. 2: *El sistema colonial tardío.* Quito: Univ. Andina Simón Bolívar.

George, Margaret. 1973. "From Goodwife to Mistress: The Transformation of the Female in Bourgeois Culture," *Science and Society* CCCVII, no. 2 (Summer), 152–177.

———. 1988. *Women in the First Capitalist Society: Experiences in Seventeenth-Century England.* Urbana: Univ. of Illinois Press.

Giordano, Eduardo. 2002. *Las guerras del petróleo.* Barcelona: Icaria.

Glade, William. 1991. "América Latina y la economia internacional, 1870–1914," in L. Bethell, ed., *Historia de América Latina,* vol. 7. Barcelona: Crítica.

Glaser, Barney and Anselm Strauss. 1967. *The Discovery of Grounded Theory*. Chicago. Aldine Press.

Glave Testino, Luis Miguel. 1986. *El virreinato peruano y la llamada "crisis general" del siglo XVII*. Lima: Univ. de Lima, Departamento Académico de Ciencias Humanas.

Global Footprint Network (GFN). 2009. *Ecological Footprint Atlas 2008*. http://www .footprintnetwork.org/download.php?id=506. Accessed Aug. 11, 2014.

Goettner-Abendroth, Heide, ed. 2009. *Societies of Peace: Matriarchies Past, Present and Future*. Toronto: Inanna Publications and Education.

Goffman, Erving. 1974. *Asylums*. Harmondsworth, UK: Penguin.

Goldstone, Jack. 2009. *Why Europe? The Rise of the West in World History, 1500–1850*. Boston: McGraw Hill.

Golte, Jürgen. 1980. *Repartos y rebeliones: Túpac Amaru y las contradicciones de la economía colonial*. Lima: Instituto de Estudios Peruanos.

Gonzalez, Ellice B. 1981. *Changing Economic Roles for Micmac Men and Women: An Ethnohistorical Analysis*. Ottawa: National Museum of Man Mercury Series, Canadian Ethnology Service Paper, no. 72.

González Echevaria, Roberto, and Enrique Pupo-Walker, eds. 1996. *The Cambridge History of Latin American Literature*, vol. 1. Cambridge, UK: Cambridge Univ. Press.

Goodwin, Crauford D.W. 1974. *The Image of Australia: British Perceptions of the Australian Economy from the Eighteenth to the Twentieth Century*. Durham, NC: Duke Univ. Press.

Gotkowitz, Laura. 2007. *A Revolution for Our Rights: Indigenous Struggles for Land and Justice in Bolivia, 1880–1952*. Durham, NC: Duke Univ. Press.

Green, Glen M., and Robert W. Sussman. 1990. "Deforestation History of the Eastern Rain Forests of Madagascar from Satellite Images," *Science* 248, no. 4952 (April 13), 212–215.

Green-Devins, Carol. 1992. *Countering Colonization: Native American Women and Great Lakes Missions, 1630–1900*. Berkeley: Univ. of California Press.

Grieshaber, Erwin P. 1980. "Survival of Indian Communities in Nineteenth-Century Bolivia: A Regional Comparison," *Journal of Latin American Studies* XII, no. 2, 223–269.

Griffiths, Naomi E.S. 1976. *Penelope's Web: Some Perceptions of Women in European and Canadian Society*. Toronto: Oxford Univ. Press.

Gwynne, Robert N., and Cristóbal Kay, eds. 2004. *Latin America Transformed: Globalization and Modernity*. London: Arnold.

Habermas, Jürgen. 1981. "Erste Zwischenbetrachtung: Soziales Handeln, Zwecktätigkeit und Kommunikation," in J. Habermas, *Theorie des kommunikativen Handelns*, vol. 1: *Handlungsrationalität und gesellschaftliche Rationalisierung*. Frankfurt: Suhrkamp.

Hall, Thomas. 2000. "Frontiers, Ethnogenesis, and World-Systems: Rethinking the Theories," in T. Hall, ed., *A World-Systems Reader: New Perspectives on Gender, Urbanism, Cultures, Indigenous Peoples, and Ecology*. Oxford: Rowman and Littlefield, 237–270.

Hamilton, Roberta. 1978. *The Liberation of Women: A Study of Patriarchy and Capitalism*. London: George Allen and Unwin.

Haude, Rüdiger. 2010. Review of Gabriel Kuhn, *Life Under the Jolly Roger. Reflections on Golden Age Piracy*. Oakland, CA: PM Press 2010. H-Soz-u-Kult, H-Net Reviews, October. http://www.h-net.org/reviews/showrev.php?id=31396. Accessed Aug. 11, 2014.

Haynes, Jonathan, and Onookome Okome. 1998. "Evolving Popular Media: Nigerian Video Films," *Research in African Literatures* XXIX, no. 3 (Autumn), 106–128.

Higham, Charles. 1993. *Trading with the Enemy. 1933–1949*. New York: Delacorte Press.

Hill, Christopher. 1991. *The World Turned Upside Down: Radical Ideas during the English Revolution*, new ed. Harmondsworth, UK: Penguin.

Hillman, Ben. 2004. "The Rise of the Community in Rural China: Village Politics, Cultural Identity and Religious Revival in a HUI Hamlet," *China Journal* LI (January), 53–73.

Hilton, Rodney H. et al. 1978. *The Transition from Feudalism to Capitalism*. London: Verso.

Hirth, Kenn, and Joanne Pillsbury, eds. 2013. *Merchants, Markets, and Exchange in the Pre-Columbian World (Dumbarton Oaks Pre-Columbian Symposia and Colloquia)*. Washington, DC: Dumbarton Oaks Research Library and Collection.

Ho, Ping-ti. 2000. *Studies on the Population of China, 1368–1953*. Beijing: SDX Joint Publishing Company.

Hoberman, Louisa S., and Susan M. Socolow, eds. 1996. *The Countryside in Colonial Latin America*. Albuquerque: Univ. of New Mexico Press.

Holland, Jack. 2006. *A Brief History of Misogyny: The World's Oldest Prejudice*. London: Robertson.

Hoppenbrouwers, Peter, and Jan Luiten van Zanden, eds. 2001. *Peasants into Farmers? The Transformation of Rural Economy and Society in the Low Countries (Middle Ages–19th Century) in Light of the Brenner Debate*. CORN Publication Series 4. Turnhout, Belgium: Brepols.

Hourani, Albert. 2007. *La historia de los árabes*. Barcelona: Vergara.

Hristov, Romeo, and Santiago Genovés. 1998. "Viajes transatlánticos antes de Colón," *Arqueología mexicana* VI, no. 33 (September–October).

Huang, Philip C. 1990. *The Peasant Family and Rural Development in the Yangzi Delta, 1350–1988*. Stanford, CA: Stanford Univ. Press.

Hufton, Olwen. 1995. *The Prospect Before Her: A History of Women in Western Europe, 1500–1800*. London: Fontana Press.

Hughes, Sarah Shaver, and Brady Hughes. 1997. *Women in World History*, vol. 2: *Readings from 1500 to the Present*. Armonk, NY: M.E. Sharpe.

Intergovernmental Panel on Climate Change (IPCC). 2009a. *Cambio climático 2007: Informe de síntesis*. http://www.ipcc.ch/pdf/assessment-report/ar4/syr/ar4_syr_sp.pdf. Accessed Aug. 11, 2014.

———. 2009b. *Climate Change 2007: The Physical Science Basis*. http://ipcc-wg1.ucar.edu /wg1/Report.

Isin, Engin F., and Bryan S. Turner, eds. 2002. *Handbook of Citizenship Studies*. London: Sage.

ISSOCO, Fondazaione Lelio e Lisli Basso, ed. 1976. *Le multinazionali in America Latina*. Roma: Coines.

Jackson, Robert H. 1997. *Liberals, the Church, and Indian Peasants Corporate Lands and the Challenge of Reform in Nineteenth-Century Spanish America*. Albuquerque: Univ. of New Mexico Press.

Jacobs, Jane. 1969. *The Economy of Cities*. New York: Vintage.

———. 1984. *Cities and the Wealth of Nations*. New York: Vintage.

Jacobsen, Nils. 1993. *Mirages of Transition: The Peruvian Altiplano, 1780–1930*. Berkeley: Univ. of California Press.

Jacques, Martin. 2009. *When China Rules the World: The Rise of the Middle Kingdom and the End of the Western World*. London: Allen Lane.

James, Cyril L.R. 1963. *Black Jacobins*, 2nd ed. New York: Vintage.

Janoski, Thomas. 2010. *The Ironies of Citizenship: Naturalization and Integration in Industrialized Countries*. Cambridge, UK: Cambridge Univ. Press.

Jaszi, Peter. 1994. "On the Author Effect: Contemporary Copyright and Collective

Creativity," in M. Woodmansee and P. Jaszi, eds., *The Construction of Authorship: Textual Appropriation in Law and Literature*. Durham, NC: Duke Univ. Press, 29–56.

Johns, Adrian. 1998. *The Nature of the Book: Print and Knowledge in the Making*. Chicago: Univ. of Chicago Press.

———. 2009. *Piracy: The Intellectual Property Wars from Gutenberg to Gates*. Chicago: Univ. of Chicago Press.

Johnson, Heather. 2004. "Subsistence and Control: The Persistence of the Peasantry in the Developing World," *Undercurrent* I, no. 1, 55–65.

Johnson-Odim, Cheryl. 2004. "Women and Gender in the History of Sub-Saharan Africa," in B.B. Smith, ed., *Women's History in Global Perspective*, vol. 3. Urbana: Univ. of Illinois Press, 9–67.

Joint Chiefs of Staff (JCS). 2000. *Joint Vision 2010*. Washington, DC.

Kahn, Mark E. 2005. "Perpetuating Patriarchy after the American Revolution," in C. Biaggi, *The Rule of Mars: Readings on the Origins, History and Impact of Patriarchy*. Manchester: Knowledge, Ideas and Trends (KIT), 249–262.

Kamen, Henry. 1971. *The Iron Century, Social Change in Europe, 1550–1660*. Worcester, MA: Trinity Press.

Kanner, Barbara Penny. 1997. *Women in Context: Two Hundred Years of British Women Autobiographers: A Reference Guide and Reader*. New York: G.K. Hall and Co.

Kastoryano, Riva. 2005. "Citizenship, Nationhood and Non-Territoriality: Transnational Participation in Europe," *PS: Political Sciences and Politics* XXXVIII, no. 4, 693–696.

Kay, Cristóbal. 1998. "Latin America's Agrarian Reform: Lights and Shadows," in P. Groppo, ed., *Land Reform. Land Settlement and Cooperatives*. Rome: FAO, 8–31.

Keim, Wiebke. 2014. "Colonialism, National-Socialism and the Holocaust. On Modern Ways of Dealing with Deviance," in A. Sitas et al., *Gauging and Engaging Deviance, 1600–2000*. Delhi: Tulika Books, 109–188.

Keller, Evelyn Fox. 1996. *Reflections on Gender and Science*. New Haven, CT: Yale Univ. Press.

Kelly, Joan. 1982. "Early Feminist Theory and the Querelle des Femmes, 1400–1789," *Signs* VIII, no. 2 (Autumn), 4–28.

———. 1984. *Women, History, and Theory: The Essays of Joan Kelly*. Chicago: Univ. of Chicago Press.

Klein, Herbert S. 1993. *Haciendas and Ayllus: Rural Society in the Bolivian Andes in the Eighteenth and Nineteenth Centuries*. Stanford, CA: Stanford Univ. Press.

Knockwood, Isabelle. 2001. *Out of the Depths: The Experiences of Mi'kmaw Children at the Indian Residential School at Shubenacadie, Nova Scotia*, 3rd ed. Black Point, Nova Scotia: Roseway Publishing.

Korzeniewicz, Roberto Patricio, and Timothy Patrick Moran. 2009. *Unveiling Inequality: A World-Historical Perspective*. New York: Russell Sage Foundation.

Krugman, Paul. 2008. *The Great Unraveling*. New York: Penguin.

Lach, Donald F. 1993 [1965]. *Asia in the Making of Europe*, vol. 3: *A Century of Advance*, books 1–4. Chicago: Univ. of Chicago Press.

Lalor, John J., ed. 1899 [1881]. *Cyclopedia of Political Science, Political Economy, and the Political History of the United States*, 3 vols. New York: Maynard Merrill.

Lane, Frederic C. 1979. *Profit from Power. Readings in Protection Rent and Violence-Controlling Enterprises*. Albany: SUNY Press.

———. 1992 [1934]. *Venetian Ships and Shipbuilders of the Renaissance*. Baltimore: Johns Hopkins Univ. Press.

Langer, Eric D. 1989. *Economic Change and Rural Resistance in Southern Bolivia, 1880–1930*. Stanford, CA: Stanford Univ. Press.

———. 2004. "Indian Trade and Ethnic Economies in the Andes 1780–1880," *Estudios interdisciplinarios de América Latina y el Caribe* XV, no. 1.

Larson, Brooke. 1995. "Andean Communities, Political Cultures, and Markets: The Changing Contours of a Field," in Larson, Brooke, and Olivia Harris, eds., *Ethnicity, Markets, and Migration in the Andes. At the Crossroads of History and Anthropology,* Durham, NC: Duke Univ. Press, 5–54.

———. 2004. *Trials of Nation Making. Liberalism, Race, and Ethnicity in the Andes, 1810–1910.* Cambridge, UK: Cambridge Univ. Press

Larson, Brooke, and Olivia Harris, eds. 1995. *Ethnicity, Markets, and Migration in the Andes. At the Crossroads of History and Anthropology,* Durham, NC: Duke Univ. Press.

Lawler, Jennifer. 2001. *Encyclopedia of Women in the Middle Ages.* Jefferson, NC: McFarland.

Lehmann, David, ed. 1982. *Ecology and Exchange in the Andes.* Cambridge, UK: Cambridge Univ. Press.

Lengermann, Patricia Madoo, and Gillian Niebrugge. 2007. *The Women Founders: Sociology and Social Theory, 1830–1930—A Text/Reader.* Long Grove, IL: Waveland Press.

Lenkersdorf, Gudrun. 2001. *Repúblicas de indios.* México: UNAM.

León Portilla, Miguel. 1989. *Visión de los vencidos: relaciones indígenas de la Conquista.* México: UNAM.

———. 1992. "Quinto Centenario: Tomar en cuenta a los otros," *Mexican Studies/Estudios Mexicanos* VIII, no. 2 (Summer), 155, 166.

Lerner, Gerda. 1979. *The Majority Finds Its Past: Placing Women in History.* New York: Oxford Univ. Press.

———. 1986. *The Creation of Patriarchy.* New York: Oxford Univ. Press.

———. 1993. *The Creation of Feminist Consciousness: From the Middle Ages to Eighteen-Seventy.* New York: Oxford Univ. Press.

LeRoy Ladurie, Emmanuel. 1975. *The French Peasantry, 1450–1660.* Berkeley: Univ. of California Press.

Lessig, Lawrence. 2004. *Free Culture: How Big Media Uses Technology and the Law to Lock Down Culture and Control Creativity.* New York: Penguin.

Levanon, Asaf, and Noah Lewin-Epstein. 2010. "Grounds for Citizenship: Public Attitudes in Comparative Perspective," *Social Science Research* XXXIX, 419–431.

Lewis, Colin M. 2009. "Las economías de exportación: América Latina c. 1870–1930." http://www.lse.ac.uk/economicHistory/pdf/Lewis/TRADUCTION-Cap-Vol%207-Lewis-260606.pdf. Accessed Aug. 11, 2014.

Li Bozhong. 1998. *Agricultural Development in Jiangnan, 1620–1850.* New York: St. Martin's Press.

Li, Wenzhi, and Taixin Jiang. 2000. *Chinese Patriarchal System and Clan-Owned Common Land (Zhongguo Zongfa Zongzu Zhi he Zutian Yizhuang).* Beijing: Social Science Academic Press.

Liang, Fangzhong. 1980. *Statistics of Population, Agricultural Land and Taxation of All Dynasties in China (Zhongguo Lidai Hukou, Tiandi, Tianfu Tongji).* Shanghai: Shanghai People's Publishing House.

Linebaugh, Peter, and Marcus Rediker. 2000. *The Many-Headed Hydra: Sailors, Slaves, Commoners, and the Hidden History of the Revolutionary Atlantic.* Boston: Beacon Press.

Litman, Jessica. 2000. *The Demonization of Piracy.* http://www-personal.umich.edu/~jdlitman/. Accessed Aug. 11, 2014.

Locke, John. 2003 [1689]. *Two Treatises of Government and A Letter Concerning Toleration.* New Haven, CT: Yale Univ. Press.

Logan, F. Donald. 1983. *The Vikings in History.* Totowa, NJ: Barnes and Noble Books.

Long, Pamela O. 2001. *Openness, Secrecy, Authorship: Technical Arts and the Culture of Knowledge from the Antiquity to the Renaissance*. Baltimore: Johns Hopkins Univ. Press.

López Austin, Alfredo, and Leonardo López Luján. 1996. *El pasado indígena*. México: Fondo de Cultura Económica.

Lowry, Bullitt, and Elizabeth Ellington Gunter, eds. and trans. 1981. *The Red Virgin: Memoirs of Louise Michel*. Tuscaloosa: Univ. of Alabama Press.

MacFarquhar, Roderick. 1997. *The Politics of China, the Eras of Mao and Deng*, 2nd ed. Cambridge, UK: Cambridge Univ. Press.

Macleod, Murdo J. 1990. "España y América: el comercio atlántico, 1492–1720," in L. Bethell, ed., *Historia de América Latina*, vol. 2: *América Latina Colonial: Europa y América en los siglos XVI, XVII, XVIII*. Barcelona: Crítica.

MacNutt, Francis Augustus. 1908. *The Five Letters of Relation from Fernando Cortés to the Emperor Charles V*. New York: Putman's.

Macy, Gary. 2008. *The Hidden History of Women's Ordination: Female Clergy and the Medieval West*. New York: Oxford Univ. Press.

Maddison, Angus. 2001. *The World Economy: A Millennial Perspective: Historical Statistics*. Geneva: OECD.

———. 1995. *Monitoring the World Economy, 1820–1992*. Paris: OECD.

Malik, Kenan. 1996. *The Idea of Race*. New York: Palgrave.

Mallon, Florencia E. 1983. *The Defence of Community in Peru's Central Highlands: Peasant Struggle and Capitalist Transition, 1860–1940*. Princeton, NJ: Princeton Univ. Press.

———. 1995. *Peasant and Nation: The Making of Postcolonial Mexico and Peru*. Berkeley: Univ. of California Press.

Mandel, Ernest. 1972. *Der Spätkapitalismus*. Frankfurt: Suhrkamp Verlag. (1979. *El capitalismo tardío*, México: Era).

Mann, Charles C. 2006. *1491. New Revelations of the Americas before Columbus*. New York: Knopf.

Mann, Michael. 1987. "Ruling Class Strategies and Citizenship," *Sociology* XXI, no. 3, 339–354.

Manning, Patrick. 2006. "African Connections with American Colonization," in V. Bulmer-Thomas, J. Coastworth, and R. Cortés-Conde, eds., *The Cambridge Economic History of Latin America*, vol. 1: *The Colonial Era and the Short Nineteenth Century*. Cambridge, UK: Cambridge Univ. Press.

Manovich, Lev. 2002. *The Language of New Media*. Cambridge, MA: MIT Press.

Marcílio, Maria Luiza. 1990. "La población del Brasil colonial," in L. Bethell, ed., *Historia de América Latina*, vol. 4: *América latina colonial: población, sociedad y cultura*. Barcelona: Crítica.

Marini, Ruy Mauro. 1986. *Dialéctica de la dependencia*. México: ERA.

Marks, Robert B. 2007. *The Origins of the Modern World. A Global and Ecological Narrative from the Fifteenth to the Twenty-First Century*. Lanham, MD: Rowman and Littlefield.

Marshall, Thomas Humphrey. 1950. "Citizenship and Social Class," in *Citizenship and Social Class and Other Essays*. Cambridge, Cambridge Univ. Press.

Martin, Emily. 1991. "The Egg and the Sperm: How Science Has Constructed a Romance Based on Stereotypical Male-Female Roles," *Signs* XVI, no. 3, 485–501.

Martínez Montiel, Luz María. 2006. *Afroamérica I: La Ruta del Esclavo*. México: UNAM-PUMC.

Masuda, Yoshio, Izumi Shimada, and Craig Morris. 1985. "Andean Ecology and Civilization: An Interdisciplinary Perspective on Andean Ecological Complementarity," in *Papers from Wenner-Gren Foundation for Anthropological Research Symposium* No. 91, Tokyo.

Mauro, Frédéric. 1990. "Portugal y Brasil: estructuras políticas y económicas del imperio, 1580–1750," in L. Bethell, ed., *Historia de América Latina*, vol. 2: *América Latina Colonial: Europa y América en los siglos XVI, XVII, XVIII*. Barcelona: Crítica.

Mayer, Enrique. 2002. *The Articulated Peasant: Household Economies in the Andes*. Boulder, CO: Westview Press.

——. 2009. *Ugly Stories of the Peruvian Agrarian Reform*. Durham, NC: Duke Univ. Press.

McFadden, Patricia. 2007. "Why Women's Spaces are Critical to Feminist Autonomy." ISIS International, http://www.isiswomen.org/index .php?option=com_content&view=article&id=630%3Awhy-womens-spaces-are -critical-to-feminist-autonomy&catid=127%3Atheme-mens-involvement-in -womens-empowerment. Accessed Aug. 11, 2014.

McGee, Harold Franklin. 1974. *Ethnic Boundaries and Strategies of Ethnic Interaction: A History of Micmac-White Relations in Nova Scotia*. Ann Arbor, MI: University Microfilms.

McGee, Harold. 1983. *Native Peoples of Atlantic Canada: A History of Indian-European Relations*. Ottawa: Carleton Univ. Press.

McLaughlin, Eleanor. 1979. "Women, Power and the Pursuit of Holiness in Medieval Christianity," in R. Reuther and E. McLaughlin, eds., *Women of Spirit: Female Leaders in the Jewish and Christian Traditions*. New York: Simon and Schuster.

McMichael, Philip. 2009. "A Food Regime Genealogy," *Journal of Peasant Studies* XXXVI, no. 1, 139–169.

McNeill, John R. 2000. *Something New Under the Sun: An Environmental History of the Twentieth Century World*. New York: Norton.

McNeill, William. 1984. *Plagues and Peoples*. New York: Anchor Books.

Menzies, Gavin. 2006. *1421: El año en que China descubrió el mundo*. México: Random House Mondadori.

Merchant, Carolyn. 1989. *The Death of Nature: Women, Ecology, and the Scientific Revolution*. San Francisco: Harper and Row.

Micklethwait, John. 2011. "Taming Leviathan. Special Report: The Future of the State," *Economist*, March 17. http://www.economist.com/node/18359896. Accessed Aug. 11, 2014.

Mies, Maria. 1986. *Patriarchy and Accumulation on a World Scale: Women in the International Division of Labour*. London: Zed Books.

——. 1998. "Decolonizing the Iceberg Economy: New Feminist Concepts for a Sustainable Society," in L. Christiansen-Ruffman, ed., *Feminist Perspectives: The Global Feminist Enlightenment: Women and Social Knowledge*. Madrid: International Sociological Association.

Miles, Angela. 1996. *Integrative Feminisms: Building Global Visions 1960–1990s*. New York: Routledge.

——, ed. 2013. *Women in a Globalizing World: Transforming Equality, Development, Diversity and Peace*. Toronto: Inanna Publications and Education

Milanovic, Branko, Peter H. Lindert, and Jeffrey G. Williamson. 2007. *Measuring Ancient Inequality*. World Bank, Washington, DC. National Bureau of Economic Research Working Paper No. 13550.

Miller, Toby et al. 2005. *Global Hollywood*, London: BFI Publications.

Moore, Jason W. 2007. *Ecology and the Rise of Capitalism*. Ph.D. dissertation, Geography, Univ. of California, Berkeley.

——. 2010. "The End of the Road? Agricultural Revolutions in the Capitalist World-Ecology 1450–2010," *Journal of Agrarian Change* X, no. 3, 389–413.

Morán, Emilio F. 2007. "The Human-Environment Nexus: Progress in the Past Decade in the Integrated Analysis of Human and Biophysical Factors," in A. Hornborg and C. Crumley, eds., *The World System and the Earth System: Global*

Socio-Environmental Change and Sustainability Since the Neolithic. Walnut Creek, CA: Left Coast Press.

Moreno, Segundo, and Frank Salomon, eds. 1991. *Reproducción y transformación de las sociedades andinas, XVI–XX*, 2 vols. Colección 500 Años. Quito: Movimiento Laicos para América Latina.

Morin, Edgar. 1977. *La Rumeur d'Orléans*. Paris: Seuil.

Morris, J. Bayard. 1928. *5 Letters of Cortés to the Emperor* London: George Routledge and Sons.

Mulder, Nanno. 2002. *Economic Performance in the Americas. The Role of the Service Sector in Brazil, Mexico and the USA*. London: Edward Elgar.

Murra, John V. 1975. *Formaciones económicas y políticas del mundo andino*. Lima: Instituto de Estudios Peruanos.

Neuwirth, Robert. 2006. *Shadow Cities: A Billion Squatters, a New Urban World*. London: Routledge.

Newson, Linda A. 2006. "The Demographic Impact of Colonization," in V. Bulmer-Thomas, J. Coastworth and R. Cortés-Conde, eds., *The Cambridge Economic History of Latin America*, vol. 1: *The Colonial Era and the Short Nineteenth Century*. Cambridge, UK: Cambridge Univ. Press.

Niveau, Maurice. 1966. *Histoire des faits économiques contemporains*. Paris: Presses Univ. de France.

Noble, David F. 1993. *A World without Women: The Christian Clerical Culture of Western Science*. New York: Oxford Univ. Press.

O'Connor, James. 2007. "¿Qué es la historia ambiental? ¿Por qué historia ambiental?" *Caminos* no 44.

O'Faolain, Julia, and Lauro Martines, eds. 1973. *Not in God's Image: Women in History from the Greeks to the Victorians*. New York: Harper and Row.

Offen, Karen. 2000. *European Feminisms, 1700–1950: A Political History*. Stanford, CA: Stanford Univ. Press.

Oliva de Coll, Josefina. 1976. *La resistencia indígena ante la conquista*. México: Siglo XXI de México.

Olsen, Kirstin. 1994. *Chronology of Women's History*. Westport, CT: Greenwood Press.

Omvedt, Gail. 1990. *Feminist Concepts*, vol. 1: *Patriarchy and Matriarchy*. Bombay: Research Centre for Women's Studies, SNDT Women's Univ., Juhu.

O'Regan, Tom. 1991. "From Piracy to Sovereignty: International VCR Trends," *Continuum: The Australian Journal of Media and Culture* IV, no. 2.

Overton, Marc. 1996. *Agricultural Revolution in England. The Transformation of the Agrarian Economy, 1500–1850*. Cambridge, UK: Cambridge Univ. Press.

Pagden, Anthony. 2001. *Hernan Cortés, Letters from Mexico*. New Haven, CT: Yale Univ, Press.

Pateman, Carole. 1989. *Democracy, Feminism and Political Theory*. Cambridge, UK: Polity Press in association with Basil Blackwell.

Paul, Daniel N. 2000. *We Were Not The Savages: A Mi'kmaq Perspective on the Collision between European and Native American Civilizations*, new 21st century edition. Halifax: Fernwood Press.

Pilon, André Francisco. 2010. *"The Right to the City": An Ecosystemic Approach to Better Cities, Better Life*. MPRA Paper No. 25572 (Munich Personal RePEc Archive), October 10. http://ideas.repec.org/p/pra/mprapa/25572.html. Accessed Aug. 11, 2014.

Platt, Tristan, 1982. *Estado boliviano y ayllu andino*. Lima: Instituto de Estudios Peruanos.

Pollard, Sidney. 1989. *Britain's Prime and Britain's Decline. The British Economy, 1870–1914*. London: Edward Arnold.

Pomeranz, Kenneth. 2000. *The Great Divergence, China, Europe and the Making of the Modern World Economy*. Princeton, NJ: Princeton Univ. Press.

Prigogine, Ilya. 2006 [1988]. *El nacimiento del tiempo*. Buenos Aires: Tusquets.

Przezworski, Adam. 2009a. "Conquered or Granted? A History of Suffrage Extensions," *British Journal of Political Science* XXXIX, no. 2, 291–321.

——. 2009b. "Constraints and Choices: Electoral Participation in Historical Perspective," *Comparative Political Studies* XLII, no. 1, 4–30.

Qian, Hang, and Zai Zheng. 1998. *Jiangnan Social Life in 17th Century*. Taipei: South Sky Press.

Red Amazónica de Información Socioambiental Georeferenciada (RAISG). 2012. *Amazonía bajo presión*. Brasil: RAISG.

Reich, Emil. 1908. *Woman through the Ages*, 2 vols. London: Methuen.

Reid, John. 2009. *Nova Scotia: A Pocket History*. Halifax: Fernwood Publishing.

Ricciutellil, Luciana, Angela Miles, and Margaret H. McFadden. 2004. *Feminist Politics, Activism, Vision: Local and Global Challenges*. London: Zed.

Rivera Cusicanqui, Silvia. 1987. *Oppressed but Not Defeated: Peasant Struggles among the Aymara and Qhechwa in Bolivia, 1900–1980*. Geneva: United Nations Research Institute for Social Development.

Roesdahl, Else. 1998. *The Vikings*, 2nd ed. London: Penguin.

Rogers, Katharine M. 1966. *The Troublesome Helpmate: A History of Misogyny in Literature*. Seattle: Univ. of Washington Press.

Romero, José Luis. 2001. *Latinoamérica. Las ciudades y las ideas*. México: Fondo de Cultura Económica.

Rose, Mark. 1993. *Authors and Owners: The Invention of Copyright*. Cambridge, MA: Harvard Univ. Press.

Rowan, Mary M. 1980. "Seventeenth Century French Feminism: Two Opposing Attitudes," *International Journal of Women's Studies* III, no. 3, May–June, 273–291.

Rubin, Miri. 1998. "The Languages of Late-Medieval Feminism," in T. Akkerman and S. Stuurman, eds., *Perspectives on Feminist Political Thought in European History: From the Middle Ages to the Present*. London: Routledge, 34–49.

Ruether, Rosemary Radford, and Eleanor T. McLaughlin. 1998. *Women of Spirit: Female Leadership in the Jewish and Christian Traditions*. Eugene, OR: Wipf and Stock Publishers.

Saari, Peggy, Tim and Susan Gall, eds. 1997. *Women's Chronology: An Annotated History of Women's Achievements*, vol. 1: *4000 B.C. to 1847*; vol. 2: *1850 to Present*. Detroit, MI: UXL.

Sala-Molins, Louis. 1987. *Le Code Noir, ou, Le Calvaire de Canaan*, Toulouse: Presses Univ. de France.

Sampson, Anthony. 1973. *The Sovereign State of ITT*. London: Hodder and Stoughton.

Sánchez Albornoz, Nicolás. 1990. "La población de la América colonial española," in L. Bethell, ed., *Historia de América Latina*, vol. 4: *América colonial: población, sociedad y cultura*. Barcelona: Crítica.

Sassen, Saskia. 2001. *The Global City*. Princeton, NJ: Princeton Univ. Press.

——. 2005. "When National Territory is Home to the Global: Old Borders to Novel Borderings," *New Political Economy* X, no. 4 (December), 523–541.

Sauer, Carl O. 2005. *La gestión del hombre en la Tierra y otros ensayos*. Selección y notas de Guillermo Castro. Panama: s.n.

Saul, John Ralston. 2008. *A Fair Country: Telling Truths About Canada*. Toronto: Viking Canada.

Schumpeter, Joseph A. 1942. *Capitalism, Socialism and Democracy*. New York: Harper and Row.

Scott, James C. 1998. *Seeing Like a State*. New Haven, CT: Yale Univ. Press.

———. 2009. *The Art of Not Being Governed*. New Haven, CT: Yale Univ. Press.

Scully, Pamela. 2004. "Race and Ethnicity in Women's and Gender History in Global Perspective," in B.G. Smith, ed., *Women's History in Global Perspective*, vol. 1, in collaboration with the American Historical Association. Urbana: Univ. of Illinois Press, 195–228.

Séjouné, Laurette. 1971. *América Latina*, vol. I: *Antiguas culturas precolombinas*. México: Siglo XXI.

Sen, Gita, and Caren Grown. 1987. *Development, Crises, and Alternative Visions: Third World Women's Perspectives*. New York: Monthly Review Press.

Serulnikov, Sergio. 2008. "The Politics of Intracommunity Land Conflict in the Late Colonial Andesö," *Ethnohistory* LV, no. 1, 119–152.

Shiba, Yoshinobu. 2000. *An Economic Historical Study on Sung Jiangnan (Songdai Jiangnan Jingjishi Yanjiu)*. Nanjing: Jiangsu People's Publishing House.

Shiva, Vandana. 1988. *Staying Alive: Women, Ecology and Development*. New Delhi: Kali for Women.

———. 1997. *Biopiracy: The Plunder of Nature and Knowledge*. Toronto: Between the Lines.

Sitas, Ari. 2004. *Voices That Reason. Theoretical Parables (Imagined South Africa)*. Pretoria: Univ. of South Africa Press.

Sitas, Ari et al. 2014. *Gauging and Engaging Deviance, 1600–2000*. Delhi: Tulika Books

Smith, Bonnie G. 2004. *Women's History in Global Perspective*, vol. 1, published with the American Historical Association. Urbana: Univ. of Illinois Press.

———. 2005. *Women's History in Global Perspective.*, vols. 2 and 3, published with the American Historical Association. Urbana: Univ. of Illinois Press.

———. 2008. *The Oxford Encyclopedia of Women in World History*. Oxford: Oxford Univ. Press.

Smith, Dorothy. 1987. *The Everyday World as Problematic: A Feminist Sociology*. Toronto: Univ. of Toronto Press.

Smith, Joan, Immanuel Wallerstein, and Hans-Dieter Evers, eds. 1984. *Households and the World-Economy*. Beverly Hills, CA: Sage.

Smith, Robert Freeman. 1991. "América Latina, los Estados Unidos y las potencias europeas, 1830–1930," in L. Bethell, ed., *Historia de América Latina*, vol. 4: *América Latina: Economía y sociedad, c. 1870–1930*. Barcelona: Crítica.

Sogyal, Rimpoche. 1996. *Destellos de Sabiduría*. Barcelona: Urano.

Sokoloff, Kenneth L., and Stanley L. Engerman. 2000. "Institutions, Factor Endowments, and Paths of Development in the New World," *Journal of Economic Perspectives* XIV, no. 3 (Summer), 217–232.

Solnit, Rebecca. 2009. *A Paradise Built in Hell: The Extraordinary Communities That Arise in Disasters*. New York: Viking Press.

Starhawk. 2002. *Webs of Power: Notes from the Global Uprising*. Gabriola Island, British Columbia: New Society Publishers.

Starnes, Colin. 2012. *Augustine's Conversion*. Waterloo, Ontario: Wilfrid Laurier Univ. Press.

Stavig, Ward, and Ella Schmidt, eds. 2008. *The Tupac Amaru and Catarista Rebellions: An Anthology of Sources*. Indianapolis: Hackett Publishing.

Stern, Steve, ed. 1987. *Resistance, Rebellion and Consciousness in the Andean Peasant World, 18th to 20th Centuries*. Madison: Univ. of Wisconsin Press.

Sumner, Claude. 1986. *The Source of African Philosophy: The Ethiopian Philosophy of Man*, in S. Uhlig, ed., *Aethiopistich Forschungen*, vol. 20. Univ. Hamburg, Abteilung Afrikanistik und Athiopistik. (Includes English translation of the Hetata by Zera Yacob and the Treatise of Walda Heywat.)

Sundaram, Ravi. 2008. "Revisiting the Pirate Kingdom," *Third Text* XXIII, no. 3, 335–345.

Sydie, R.A. 1994. *Natural Women, Cultured Men: A Feminist Perspective on Sociological Theory.* Vancouver: Univ. of British Columbia Press.

Tandeter, Enrique. 1995. "Población y economía en los Andes (siglo XVIII)," *Revista Andina* XXV, no. 1, 7–22.

Tauger, Mark B. 2011. *Agriculture in World History.* London: Routledge.

Taylor, Peter J. 1999. *Modernities: a Geohistorical Introduction.* Cambridge: Polity.

——. 2004. *World City Network.* London: Routledge

——. 2013. *Extraordinary Cities: Millennia of Moral Syndromes, World-Systems and City-State Relations.* Cheltenham, UK: Edward Elgar.

Taylor, Peter J. et al. 2010. "Explosive City Growth in the Modern World-System: An Initial Inventory Derived from Urban Demographic Changes," *Urban Geography* XXXI, no. 7, 865–884.

Taylor, Peter J. et al., eds. 2011. *Global Urban Analysis: A Survey of Cities in Globalization.* London: Earthscan

Thoen, Erik. 2001. "A Commercial Survival Economy in Evolution. The Flemish Countryside and the Transition to Capitalism (Middle Ages–19th Century)," in P. Hoppenbrouwers and J.L. van Zanden, eds., *Peasants into Farmers? The Transformation of Rural Economy and Society in the Low Countries (Middle Ages–19th Century) in Light of the Brenner Debate,* CORN Publication Series 4. Turnhout, Belgium: Brepols, 102–157.

Thompson, Edward P. 1974. *The Making of the English Working Class.* Harmondsworth, UK: Penguin.

——. 1977. *Whigs and Hunters: The Origins of the Black Act.* London: Allen Lane.

——. 1989. *Tradición, revuelta y consciencia de clase.* Barcelona: Crítica.

Thompson, Grahame. 1997. "'Globalization' and the Possibilities for Domestic Economic Policy," *Internationale Politik und Gessellschaft,* no. 2.

Thompson, Kenneth. 1998. *Moral Panics.* London: Routledge.

Thurner, Mark. 1997. *From Two Republics to One Divided: Contradictions of Postcolonial Nationmaking in Andean Peru.* Latin America Otherwise: Languages, Empires, Nations. Durham, NC: Duke Univ. Press.

Tilly, Charles. 1998. *Durable Inequality.* Berkeley: Univ. Of California Press.

Tucker, Richard P. 2000. *Insatiable Appetite: The United States and the Ecological Degradation of the Tropical World.* Berkeley: Univ. of California Press.

Tucker, Ruth A., and Walter Liefeld. 1987. *Daughters of the Church: Women and Ministry from New Testament Times to the Present.* Grand Rapids, MI: Academie Books.

Turok, Ivan. 2009. "The Distinctive City: Pitfalls in the Pursuit of Differential Advantage," *Environment and Planning A* 41, no. 1, 13–30.

UNCTAD (United Nations Conference on Trade and Development). 2010. *World Investment Report,* Geneva: UNCTAD.

Urioste, Miguel et al., eds. 2007. *Los nietos de la reforma agraria: Tierra y comunidad en el altiplano de Bolivia.* La Paz: Fundación TIERRA y CIPCA.

Urteaga, Horacio H. 1916. "Instrucción del Inca Don Diego de Castro Titu Cusi Yupanqui al Licenciado don Lope García de Castro," in *Colección de libros y documentos relativos a la historia del Perú,* vol. 2: *Relación de la Conquista del Perú y hechos del Inca Manco II.* Lima: Imprinta y Librería San Martín y Compañía.

Vallée, Brian. 2007. *The War on Women: Elly Armour, Jane Hurshman, and Criminal Violence in Canadian Homes.* Toronto: Key Porter.

Van Bavel, Bas. 2010. *Manors and Markets. Economy and Society in the Low Countries, 500–1600.* Oxford: Oxford Univ. Press.

Van Bavel, Bas, and Richard W. Hoyle, eds. 2010. *Rural Economy and Society in North-Western Europe, 500–2000. Social Relations: Property and Power*. Turnhout, Belgium: Brepols.

Van der Linden, Marcel. 2008. *Workers of the World: Essays toward a Global Labor History*. Leiden: Brill.

Van der Ploeg, Jan Douwe. 2010. "The Peasantries of the Twenty-First Century: The Commoditisation Debate Revisited," *Journal of Peasant Studies* XXXVII, no. 1, 1–30.

Vanhaute, Eric. 2008. "The End of Peasantries? Rethinking the Role of Peasantries and Peasant Families in a World-Historical View," *Review (Fernand Braudel Center)* XXXI, no. 1, 39–59.

———. 2011. "Peasants and Depeasantization," in S. Babones and C. Chase-Dunn, eds., *Routledge International Handbook of World-Systems Analysis*. New York: Routledge.

Vanhaute, Eric et al. eds. 2011. *Rural Economy and Society in North-Western Europe, 500–2000. Making a Living: Family, Income and Labour*. Turnhout, Belgium: Brepols.

Vaughan, Genevieve. 2007. *Women and the Gift Economy: A Radically Different Worldview Is Possible*. Toronto: Inanna Publications and Education.

Vaupel, James W., and Joan P. Curhan. 1974. *The World's Multinational Enterprises*. Cambridge, MA: Harvard Univ Press.

Verger, Antoni. 2003. *El sutil poder de las transnacionales*. Barcelona: Icaria.

von Werlhof, Claudia. 1984. "The Proletarian is Dead: Long Live the Housewife?" in J. Smith et al., *Households and the World-Economy*. Beverly Hills, CA: Sage Publications, 131–147.

———. 2004. "Using, Producing and Replacing Life? Alchemy as Theory and Practice in Capitalism," in I. Wallerstein, ed., *The Modern World-System in the Longue Durée*. Boulder, CO: Paradigm Publishers, 65–78.

———. 2007. "No Critique of Capitalism without a Critique of Patriarchy! Why the Left Is No Alternative," *Capitalism, Nature, Socialism* XVIII, no. 1 (March), 13–27.

Wagner, Sally Roesch. 2004. "The Indigenous Roots of United States Feminism," in L. Ricciutellil, A. Miles, and M.H. McFadden, eds., *Feminist Politics, Activism, Vision: Local and Global Challenges*. London: Zed, 267–284.

Walby, Sylvia. 1990. *Theorizing Patriarchy*. Oxford: Blackwell.

———. 2009. *Globalization and Inequalities: Complexity and Contested Modernities*. London: Sage.

Waldmann, Peter. 2008. "Politische und kriminelle Gewalt in Lateinamerika," presentation at Conference of the Swiss Society of Americanists, *Zwischen Neoliberalismus, Dritten Weg und Neopopulismus: Diagnosen der politischen Wende in Lateinamerika*. Univ. of Fribourg, March 14–15.

Wallerstein, Immanuel. 1974a. *The Modern World-System: Capitalist Agriculture and the Origins of the European World-Economy in the Sixteenth Century*. New York: Academic Press.

———. 1974b. "The Rise and Future Demise of the World Capitalist System: Concepts for Comparative Analysis," *Comparative Studies in Society and History* XVI, no. 4, 387–415.

———. 1979. *The Capitalist World-Economy*. Cambridge, UK: Cambridge Univ. Press.

———. 1980. *The Modern World-System*, vol. 2: *Mercantilism and the Consolidation of the European World-Economy, 1600–1750*. New York: Academic Press.

———. 1984a. "Cities in Socialist Theory and Capitalist Praxis," *International Journal of Urban and Regional Research* VIII, no. 1 (March), 64–72.

———. 1984b. *Politics of the World-Economy: The States, the Movements, and the Civilizations*. Cambridge, UK: Cambridge Univ. Press.

——. 1989. *The Modern World-System,* vol. 3: *The Second Era of Great Expansion of the Capitalist World-Economy, 1730–1840s.* San Diego: Academic Press.

——. 1999. "Ecology and Capitalist Costs of Production: No Exit," in W.L. Goldfrank et al., *Ecology and the World-System, Studies in the Political Economy of the World-System,* vol. 21. Westport, CT: Greenwood Press, 3–12.

——. 2000. *The Wallerstein Reader.* New York: New Press.

——. 2003. "Citizens All? Citizens Some! The Making of the Citizen," *Comparative Studies in Society and History* XLV, no. 4, 650–679.

——. 2004. *World-Systems Analysis. An Introduction.* Durham, NC: Duke Univ. Press.

Walls, Martha Elizabeth. 2010. *No Need of a Chief for this Band: The Maritime Mi'kmaq and Federal Electoral Legislation, 1891–1951.* Vancouver: Univ. of British Columbia Press.

Wang, Qisheng. 2003. *Comrades, Control and Contention of the Kuomintang, 1924–1949 (Dang yuan, dang quan yu dang zheng: 1924–1949* nian Zhongguo guo min dang de zu zhi xing tai). Shanghai: Shanghai Bookstore Publishing House.

Weaver, J.C. 2006. *The Great Land Rush and the Making of the Modern World, 1650–1900.* Montreal: McGill Univ. Press.

Weber, Adna Ferrin. 1899. *The Growth of Cities in the Nineteenth Century America.* New York: Macmillan.

Weber, Max. 1922. *Wirtschaft und Gesellschaft.* Tübingen: Mohr

——. 1991, *From Max Weber: Essays in Sociology,* H.H. Gerth and C. Wright Mills, eds. New York: Oxford Univ. Press.

Weiss, Linda. 1997. "Globalization and the Myth of the Powerless State," *New Left Review* 225 (September/October), 3–27.

——. 1998. *The Myth of the Powerless State: Governing the Economy in the Global Era.* Cambridge, UK: Polity Press.

Wiesner-Hanks, Merry. 2007. "World History and the History of Women, Gender and Sexuality," *Journal of World History* XVIII, no. 1, 53–67.

Williamson, John. 1990. "What Washington Means by Policy Reform." Washington: Peterson Institute for International Economics.

Woodmansee, Martha, and Peter Jaszi, eds. 1994. *The Construction of Authorship: Textual Appropriation in Law and Literature.* Durham, NC: Duke Univ. Press.

World Bank. 2008. *World Development Indicators.* Washington, DC: World Bank.

Wright, Gavin. 2006. *Slavery and American Economic Development.* Baton Rouge: Louisiana State Univ. Press.

WWF (World Wildlife Fund). 2010. *Planeta Vivo Informe 2010, Biodiversidad, biocapacidad y desarrollo,* http://www.magrama.gob.es/es/ceneam/recursos/materiales/conservacion-medio-ambiente/planeta-vivo-informe-2010.aspx. Accessed Aug. 11, 2014.

Yepes Del Castillo, Ernesto. 1972. *Peru: 100 años de desarrollo capitalista (1820–1920).* Lima: Instituto de Estudios Peruanos.

Zinsser, Judith, and Bonnie S. Anderson. 2004. "Women in Early and Modern Europe: A Transnational Approach," in B.G. Smith, ed., *Women's History in Global Perspective,* vol. 3. Urbana: Univ. of Illinois Press, 111–144.

About the Author

Immanuel Wallerstein is Senior Research Scholar at Yale University and former President of the International Sociological Association. He is the author of *The Modern World-System* (4 vol.) as well as, most recently, co-author of *Does Capitalism Have a Future?*